Henry Brewster Stanton

Random Recollections

Vol. 3

Henry Brewster Stanton

Random Recollections
Vol. 3

ISBN/EAN: 9783337217440

Printed in Europe, USA, Canada, Australia, Japan

Cover: Foto ©Suzi / pixelio.de

More available books at **www.hansebooks.com**

RANDOM RECOLLECTIONS

BY

HENRY B. STANTON

NEW YORK
HARPER & BROTHERS, FRANKLIN SQUARE
1887

Entered according to act of Congress, in the year 1885, by
HENRY B. STANTON,
in the office of the Librarian of Congress, at Washington, D. C.

Entered according to act of Congress, in the year 1886, by
HENRY B. STANTON,
in the office of the Librarian of Congress, at Washington, D. C.

Copyright, 1887, by HARPER & BROTHERS.

Printed by Wynkoop, Hallenbeck & Co.

PREFACE TO THE THIRD EDITION.

Though no portions of the first and second editions of this work were on sale, they were soon exhausted in supplying calls on me for copies. The requests in numerous newspapers and letters that I would place the book where it could be purchased, amounted almost to a rebuke for my not having done this. In compliance with this desire, I have spent a few weeks in preparing a third edition, which will be issued and sold by a book-publishing house. The new matter in this third edition makes the volume about two thirds larger than the second edition, and about three times as large as the first.

This production is neither a history, a biography, nor an autobiography, but is exactly what it professes to be, namely, some " random recollections " of the writer. It will be well to read it from that point of view. Such value as this draft on my memory may possess is mainly due to the fact that in describing events and men I have usually told only what I personally knew of them; and, perhaps better than all, I have tried to stop when I was done.

H. B. S.

Tenafly, N. J., *September*, 1886.

NOTE BY THE PUBLISHERS.

Henry B. Stanton, the author, died suddenly on January 14th, 1887, in New York. He was busy correcting the proofs of this book the day before he died. H. & B.

CONTENTS.

CHAPTER I.

The Author's Birthplace.—Pachaug, Connecticut.—Jewett City.—The Author's Ancestry.—Thomas Stanton, the Indian Interpreter, and William Brewster, the Pilgrim Father.—Indian Tribes in New London County.—Sachems Uncas, Sassacus, and Miantonomoh.—Extermination of the Pequods in 1637.—Benedict Arnold.—Massacre at Groton Heights in 1781.—The Stantons who Fell there.—War of 1812-15.—Commodores Hardy, Decatur, and Perry.—Bombardment of Stonington.—Perry Describes his Victory on Lake Erie.—"Don't Give up the Ship."—Bitter Politics and Blue-Laws.......................Page 1

CHAPTER II.

Puritan "Meeting-house" at Pachaug.—Freezing as a Means of Grace.—Musical Instruments and Timepieces.—The Clergy.—Doctors Hart, Bellamy, Hopkins, and Lorenzo Dow.—The Burroughses.—The Westminster Catechism.—Connecticut Calvinism *vs.* Rhode Island Liberalism.—The Deacon's Horse-race on Sunday.—Schools, Teachers, and Books.—Nathan Daboll, the Arithmetician.—George D. Prentice, Poet, Wrestler, and Founder of the *Louisville Journal.*—Celebration on July 4, 1824, at Jewett City.—Toast to Henry Clay.—La Fayette at Jewett City in 1825.. 11

CHAPTER III.

Journey to Rochester in April, 1826.—New York City had 150,000 Souls.—Tammany Hall.—The Bucktails.—The City Hall.—Albany's Population, 15,000.—The Old Capitol.—Legislative

Leaders: Young, Root, Frank Granger, Colden, Livingston, Silas Wright, Tallmadge. — Governor De Witt Clinton, the Magnificent. — The Erie Canal just Completed. — Utica. — Syracuse. — Rochester in 1826. — Anti-Masonic Excitement. — Thurlow Weed's Dingy Newspaper, Shabby Dress, and Empty Pocket. — Henry O'Reilly Issues at Rochester, in 1826, the First Daily Journal West of the Hudson and Delaware Rivers. — Edmund Kean, the Tragedian, Performs in the "Iron Chest" at Rochester. — Sam Patch Twice Leaps the Genesee Falls and is Drowned. — Gerrit Smith and Fanny Wright Speak at Rochester. — Samuel Wilkeson Constructs the Harbor at Buffalo............Page 21

CHAPTER IV.

Horatio Seymour when a Cadet; his Father, Henry Seymour. — The "Immortal Seventeen" Senators. — Marcy, Flagg, Bouck in 1826-27. — Death of De Witt Clinton in 1828; Martin Van Buren and Benjamin F. Butler's Eulogiums on Him; their Drift and Purpose. — Van Buren at Rochester in 1828; His Variegated Dress. — Roscoe Conkling's Style. — Presidential Struggle between Adams and Jackson in 1828. — Van Buren Runs for Governor to Help Jackson, and is Chosen. — Smith Thompson and Solomon Southwick also Candidates. — Jackson Elected President. — Van Buren Appointed Secretary of State. — Young Men's State Convention at Utica in 1828; the First ever Held in the Union; William H. Seward Presides; his Unexpected and Embarrassing Nomination for Congress in 1828; he Declines to Run.................................... 29

CHAPTER V.

Courts and Counsellors at Rochester in 1827-30. — Daniel D. Barnard. — Addison Gardiner. — Samuel L. Selden. — Occasional Visitors. — Elisha Williams. — John C. Spencer. — Daniel Cady. — Henry R. Storrs. — Millard Fillmore. — William H. Seward and others. — Thurlow Weed Chosen to the Assembly in 1829. — "A good enough Morgan till after the Election." — Weed Founds the Albany *Evening Journal* in April, 1830. — The State Mends William L. Marcy's "Pantaloons." — The Patch a Campaign Issue when he Ran for Governor. — John W. Taylor, of Saratoga, and the Missouri Compromise. — Marcy and Silas Wright on its Repeal.—The Wilmot Proviso.—Marcy and Wright Compared.—The Rochester Clergy in 1830.—Charles G. Finney, the Famous Evangelist.—His Pulpit Oratory............Page 35

CHAPTER VI.

The Author Goes to Lane Seminary in 1831.—President Lyman Beecher Tried for Heresy at Cincinnati.—Henry Ward Beecher Says his Father is "Plagued Good at Twisting."—New and Old School Theological Magnates.—"In Adam's Fall we Sinned all."—Dr. Beman's Parody.—Dr. Beecher's Eccentricities.—First Anti-slavery Speech.—James G. Birney, and General Birney, his Son.—"Boys, Keep your Eye on that Flag."—First Mob.—Anti-slavery Debate at Lane in 1834.—Its Consequences.—Early Anti-slavery Career.—The Author Addresses the Massachusetts Legislature on Freedom, in 1837.—The Epoch of Mobs.—East Greenwich.—Utica.—Boston.—Newport.—Providence.—Bishop Clark of Rhode Island.—Methodist Church Burned.—Pennsylvania Hall Burned.—Quaker Meeting-house Sacked in Portland.—John Neal, the Poet, Puts the Mob down.—Senator William Pitt Fessenden.—"I am that Person."—Mob in Norwich, Connecticut.—Mobbed in many States.—Never in Vermont... 43

CHAPTER VII.

John G. Whittier and the Author Visit Gettysburg for Anti-slavery Lecturers.—Whittier's Services to Liberty.—Caleb Cushing a Candidate for Congress in 1838.—Whittier Gets a Letter that Averts Cushing's Defeat.—Origin of the Republican Party.—Peculiar Honors paid to John Quincy Adams in 1837.—Author at Washington in 1838.—Adams and the Right of Petition.—Speaker Polk.—Latimer's Case.—The Reel on Mr. Adams's Desk.—Vice-President Dick Johnson Compared with Van Buren as a Presiding Officer.—The Lions in the Senate in 1838.—Foreshadowing the Methods for Overthrowing Slavery.—The Author's Early Newspaper Productions.—Sylvester Graham, the Dietetic Reformer; his System................... 56

CHAPTER VIII.

Abolitionists and the Constitution.—Anti-slavery Leaders: Garrison and others in Boston; Tappan and others in New York;

Smith and others in Central New York; Lovejoy and others in the Western States.—Celebrated Women: Prudence Crandall; Mrs. Child; The Grimkes; Mrs. Mott; Lucy Stone; Harriet Beecher Stowe; Elizabeth Cady Stanton; Susan B. Anthony.—Leading Colored Men; Frederick Douglass; Robert Purvis.—Eccentricities of Abolitionists.—A Motley Group in Boston.—Father Lampson and his Scythe-snath.—Crazy George Washington Mellen.—Disturbing Religious Meetings.—Stephen S. Foster Imitates George Fox.—Charles C. Burleigh's Vile Garments Torn off and Carried away.—Rev. Dr. Channing Eulogizes Burleigh's Oratory.—Controversy between Garrison and Wendell Phillips.—Lord Timothy Dexter........................Page 64

CHAPTER IX.

Tour in Europe in 1840.—Current Description of Author's Travels.—The Main Object of the Tour.—World's Anti-slavery Convention in London.—Leading Members.—Distinguished Women.—Haydon's Large Painting of the Convention; his Anecdote of the Iron Duke.—House of Peers.—Scotch Church Debate.—Brougham Speaks.—Melbourne, the Premier.—Lord Lyndhurst, a Boston-born Boy.—Wellington Speaks on an Irish Question.—Earl Grey Enters.—The Reform Bill of 1832.—Grey's Warning to the Peers to Set their Houses in Order.—Sydney Smith and Dame Partington.—Gorgeous Pageant at the Funeral of Earl Durham, Son-in-law of Grey, and the Persecuted Ex-Governor of Canada.. 74

CHAPTER X.

The House of Commons.—Debate on Canada.—Macaulay's Speech.—Lord John Russell.—The Lions of the House.—O'Connell Aims a Stinging Arrow at Disraeli, the Future Beaconsfield.—Stanley, the Inchoate Earl Derby, Collides with Howick, Son and Heir of Earl Grey.—Sir Robert Peel Compared with Clay, Calhoun, and Webster.—Gladstone, "The Rising Hope of the Stern and Unbending Tories."—Talfourd.—Bulwer's Dandy Dress.—Anecdote of Brougham and Buxton.—Clarkson's Description of Wilberforce's Oratory.—Manners in the English Commons and the American Congress Compared.—The Englishman's H.—Oratory in America and Great Britain.—American Snobbery.—Joseph H. Choate and William E. Forster before

the Union League Club.—Dean Stanley, Canon Farrar, Sergeant
Ballantyne, and Matthew Arnold Facing American Audiences.—
How they Appeared...................................Page 82

CHAPTER XI.

Westminster Hall.—The Courts: Lords Cottenham, Denman, and
Abinger, Sir Frederick Pollock, and other Members of the
Bench and Bar —In France.—Deputy Isambert and Advocate
Cremieux.—The Great Napoleon's Mausoleum in Preparation
on the Banks of the Seine.—Napoleon, "the Pretender," Seized
while Raising a Rebellion at Boulogne.—Return to England.—
London in a Fog.—William the Conqueror and Battle Abbey.—
Runnymede and Magna Charta.—Bosworth Field and Richard
III — Cromwell's Schoolhouse, Mansion, and Farm.—Judge
Jeffreys and the Bloody Assizes.—William III. and the Battle
of the Boyne.—Old Sarum, the Model Rotten Borough.—The
Chartists and their Creed.—Main Cause of their Failure.... 92

CHAPTER XII.

Some British Poets.—Thomas Campbell.—In the London Convention he Ridicules American Poets. — He is Answered.—
Ebenezer Elliott.—James Montgomery —Lord Byron's Widow.
—His Daughter, Ada Augusta —Thomas Carlyle. — He Calls
Victor Hugo a Humbug, and Criticises Emerson.—In Scotland.
—Rev. Doctors Chalmers and Wardlaw as Pulpit Orators.—The
Manager of the *Edinburgh Review* Presides over an Anti-Slavery
Meeting. — Sydney Smith Preaches a Sermon. — Lord Francis
Jeffrey on Law Reform, the New York Revised Statutes, and
Jeremy Bentham, the Codifier —The Field of Culloden.—
Charles Edward Stuart.—Clarkson's Opinion of the Four Stuarts
and the Four Georges.—In Ireland.—O'Connell on the Repeal
of the Union.—John Randolph Said he was the First Orator in
Europe.—Other Famous Men and Places.—Return to America.
—Admitted to the Boston Bar...   102

CHAPTER XIII.

The Law —Boston Bench and Bar.—Judges Story, Sprague, and
Shaw.—Jeremiah Mason.—Daniel Webster.—Rufus Choate.—
Their Triumphs in the Criminal Cases of Avery, the Knapps,
and Tirrell.—Samuel Hoar.—He is Sent to South Carolina to

A*

Test the Constitutionality of Laws Imprisoning Free Colored Seamen.—Expelled from the State by Force.—Mr. Hoar's Fee as a Referee.—Choate before Juries.—Shaw on the Bench.—Choate's Stimulants, Hot Coffee and Hot Water.—Tirrell's Two Celebrated Trials for Murder and Arson.—Parker, the Prosecuting Attorney.—Somnambulism the Defence.—George Head's Manufactured Testimony, and Rufus Choate's Marvellous Oratory, Twice Save Tirrell's Life.....................Page 110

CHAPTER XIV.

The Law.—Several Novel Cases.—Libel Suit at Taunton.—The Vivid "Dream."—Criminal Prosecution for Libel at New London.—John T. Wait and Lafayette S. Foster for the State.—The Daniels's Case at Boston.—Charles G. Loring and Benjamin R. Curtis Counsel for the Defendant.—Choate for Plaintiffs.—A Patent Suit.—Charles Sumner, Benjamin F. Hallett, and Horace E. Smith Counsel.—Joel Prentiss Bishop, the Law-writer.—John P. Hale as Lawyer and Senator.—Theodore Parker under Indictment.—Hale his Counsel.—Parker on Fish and Phosphorus 122

CHAPTER XV.

The Law.—Bench and Bar of the Empire State.—Kent, Spencer, and other Eminent Jurists.—Four Great Lawyers of Columbia County.—The Power of Elisha Williams over a Jury.—Henry R. Storrs.—Lawyers and Trials at Rochester.—Selleck Boughton.—Jesse Hawley, the Land Surveyor, Foreshadowing the Erie Canal.—Charles M. Lee.—General "Mad" Anthony Wayne's Storming of Stony Point Saves a Counterfeiter from the State Prison.—John Griffin, the Rough Judge of Allegheny County, Sits down on a Dandy Attorney.—Alvan Stewart.—Some Albany Lawyers.—The Famous Firm of Hill, Porter, & Caggar.—Quirk, Gammon, & Snap.—Eseck Cowan's Rare Law Library.—Marcus T. Reynolds.—Samuel Stevens.—Daniel Cady.—Joshua A. Spencer 129

CHAPTER XVI.

The Law.—The Corning and Burden Spike Case.—Seward, Blatchford, and Stevens Counsel.—Reuben H. Walworth, Ref erce.—Jarndyce vs. Jarndyce.—Clients Erect Federal Buildings at Buffalo and Oswego, and Sue the Government.—Speaker Grow, R. E. Fenton, and William Steele Holman Intervene.—Captain Cornelius Vanderbilt and the Fist Fight.—His Son, Cornelius Jeremiah, is Sued, and Blows his Brains out.—The Controversy over the Commodore's Will.—The Spencers.—John C. Spencer.—His Acute Legal Mind.—Interview with his Son, who was Executed for Alleged Mutiny on Board *The Somers*.—Chief-justice Ambrose Spencer.—John C. Spencer Concocts the Canal Bill of 1851........................Page 141

CHAPTER XVII.

Dr. Samuel B. Woodward and Senator Albert H. Tracy.—Close Resemblance to Washington and Jefferson.—Webster and the Conscience Whigs in Faneuil Hall in 1846.—Crittenden on Clay and Webster.—Clay before the Supreme Court.—Mrs. James Madison.—John Sargeant.—Chief-justice Taney.—Clay in the Senate.—A Galaxy of Talents.—"Biddle and the Bank."—The Sub-Treasury Question.—Clay's Speech in New York.—His Personal Magnetism.—His Funeral Pageant.—A Cluster of Political Rivals.—George P. Barker.—Sanford E. Church.—Church in the New York Assembly in 1842.—Hoffman, Dix, Seymour, and other Members.—Church makes Barker Attorney-General.—Anecdote of Church and James W. Nye at the Buffalo Convention in 1848............................ 148

CHAPTER XVIII.

Democratic National Convention of 1844.—Van Buren, Polk, and Cass.—Polk Nominated for President.—Wright Nominated for Vice-President.—He Declines.—First Use of the Morse Telegraph.—Polk's Duplicity in Forming his Cabinet.—Marcy, Secretary of War.—The Barnburners Angry.—Death of John Quincy Adams.—The Barnburner Revolt of 1847-48.—"The Assassins of Silas Wright."—List of Barnburners and Hunkers.—Utica Convention of 1848.—Young, Cambreling, and Tilden Present.—Cass and Taylor Rival Candidates for President.—Convention at Buffalo in 1848.—B. F. Butler's Speech.—"D—n his Turnips!"—Van Buren Nominated for President, and Charles Francis Adams for Vice-President.—The Barnburner Revolt

Defeats Cass and Elects Taylor.—Reunion of the New York Democracy in 1849.—The Election and its Results....Page 157

CHAPTER XIX.

The Author Elected to the New York Senate in 1849.—The Canal Bill.—Twelve Senators Resign to Defeat it.—Re-elected in 1851.—The Bill Passes.—The Court of Appeals Pronounce it Unconstitutional.—The Author's Seat Contested.—Dinner at the Astor House.— Speech of Seward and another.— Thurlow Weed.—The Midnight Call.—The Contest Squelched.—Weed's Hand in it.— Members and Measures in the Senate.— Hamilton Fish Elected United States Senator.—James W. Beekman Bolts Fish.—Notices of Hoffman, Loomis, Seymour, Dix, Van Buren, Marcy, and Dickinson.—John Van Buren and the Apple-woman; his Ill-health; the Water-cure Establishment; his Death at Sea 166

CHAPTER XX.

Whig National Convention of 1852.—Webster's Sad Appearance.—General Scott Nominated for President.—Democratic National Convention of 1852. — Cass, Buchanan, Marcy, Douglas, and Dickinson Aspirants.—An Unexpected Interview by the Virginians.—New York Delegation in Private Conference.—Threats to Throw Seymour out of the Window.—Marcy and Dickinson Slaughter each other. — Pierce Nominated.—Dean Richmond's "Finality."—Pierce's Cabinet.—Dix Cheated, and Marcy Called.—Pierce Approves the Missouri Compromise Repeal.—Rends the Democratic Party Asunder.—Republican Party Formed in 1855–56.—Fremont Nominated for President.—James G. Blaine.—Notices of Horace Greeley, Gerrit Smith, John Jacob Astor, John Brown, and Martin Van Buren.—Brown Handles a Rifle, and Hits the Bull's-eye.—Van Buren Predicts the Overthrow of Slavery amid Convulsions.................................. 179

CHAPTER XXI.

William H. Seward as Senator.—Seward on Weed.—Seward Unbending. — Seward and Judge Sackett. — Weed the "State Fifer."—Seward and Conkling.—Conkling Elected to Congress in 1858.—Seward on Greeley.—John Sherman, Candidate for Speaker.—Tom Corwin as an Orator.—The Jewish Rabbi Prays.

—Henry Winter Davis.—Pennington Chosen Speaker.—Slidell's Bill to Purchase Cuba.—Wade and Toombs in Close Contact.—"Land for the Landless *versus* Niggers for the Niggerless."—Scene in the Senate in 1859 between Benjamin and Seward.—Seward Smokes Benjamin's Cigar.—Scene in the Senate in 1834 between Clay and Van Buren.—Van Buren Takes a Pinch of Clay's Snuff..Page 193

CHAPTER XXII.

Turbulent Scenes in the House in 1859, 1860.—Grow Knocks Keitt Down.—Crawford Threatens Thad. Stevens.—Tribute to Stevens.—Stephen A. Douglas; his Re-election to the Senate over Abraham Lincoln in 1859.—His Reception in the Senate.—Pro-Slavery Democrats Assail him.—Seward Preparing for the Chicago Convention of 1860.—Deluded as to his Strength.—The Senators Opposed to him.—Corwin and Lincoln Speak in New England Early in 1860.—New-Yorkers who Oppose Seward at Chicago.—Lincoln Nominated.—Scene at Auburn when the News Came.—Seward Embittered.—Crushed Presidential Aspirations of Seward, Greeley, Clay, and Webster.—Ira Harris Chosen Senator in 1861.—Defeat of Greeley and Evarts.—Rufus King's Chair in the Senate.—Its Distinguished Occupants.. 207

CHAPTER XXIII.

Lincoln's Cabinet.—Chase Pushed in.—David Davis, Confidential Adviser of Lincoln.—Mrs. Lincoln "Sub-President."—Notices of Seward, Chase, Cameron, Bates, Blair, and Welles.—Bickerings in the Cabinet.—Chase and Seward Grapple.—Bray Dickinson and Marcus Curtius.—Down in Dixie in April, 1861. —Narrow Escape from Secessionists.—General Butler and his Troops.—Colonel Jones and his Regiment Going through Baltimore.—First Blood of the War.—Notice of Edwin M. Stanton, the War Secretary... 220

CHAPTER XXIV.

Mr. Lincoln and Dr. McPheeters.—Lincoln's Story.—Roscoe Conkling and Noah Davis Candidates for the Senate in 1867.—Conkling Elected.—Defeat of Morgan by Fenton for the Senate in 1869.—Escape of Marshall O. Roberts from the Lobby.—Democratic National Convention of 1868.—Seymour Favors

Chase.—Vallandigham's Course.—Seymour Nominated.—Grant Elected.—Seymour Urged to Accept the Senatorship in 1875; Refuses; Why.—Seward's Trip around the World.—Death of Seward in 1872.—R. B. Hayes Running for Governor of Ohio in 1875.—Senator Thurman's Singular Prediction.—Conkling and Platt Resign from the Senate, and Lapham and Miller Succeed them in 1881.—Conkling's Success at the Bar.......... Page 234

CHAPTER XXV.

Samuel J. Tilden; his Triumph over the Canal Ring and the Tweed Ring; his Sudden Death; his Note to the Author about "Random Recollections."—State Convention of 1874, when he was Nominated for Governor.—*The* (N. Y.) *Sun's* Editorial Article.—Tilden Elected.—The Presidential Contest of 1876.—Tilden Dies of Heart Disease.—Ex-Governors Clinton, Wright, Marcy, and Fenton Fall by the same Malady under Peculiar Circumstances.—Notice of Robert L. Stanton, D.D.; his Death in Mid-Ocean in May, 1885.—The Presbyterian General Assembly's Tribute to his Memory............................. 244

CHAPTER XXVI.

American Journalism.—Its Rank as a Profession.—Earliest Newspapers.—First Daily Paper.—*Philadelphia Advertiser.*—*Boston Centinel.*—*National Gazette.*—Controversy of Washington and Jefferson over Freneau.—Early Dailies in New York City.—Three Famous Editors.—Bitter Tone of the Press.—List of Distinguished Contributors.—Duels.—Early Journalism in New England.—Rude Methods of Collecting News and Circulating Papers.—Post-riders and Reporters.—The Deacon and the Mohawks.—Dailies in New York, Albany, and Rochester in 1826.—The *Rochester Advertiser* the First Daily Issued West of the Hudson and Delaware Rivers.—Henry O'Reilly.—*Cincinnati Gazette* and Charles Hammond.—*Louisville Journal* and George D. Prentice.—List of Celebrated Contributors in that Era.—Later Editors.—Charles A. Dana.—Henry J. Raymond.—John G. Whittier.—George William Curtis..................... 252

CHAPTER XXVII.

American Journalism.—Vice-President Wilson and Charles Francis Adams.—James and Erastus Brooks.—The *New York Express.*—

Lewis Tappan and David Hale.—The *Journal of Commerce.*—
Early Modes of Getting News. — William Cullen Bryant and
William H. Leggett.—*New York Evening Post.*—Courage of *The
Post.*—President Van Buren.—James Watson Webb.—The *Courier and Enquirer.*—Famous Duels of Cilley, Graves, Webb, and
Marshall.—Greeley's Comments.—Benjamin Day.—*The* (N. Y.)
Sun.—James Gordon Bennett.—The *New York Herald.*—"It
Does Move."—Brave Editors and Journals. — Joseph Tinker
Buckingham and the *Boston Courier.*—Charles King and the
New York American. — Charles Hammond and the *Cincinnati
Gazette.*—James G. Birney.—Gamaliel H. Bailey.—Elijah Parrish Lovejoy.—Cassius M. Clay .... Page 265

CHAPTER XXVIII.

American Journalism.—Religious Newspapers.—Albany Journals
and Editors: *The Argus, Atlas,* and *Evening Journal;* Croswell,
Weed, Cassidy, Van Dyck, Shaw, Dawson, Wilkeson.—Names
of Thirty Persons whose Obituary Notices were Written by the
Author in Various Journals.—Death of Gerrit Smith in December, 1874. — Several State Conventions. — Tweed Exposes his
Persecutors at Rochester in 1871.—Conkling and Fenton Cross
Swords at Syracuse in 1871.—Tilden Nominated for Governor
in 1874, Robinson in 1876, Cornell and John Kelly in 1879.—
Speech-Making and Reporting.—Meeting at Providence in 1856.
—The *New York Times.*—Isaac Hill and the *Concord Patriot.*—
John M. Niles and the *Hartford Times.* — Newspaper Correspondents Writing Speeches for Senators and Congressmen, and
Reports for Committees, and Messages for Governors.—Press
Club Receptions in 1885. — Extract from President Amos J.
Cumming's Speech; he is Elected to Congress in November,
1886.—The Great Newspaper District he Represents....... 278

CHAPTER XXIX.

Conclusion.—Retrospect.—Extract from Thomas Moore's "Oft in
the Stilly Night.".................................. 289

INDEX OF NAMES................................... 291

RANDOM RECOLLECTIONS.

CHAPTER I.

The Author's Birthplace.—Pachaug, Connecticut.—Jewett City.—The Author's Ancestry.—Thomas Stanton, the Indian Interpreter, and William Brewster, the Pilgrim Father.—Indian Tribes in New London County.—Sachems Uncas, Sassacus, and Miantonomoh.—Extermination of the Pequods in 1637.—Benedict Arnold.—Massacre at Groton Heights in 1781.—The Stantons who Fell there.—War of 1812–1815.—Commodores Hardy, Decatur, and Perry.—Bombardment of Stonington.—Perry Describes his Victory on Lake Erie.—"Don't Give up the Ship."—Bitter Politics and Blue-Laws.

I was born on June 27, 1805, on the margin of the River Pachaug, in the part of Preston which, in 1815, became Griswold, county of New London, Connecticut. I dwelt in the little hamlet of Pachaug till 1814, when my father removed to Jewett City, in the same township, a pretty village, situated just where the Pachaug empties its pellucid waters into the more stately Quinnebaug, on whose banks I lived till the spring of 1826. These two beautiful streams flow along together some five miles southwesterly, till the Shetucket, which had already captured the Willimantic, comes pouring down from the north, and gives them its own name, and leads them a rippling dance to Norwich. Here the Yantic, having previously taken in small rivulets in the northwest, tumbles heedlessly over fantastic rocks, and joins the Shetucket. These five rivers and their accessories, after working their way towards the sea by turning the wheels of hundreds of factories, form the Thames in front of Norwich, and it marches off with its Indian tributaries in lordly style. After greeting Fort Griswold and New London, the Thames falls into Long Island Sound just below the Pequod House, and is seen no more.

My father was Joseph Stanton. He was born in Washington County, R. I., on the shores of the Atlantic, whence he went in his early days to Preston, to begin a mercantile career. He had a distinguished ancestry. His father was an officer in the Revolutionary War, under his eldest brother, who was a young lieutenant in the army of General Wolfe that conquered Canada from France in 1759. He was subsequently a colonel in the Revolution, and a senator and representative in Congress from Rhode Island for many years. Another of the ancestral line was an officer in the forces that wrested Louisburg from the French in 1745, their stronghold in North America. From my father this line is traced directly upward to Thomas Stanton, who was born in England in 1615, and came to New England in 1635. He was learned for those days; became famous as a negotiator with the Indians, whose dialects he thoroughly mastered; was appointed by the Commissioners of the United Colonies Indian Interpreter-general for New England; was a judge of the New London County Court, and deputy for ten years to the General Court. He died in 1677.

My mother was Susan Brewster, born in Preston. Her father was Simon Brewster, who died in Griswold, August 16, 1841, aged ninety years, three months, and fifteen days. He was a wealthy farmer and a magistrate. He was one of the defenders of Fort Griswold when it was stormed by Benedict Arnold. The line of the Brewsters goes straight upward from my mother to William Brewster, who was born at Scrooby, England, in 1560; was educated at Cambridge, entered the diplomatic service of Queen Elizabeth, was imprisoned at Boston a long time for non-conformity, and came to America by the way of Holland, in the *Mayflower*, and landed on Plymouth Rock, December 22, 1620. Here he ministered as the ecclesiastical head of the Pilgrim colony till his death, on April 16, 1644, aged eighty-four years. He is a prominent figure in the picture of the embarkation of the Pilgrims, which hangs in the rotunda of the Capitol at Washington.

Thus my paternal line goes back in this country two hundred and fifty years, and my maternal line two hundred and sixty-five years, which, I think, entitles me to call myself a native American.

My parents were married at Pachaug, on January 25, 1803.

My father was an enterprising country merchant, a shipper of goods to and from the West Indies, and a woollen manufacturer. He was a political leader of the Jefferson school, thoroughly versed in military matters, courtly in manners, and of indomitable courage. He died at New York, in 1827. My mother was of the Puritan stock, intelligent, high-spirited, and pious. She died at Rochester, N. Y., in 1853.

In early times three great tribes clustered in New London County, viz., the Pequods, the Mohicans, and a branch of the Narragansetts. In my youth quite a body of Mohicans dwelt near my home, while a liberal sprinkling of Narragansetts and a bare trace of Pequods remained.

In 1637 the Pequods had a palisade fortress at Mystic, six miles from Pachaug. Warlike and cruel, they had long been the scourge of Connecticut, and it was resolved to exterminate them. Their sachem was the bloody Sassacus. The hypocritical Uncas was the chief of the Mohicans. "Uncas Rock" is still a famous landmark, overlooking the Yantic Falls, near Norwich. The chief of the Narragansetts was the generous Miantonomoh, one of the noblest and most unfortunate of his race. He was the nephew of the great Canonicus, the sachem who saved the Plymouth Pilgrims from destruction, and succored Roger Williams when he was banished from Massachusetts.

In May, 1637, Captain John Mason, with ninety white soldiers, seventy Mohicans, under the lead of Uncas, and several hundred Narragansetts, commanded by Miantonomoh, attacked the Pequods at dead of night in their stronghold at Mystic. The battle was desperate. It became a massacre. The assailants set fire to the birch-bark wigwams within the palisades. The swamp was soon a lake of flame, devouring men, squaws, and papooses, while those who attempted to flee were shot or pierced with arrows.

A few escaped, and never rested foot till they reached the Mohawk beyond Albany. A handful received quarter from the gentle Miantonomoh. It was the end of the once powerful Pequods.

And now for the sad fate of Miantonomoh. In 1643 he was attacked by Uncas. Their tribes had a fierce struggle on Sachem's Plain, just west of Norwich. Miantonomoh was defeated. Heartless white commissioners delivered him into the hands of Uncas, who took his victim to the field where the day had gone against him, and, near the "Uncas Rock," he cut from the shoulder of the unflinching Miantonomoh a slice of flesh, broiled it before his eyes, devoured it, and said, "It is the sweetest meat I ever ate." He then despatched the fallen sachem with his own tomahawk. In 1844, two hundred years after this barbarous deed, Connecticut rendered tardy homage to the intrepid Miantonomoh by erecting a monument to his memory at the spot where he met his cruel death.

In the last century a dirge was composed to the memory of Miantonomoh, and set to a plaintive melody. In my childhood we had a negro slave whose voice was attuned to the sweetest cadence. Many a time did she lull me to slumber by singing this touching lament. It sank deep into my breast, and moulded my advancing years. Before I reached manhood I resolved that I would become the champion of the oppressed colored races of my country. I have kept my vow.

Benedict Arnold was born in Norwich, in 1740. In my youth I often passed the house where he first saw the light, and once ventured timidly within. It cowered, among gloomy trees, away from the street, as if ashamed to face the sunshine. Arnold having failed to deliver West Point to the British, they fitted out an expedition, under his command, to Eastern Connecticut, in the fall of 1781. He burned New London, and expressed malignant regrets that he could not lay his native town in ashes. He attacked Fort Griswold, on Groton Heights, and massacred a large portion of the garrison. Colonel William Ledyard, the intrepid commander, the brother of the famous traveller, was thrust through with his own sword after he had surrendered. The wounded were thrown into carts, which, by their own weight, plunged, with their writhing freight, furiously down the rocky declivity towards the Thames. A shapely monument now crowns the Heights. On marble tablets at its base are engraved the names of the one hundred and more who were slain on that bloody day. Among them are four Stantons, my kindred. My Grandfather Brewster participated in this deadly affray, but came out uninjured. I scarcely need add that the people of my county were taught to detest the cowardly caitiff Benedict Arnold.

As New London was rather a fighting county, I will dispose of the war of 1812–1815 before touching on a few topics that occurred earlier. In 1813 Commodore Stephen Decatur, the lion of our navy, undertook to go to sea with his fleet through the eastern end of Long Island Sound. Commodore Hardy, who had been the captain of Nelson's flag-ship at Trafalgar, where the great admiral fell, chased Decatur into

New London with a superior force. Well do I remember the prodigious sensation this caused in the rural towns. Hardy blockaded Decatur's fleet more than a year, ravaging the coast by incursions on shore at safe points, frightening the women with the thunder of his guns, and keeping the militia of the county constantly on the alert. The division of my father was at the front nearly half the time. As became a stanch Madisonian, he was busy drilling the militia for home service and in raising volunteers to go to Canada, and in composing songs adapted to the exigency. I recall scores of these doggerel verses. One gory ballad rang out:

"Brave boys, don't be afraid or skittish,
But go and learn to fight the British."

The aforesaid "boys" were told not to dread the Red Coats, for—

"If you'll boil a lobster in a stew,
He'll look as red and gay as they do."

On a sunny day in September, 1814, I went to Mrs. Ephraim Tucker's, a couple of miles from home, to play. Her husband, a lieutenant in my father's division, was at the seaside. Soon we heard the boom of Hardy's guns floating up from Stonington Point. Mrs. Tucker and I were seated on the doorsteps. An infant lay in her lap. Boom! boom! boom! went the cannon for hours. Tears stole down her ashen cheeks, and she shook like an aspen-leaf. I was nine years old. In my boyish way I tried to comfort her by telling her that my father would see to it that Mr. Tucker was not hurt. The attack at Stonington was a fiasco. Hardy's firing was wild.

In the Fremont campaign of 1856 I went to Norwich to address a mass-meeting. It occurred to me to run out to Pachaug, which I had not visited for a long period. I seated myself on the doorsteps of the Tucker house, now occupied by strangers. My eye rested on the cemetery which crowned the neighboring hill, where lay in dread repose the generation I had known in my youth. I mused deeply on events that had transpired in the forty-two years that had passed since I sat there before. Such thoughts and scenes rarely come to us except in the visions of the night.

At the close of the war I visited relatives of the name of Hazard, at Westerly, R. I., near the old Stanton homestead. Commodore Oliver Hazard Perry, my father's cousin, was born in that county. One day the hero of the battle of Lake Erie suddenly dropped in at the Hazards'. His visit elicited a burst of enthusiasm. His dashing manners and brilliant uniform filled me with visions of naval glory, and I wanted him to take me to sea. He bore a striking resemblance to the portraits and statues of him which I saw in riper years.

I longed to see the ocean, and hear the beating of its great heart. My father, in company with the commodore, took me to Watch Hill, near the mouth of Pawkatuc River. We arrived late in the evening. The sky was clear, the wind was brisk, the full moon was playing on the waves. I did not sleep a wink. All night I sat at the window and gazed at the whitecaps of the billows, or lay on the bed listening to the roar of the breakers.

"Time writes no wrinkles on thine azure brow;
Such as creation's dawn beheld thou rollest now."

Perry described to us the victory on Lake Erie; how Lawrence's dying words, "Don't give up the ship!" streamed from the fore, and how he went in an open boat from one of his disabled ships to another, the cannon-balls of the enemy whizzing around him, and there hoisted again the Lawrence motto, which waved defiantly till the English surrendered.

The politics of this epoch was extremely bitter. I have witnessed three such eras—the Madisonian, in Connecticut; the Anti-masonic, in Western New York; and the persecution of the Abolitionists everywhere; and I hardly know which was the most acrimonious. Leaving the two latter to take their turn, I will say a few words about the first.

In Madisonian days schoolboys pulled hair and grown men drew swords. I took a hand in the first-mentioned pastime, understanding just about as much of the merits of the encounter as the mass of voters do nowadays in Presidential contests. As to deadly weapons, I saw my father, in 1812 or 1813, drive out of his grounds at Pachaug, sword in hand, a whole company of Federalist militia, who had come there to insult him. The lawsuit which followed cost him a round sum. Smaller fights were often ludicrous. The standing menace of one old Federalist, when heavily loaded with cider-brandy, was, "I will not say that every Democrat is a horse-thief, but I do say that every horse-thief is a Democrat." A sturdy Democrat, who had smelt powder at the seaside, taught me to stand on a chair and say, "The Hartford Convention

1*

was hatched in the purlieus of hell!" What purlieus meant, and what the Hartford Convention was, I did not know, and I presume my admiring auditors were in the same predicament. After much delay a new Democratic journal came to town. Its motto was from Shakespeare's Henry VIII., "Be just, and fear not." Shakespeare's name was appended. A warm Madisonian wiped his spectacles. His eyes fell on the motto. He read it through without a pause, "Be just and fear not Shakespeare." Lifting his fist, he exclaimed, "I'll let 'em know I don't fear Shakespeare or any other Federalist." All through Connecticut, in those turbulent years, inflamed partisans rent families, churches, and neighborhoods asunder. Vituperation furnished the staple of political discussion.

The Congregationalists, or "the Standing Order," as they were called, had long been the established Church of Connecticut. In 1818 portions of the Federalists of other denominations united with the Democrats, and defeated the Federal party. The last trace of the Blue Law dynasty soon disappeared. It was one of the bitterest political conflicts I ever saw. An amendment of the constitution finally placed all sects on a basis of political equality.

CHAPTER II.

Puritan "Meeting-house" at Pachaug.—Freezing as a Means of Grace.—Musical Instruments and Timepieces. — The Clergy.—Doctors Hart, Bellamy, Hopkins, and Lorenzo Dow.—The Burroughses.—The Westminster Catechism.—Connecticut Calvinism *vs.* Rhode Island Liberalism.—The Deacon's Horse-race on Sunday.—Schools, Teachers, and Books.—Nathan Daboll, the Arithmetician.—George D. Prentice, Poet, Wrestler, and Founder of the *Louisville Journal.*—Celebration on July 4, 1824, at Jewett City.—Toast to Henry Clay.—La Fayette at Jewett City in 1825.

Our Congregational house of worship stood on a lawn, surrounded by oaks, on the banks of the Pachaug. It was constructed of wood, according to the severest order of Puritan architecture—large, square, with two stories of glaring windows on four sides, the pulpit a perch, the galleries ample, the pews boxes, except the negro-pew, which was a pen near the ceiling. Opposite the front entrance was the whipping-post, near by were the stocks, while on a distant hill grinned the skeleton of a gallows. In my childhood I saw a wretch scourged at the post, a drunkard writhing in the stocks, and a negro executed on the gallows. These exhibitions have sufficed me for a lifetime.

For many years we had no fires in the church in the winter, and we worshipped God and shivered over the Westminster Catechism till the congregation came to the conclusion that freezing was not a means of grace, and two huge stoves were brought in. We had fine singing, but no musical instrument except the chorister's pitchpipe. Ere I left Griswold I saw the gallery desecrated by a bass-viol. We had no clock wherewith to time the sermon, though the minister had an hour-glass in the pulpit. One of the early clergymen of Pachaug used to pray fifty or sixty minutes by the glass, the audience all standing. Now I am on timepieces, I will add that I doubt if, when I was born, there were five gold watches in the county. How changed! In this progressive age every boy claims one as soon as he has learned to swear. Silver Swiss watches were common; the poor resorted to sun-dials, and the affluent had eight-day brass clocks in their parlors, counting the passing hours with owl-like gravity. The pitchpipe reminds me that I recollect seeing only two pianos in my county, though harps and harpsichords were not infrequent, and there was a surfeit of drums, fifes, fiddles, bugles, and trumpets, as befitted a martial people.

There was rare stability in the ecclesiastical affairs of Pachaug. Three Congregational ministers were settled there in unbroken succession from 1720 to 1830, viz., Hezekiah Lord, Levi Hart, and Horatio Waldo. Dr. Hart was the son-in-law of the famous Dr. Joseph Bellamy, the rival of Jonathan Edwards, and he was the friend of the celebrated Dr. Samuel Hopkins, the founder of the Hopkinsian sect. Drs. Bellamy and Hopkins often preached in Pachaug. Dr. Hart died in October, 1808, an event I remember as distinctly as if it had happened yesterday. His venerable form, arrayed in the clerical dress of the Revolution, rises before me as I write this line. This fact is perhaps worthy of notice as showing that octogenarians may recall things that occurred when they were three years old.

A few words about other clerical celebrities. The echo of Whitefield's fame lingered among my native hills. My grandmother told me of the mellow accents of his voice, now soft as a flute, anon swelling like a bugle; of his dramatic gestures and thrilling appeals, which swayed great audiences as if swept by the wings of the tempest, and how he rode at full gallop from town to town to meet engagements, the skirts of his silk gown streaming behind on the wind. I have bent reverently over the sepulchre of the peerless preacher in Newburyport. The Baptists were occasionally represented in our town by their two great lights, the Rev. Silas and Roswell Burroughs, of Stonington, kinsmen of the families of that name who were subsequently conspicuous in the politics of Western New York. The strangest and widest known of all was Lorenzo Dow, a Methodist, who had travelled the world over, and lived near Griswold, where he often preached and drew crowds. He looked like Joe Jefferson, in "Rip Van Winkle." His sermons were sharply anti-Calvinistic, and his illustrations the quaintest imaginable, while his manners overstepped all ordinary bounds. When discoursing he bestrode the pulpit, sat on the stairs, or walked through the aisles. One characteristic anecdote must suffice. It was in the height of the summer solstice. An aged matron occupied a conspicuous seat. She wore a tall cap with a wide border, which rose and fell under the impulse of a broad fan in a style so odd that the boys kept tittering. Mr. Dow endured it for a while, and then, pausing in his sermon and pointing his finger at the venerable lady, exclaimed, "Oh, God, send an arrow of conviction from heaven straight through that old woman's cap into her heart!" The fan was folded, the boys subsided, and the discourse went on.

My native town was only one remove from Rhode Island. We boasted of our supposed superiority in knowledge and virtue over the neighboring commonwealth. If we saw a tramp, or a rickety wagon drawn by a spavined horse, passing through Griswold, we spoke of them as from what we sneeringly called "t'other state," where the people were Baptists and Methodists, and took walks on Sunday instead of whipping their cider-barrels for working on that day. Our few inhabitants who dared to use a stronger term than "darnation" would talk of "banishing a bad man off the face of the earth into the State of Rhode Island." We were taught to look with shivering dread at the boys whose parents came from that state to work in our factories, because of their ignorance of the Westminster Catechism. One of them was lured into the Pachaug school. The master was examining the pupils in the Catechism. Following the text, he asked the heathen from "t'other state" if there were more gods than one. The barbarian petrified us with the flippant answer, "I don't know how many you've got up here in Connecticut; we ha'int got none down in Rhode Island."

The liberals of the land of Roger Williams would

sometimes play pranks on the Puritans along the Pachaug and Quinnebaug rivers. Our Sabbatarian laws were extremely strict. The deacons, tithing-men, and other officials in Church and State, could arrest any person found riding on Sunday, unless he were going to "meeting" or for a physician. A dashing Rhode-Islander, who owned a spirited gelding, had a manufacturing job in Jewett City. The road to his Rhode Island home ran past the Pachaug church. One Sunday he started from Jewett City for his paternal abode on his gay horse. Ere he reached Pachaug one of the deacons mounted his mare and pursued him, crying, "Stop! stop!" They came tearing at full gallop in among the oak-trees which surrounded the church just as the congregation was gathering on the broad green sward. The deacon chased the Rhode-Islander round and round the venerable edifice, each lashing his steed with a rawhide, the deacon shouting, "Stop your horse! you are breaking the Sabbath!" the Rhode-Islander responding, "I have told you a dozen times that I will not trade horses with you on a Sunday, and you ought to be ashamed to keep on violating the Sabbath by proposing it." The crowd on the green viewed the spectacle with amazement. The deacon's mare was all of a foam, and he abandoned the pursuit. He was fond of horses, and something of a jockey, and many of the congregation long believed that on that Sunday he was urging a horse-trade with the Rhode-Islander.

I have spoken of the oaks that surrounded the Pachaug church. I was aware that the large things of youth look small in riper years. I had seen many large oaks in this country and Europe, when, in 1868, being near Pachaug, I thought I would run over and measure those oaks, which I had not seen in a long while, but had never been able to get wholly out of my head. Alas! the biggest had sunk under the weight of age, and the next biggest had succumbed to an autumn gale. I measured the two largest that remained. The trunk of the smallest of these averaged sixteen feet in circumference, and from tip to tip of its longest limbs it measured through the body one hundred and ten feet. The trunk of the largest averaged eighteen and a half feet in circumference, and from tip to tip of its longest limbs it measured through the body one hundred and twenty feet. These were not "the babes of the woods." Nobody knew anything of the age of these patriarchs.

Well do I remember the little red schoolhouse in which I learned the A B C's. The sun glared upon it in summer, and the snow blockaded it in winter. The great fireplace blazed with hickory logs from November to April. Consequently, the youngsters who sat on the low, hard benches near the hearth were roasted, while the big boys and girls, who occupied the back benches, near the rattling windows, shivered with cold. Our ordinary text-books were "Webster's Spelling-book," "Daboll's Arithmetic," "Murray's Grammar," "Morse's Geography," "Flint's Surveying," "Tytler's History," "Belknap's Biographies," the "American Preceptor," and the never-to-be-forgotten "Westminster Catechism." We had no maps, atlases, blackboards, or any of the modern aids and appliances for the acquisition of knowledge. We lost less by this than many imagine. Learning is like gold. Those who get it the hardest generally keep it, while from those to whom it comes without the asking it is liable to slip away. The most of what I obtained in the red schoolhouse at Pachaug and the rickety building at Jewett City in youthful days stays with me yet. Aside from school-books, Bibles, psalm-books, and the professional books of the clergy, the physicians, and our one lawyer, I presume all the volumes in this rather wealthy town did not exceed one hundred and fifty. I went through the whole of them more than once.

Nathan Daboll, the arithmetician, was a native of our county. Of course, we thought he was the greatest mathematician in the world. One day we heard he was about to pass the red schoolhouse. We were marshalled out to greet him, the pupils all in a row, and the master at the head of the line. Mr. Daboll approached on a venerable gray horse, his white beard touching the pommel of the saddle. We gave him a low bow; he lifted his aged hat, smiled benignly, and rode on. He had taught school in Griswold.

One of my teachers was George D. Prentice, the poet, who was born within a stone's-throw of me. He is better known as the witty editor of the *Louisville Journal*, now the *Courier-Journal*, managed by Henry Watterson. Many were the literary favors I received from Prentice. He was a graduate of Brown, an admirable instructor, a ripe scholar, had a wonderful memory, and was a skilful wrestler I have seen him, on a wager, read two large pages in a strange book twice through, and then repeat them without a miss. The champion wrestler of the county met Prentice casually in the bar-room of the Jewett City hotel. The champion was a stalwart fellow, tall, athletic, and weighed fifty per cent. more than Prentice. The floor was hard, and the ceiling was high. They clinched. The struggle was desperate. The champion went under rather lightly. He insisted upon another hold. No sooner were they ready than Prentice threw the champion clear over his shoulders, bringing him to the floor with a thud that made the house jar, and beating all the breath out of his body.

Prentice studied law at Griswold. He wore a pistol, but had no use for it there. When he went to Louisville, and took up the editorial pen, the pistol came into play.

When I dwelt at Cincinnati, in 1832-1835, the great daily of the Southwest was the *Journal*, founded in 1830, by Prentice, and conducted by him till his death, in 1870. It was the leading Whig organ in the Western States during the existence of that party. As an editor he was full of wit and fire, and his paragraphs exploded like nitro-glycerine, he fighting out his quarrels with pen or pistol, as the case required. Long ago I wrote a little for Prentice's *Journal*. The last time I saw Prentice was in 1859, at New York, where he had come to publish a volume of his witty sayings. I noticed his arrival at the Astor. Though we had not met for a third of a century, he instantly recognized me when I called him by name. Years only added to the zest with which we talked of the events of youth.

In passing through Jewett City, the industrious

Pachaug River propelled the wheels of a dozen mills. Among them was a woollen factory, erected, at the opening of the century, by a Mr. Schofield, an Englishman, who brought his machinery from beyond the Atlantic. It was said that threats were made to kill him, in order to crush this then scarcely-born species of industry. England has since learned to accomplish the same end by prostrating the protective tariffs of her rivals. My father was, ultimately, the partner of Schofield. At the same time he manufactured machinery and owned three country stores. The years I spent in these stores and factories gave me a close acquaintance with merchandise and machinery. The latter served me an excellent purpose in later times, when I became a patent-lawyer, and tried patent-suits in the courts.

We always celebrated the Fourth of July in Jewett City. We had our dinner, read the Declaration of Inpendence, drank our lemon-punch, gave the thirteen regular toasts, and then called for volunteers; that is to say, the full-grown men did this. I was brought up to admire Henry Clay. In 1824 Clay, Crawford, Adams, and Jackson were running for the presidency. The Fourth of July brought its celebration. Captain Charles Fanning, my great-uncle, who had fought through the Revolution, was to preside at the dinner. Clad in the garb of the previous century, and crowned with a flowing wig, Captain Fanning sat at the head of the table, gave the regular toasts, and asked for volunteers. I sprang to my feet, delivered a speech about an inch long, and gave, " Henry Clay: the eloquent champion of domestic manufactures and internal improvements." My prim old uncle stared at me with amazement. The Clay men clinked their glasses, pounded the table, and I sat down covered with confusion and applause. This was the first of the sixteen Presidential campaigns in which I have delivered speeches; sometimes not a few.

In 1825 General La Fayette, in his last visit to this country, passed through Jewett City on his way from New York to Boston. We had short notice of his coming. The whole village turned out to greet him. Captain Fanning, who had fought under him at Monmouth, and had taken a hasty breakfast with him just as the battle was commencing, did the honors of the present occasion. La Fayette and Fanning had not met in nearly forty-five years, and the latter was wondering if the marquis would recognize him. The coach drove up. It was late in the evening. The marquis alighted, with his son and other companions, and entered the hotel. Captain Fanning stood in the parlor without moving. La Fayette gazed intently at him for a moment, then walked straight up to him, and, throwing his arms around him, French fashion, exclaimed, "Captain Fanning! God bless you, my old comrade!"

CHAPTER III.

Journey to Rochester in April, 1826.—New York City had 150,000 Souls.—Tammany Hall.—The Bucktails.—The City Hall.—Albany's Population, 15,000.—The Old Capitol.—Legislative Leaders: Young, Root, Frank Granger, Colden, Livingston, Silas Wright, Tallmadge.—Governor De Witt Clinton, the Magnificent.—The Erie Canal just Completed.—Utica.—Syracuse.—Rochester in 1826.—Anti-Masonic Excitement.—Thurlow Weed's Dingy Newspaper, Shabby Dress, and Empty Pocket.—Henry O'Reilly Issues at Rochester, in 1826, the First Daily Journal West of the Hudson and Delaware Rivers.—Edmund Kean, the Tragedian, Performs in the "Iron Chest" at Rochester.—Sam Patch Twice Leaps the Genesee Falls and is Drowned.—Gerrit Smith and Fanny Wright Speak at Rochester.—Samuel Wilkeson Constructs the Harbor at Buffalo.

EARLY in April, 1826, I started for the "Far West," even to the Genesee country, which seemed then farther off than Alaska does now. My route was by Long Island Sound, the Hudson River, and Erie Canal, which had been completed the October previous. I arrived at New York in the morning. It then contained a population of one hundred and fifty thousand. I rushed into Broadway. All the world seemed to be there. I stared at the tall houses, and everybody I didn't run into ran into me. I was specially attracted by the omnibuses, as I have seen to be the case with other immigrants in later years. They were bound for such far-off villages as Greenwich and Chelsea, which, I subsequently learned, were located, one near the foot of Tenth Street, and the other at Eighteenth Street, on the west side. My father had taken Major Mordecai M. Noah's newspaper, and I knew about Tammany Hall and the Bucktails. I sought the famous building. I stood before it. I remembered the couplet:

> "There's a barrel of porter in Tammany Hall,
> And the Bucktails are swigging it all the day long."

I confronted the City Hall. To my youthful eye it seemed an architectural marvel. Well, to this day it is one of the most unique specimens of its order in the country.

I reached Albany in the forenoon. Its population was fifteen thousand. I repaired to the Capitol. It filled me with wonder. I thought it equal to the edifice which crowned Capitoline Hill in ancient Rome. I was bewildered when I learned that it cost $110,000. The Tweed style of doing this sort of a thing had not then been discovered. There it stood—its massive walls; its fluted columns; its towering dome, surmounted by the statue of Justice bearing aloft the scales. I entered the Assembly Chamber, and listened to an angry debate between Samuel Young, Erastus Root, and Francis Granger, then among the renowned politicians of New York. Granger was the attraction of the ladies' gallery. Dressed in a bottle-green coat with gilt buttons and brilliant appurtenances, he was a model of grace and beauty. I went into the Senate Chamber, and heard a discussion about the canals by Cadwallader D. Colden, Peter R. Livingston, and Silas Wright. Lieutenant-governor

James Tallmadge, who had won distinction in Congress in the Missouri controversy, filled the chair. These things and these men looked large to me then. Years afterwards, when a member of the same body, and standing behind the scenes, they dwindled in magnitude.

I saw the governor in the Executive Chamber. De Witt Clinton was one of the most magnificent men that ever stood on the soil of New York. He was then in the height of his grandeur and glory. The Erie Canal, his greatest achievement, had been finished the previous fall, and he had come from Buffalo to Albany, and thence to New York, in the canal-boat *Seneca Chief*, through an unbroken succession of cheers and the booming of cannon. Amid many imposing ceremonies, a barrel of water brought from Buffalo to New York was emptied into its harbor, and then another barrel was carried from New York to Buffalo, and poured into its harbor, and thus was Lake Erie wedded to the Atlantic Ocean. Mr. Clinton then ranked among the foremost statesmen in the nation.

The canal not being wholly free of ice, I went by stage-coach to Utica. The tributaries of the Mohawk River not having been then denuded of their protecting forests, its banks were full. On arriving at Utica I could say with Tom Moore,

"From rise of morn to set of sun,
I've seen the mighty Mohawk run."

Utica was a gem of a city, with four thousand five hundred souls. There I took the packet-boat for

Rochester. We passed through Syracuse in a drizzling rain. It contained about two thousand five hundred people, and was just scrambling out of its salt-pits, covered with mud and slime. By-the-by, I supposed that the Erie Canal was a pellucid stream like my own Pachaug. I found it the muddiest ditch I ever saw. We shot into Rochester through the aqueduct across the Genesee as the sun was peeping over the shoulders of the hills in Brighton. The aqueduct seemed to me equal to those famous structures which supplied old Rome with water.

In April, 1826, Rochester was a little town of three thousand five hundred inhabitants, clinging to both banks of the Genesee River. In the centre of the village roared the Falls, one hundred feet high. It already showed premonitory symptoms of its coming beauty and greatness. It was growing with marvellous rapidity. Stumps of trees were standing in its principal streets, and the woodman's axe was hewing down the forest to make room for other streets.

In September, 1826, William Morgan was abducted from Canandaigua, carried through Rochester, and incarcerated in Fort Niagara, which had been abandoned by the government. Then broke out the Anti-masonic excitement, which convulsed Western New York for many years. These bitter controversies tore society all in pieces. Their history has been written again and again, and I shall not repeat a line of it, although I was a witness of the whole of it. The statement of Thurlow Weed, published since his death, in regard to the fate of Morgan, is, no doubt, substantially true. I knew all the principal characters mentioned in that statement. I have seen many sharp political and social contests in my day, but, viewed in some aspects, I think the Anti-masonic feuds excelled them all.

When I came to Rochester, in April, 1826, Mr. Weed was the editor of a dingy weekly Clintonian newspaper, called the *Monroe Telegraph*. He had been a member of the Assembly the year before. He was one of the poorest and worst-dressed men in Rochester. He dwelt in a cheap house, in an obscure part of the village. In the western counties of the state, however, he was then as great a power in politics, perhaps, as at any subsequent period of his life. He was often sent by his associates on missions of grave importance into various states. He sometimes had to borrow clothes to give him an appearance befitting his talents. I was standing one day in the street with Mr. Weed and Frederick Whittlesey, who was afterwards Vice chancellor and Judge of the Old Supreme Court, when up came Weed's little son, and said, "Father, mother wants a shilling to buy some bread." Weed put on a queer look, felt in his pockets, and remarked, "That is a home appeal, but I'll be hanged if I've got the shilling." Whittlesey drew out a silver dollar, gave it to the boy, and said, "Take that home to your mother." He seized the glittering prize, and ran off like a deer. I don't mention these things to the discredit of Mr. Weed, but to his honor. It was rare that a man who was so poor should be so great. Spattered with ink, and with bare arms, he pulled at the old hand-press of the *Telegraph*, and at a rickety table that would have been dear at fifty cents he wrote those sparkling paragraphs which, in later years, made the *Albany Evening Journal* famous.

In the fall of 1826 Luther Tucker & Co. established in Rochester the earliest daily journal issued between the Hudson and Delaware rivers and the Pacific Ocean. It was entitled the *Rochester Daily Advertiser*, and was edited in a spirited manner by Henry O'Reilly. It continues to the present day as the *Advertiser and Union*. Soon after it was started the *Advertiser* became a Democratic exponent, and for many months a good share of Weed's and O'Reilly's time seemed to be devoted to firing red-hot shot at each other. Having been inducted into the mystery of newspaper scribbling about two years before by my townsman, George D. Prentice, I took a hand occasionally in those pen-and-ink contests.

We had a little theatre at Rochester, managed by an Englishman named Williams, who had played subordinate parts to Edmund Kean in London. Kean stopped at Rochester, with one or two companions, on his way to Niagara Falls for rest. Williams was always in debt, and generally in the hands of the sheriff. He saw Kean at the hotel, and implored him to play one night and help him out of difficulty. Please remember this was the original Kean, the real Kean, the great Kean; not the feeble imitation which appeared in his son, Charles Kean. The peerless actor yielded to the importunities of Williams. Ample time for preparation was given; the price of seats was put far above the current rates in New York; the play was "The Iron Chest," Kean, of course, taking the part of Sir Edward Mortimer. The *élite* of

Monroe and one or two adjoining counties crowded the house in every part. The affair was a grand success. At the close of the performance we got a speech out of Kean, and Williams got out of the hands of the sheriff.

Sam Patch, the famous jumper and diver, came to Rochester in November, 1829, and proposed to leap from the Falls in the heart of the village. On the day fixed Sam appeared. The banks of the river, as far as the eye could reach, were lined with spectators. He was dressed in a suit of white, and I will state, for the benefit of other fools of the same class, that, before he leaped, he placed his hands firmly on his loins, then sprang from the shelving rock, and went down straight as an arrow. He came up feet foremost, and swam ashore amid the shouts of thousands. A few days later he proposed to leap again. He erected a scaffold twenty-five feet high on the brink of the Falls, making the descent one hundred and twenty-five feet. On the day named another immense throng assembled. Mr. Thurlow Weed and I happened to meet at the foot of the scaffold. Patch came, dressed as before, and apparently under the influence of liquor. As he ascended the scaffold Weed left, but I remained. He made a ridiculous speech, and then jumped. As he went down his arms were all in a whirl, and he struck the water with a stunning splash. The crowd waited for hours. He did not rise. The next spring the mangled remains of the poor wretch were found at the foot of the Falls at Carthage, four miles below Rochester.

Gerrit Smith, at Rochester, in 1827 or 1828, delivered a Colonization address in the Court-house. Then thirty years of age, in glowing health, and with a voice that was pronounced superior in melody to Henry Clay's, he was a noble specimen of manly dignity and beauty. He was master of a theme that attracted the attention of philanthropists and statesmen. It was in that year, I believe, that, in the same building, I heard a speech from a very different orator, on quite a dissimilar subject. This was the famous Fanny Wright, who advocated views concerning woman which were then novel, but have since become familiar. She spoke with grace and ability, but was hardly as beautiful as the engraving in vol. i. of "The History of Woman Suffrage."

When I passed through Albany in 1826 I saw in the Senate Samuel Wilkeson, of Buffalo, one of the most remarkable of the pioneers that built up western New York. Buffalo then contained only four thousand five hundred people, but was rapidly increasing in population, trade, and wealth. Judge Wilkeson, eagle-eyed and lion-hearted, possessed keen sagacity and indomitable enterprise, and, though not versed in the lore of the schools, he had what no amount of learning can supply—an original, creative genius. He was the founder of the commercial prosperity of Buffalo. He constructed its harbor, and thus made it the terminus of the Erie Canal and the outlet of the trade of the upper lakes. The city recognizes its obligations to the man to whom it is so largely indebted for its early growth and present greatness.

CHAPTER IV.

Horatio Seymour when a Cadet; his Father, Henry Seymour. — The "Immortal Seventeen" Senators. — Marcy, Flagg, Bouck in 1826-1827.—Death of De Witt Clinton in 1828; Martin Van Buren and Benjamin F. Butler's Eulogiums on Him; their Drift and Purpose.—Van Buren at Rochester in 1828; His Variegated Dress.—Roscoe Conkling's Style.—Presidential Struggle between Adams and Jackson in 1828. — Van Buren Runs for Governor to Help Jackson, and is Chosen. — Smith Thompson and Solomon Southwick also Candidates.—Jackson Elected President.—Van Buren Appointed Secretary of State.— Young Men's State Convention at Utica in 1828; the First ever Held in the Union; William H. Seward Presides; his Unexpected and Embarrassing Nomination for Congress in 1828; he Declines to Run.

I saw Horatio Seymour when he was quite young. Captain Alden Partridge, who had been professor and superintendent at West Point, established, in 1820, a private military school in Vermont, whence he removed it to Middletown, Conn. One summer he made a tour of the latter state with his cadets. They visited Jewett City, where I was. Horatio Seymour was one of them. They were a bright bevy of blooming boys, carrying little guns, and dressed in gray jackets, white trousers, and jaunty caps, and they manœuvred with the pride and precision of veterans. A Revolutionary officer, in whose house I felt at home, gave them a reception, and I made bold to shake hands with all of them. Many years later, when I met Mr. Seymour in the Assembly at Albany, he spoke of his tour to Jewett City as a cadet. We exchanged smiles over our early acquaintance, though probably neither of us had heard of the existence of the other since the casual handshake on the banks of the Quinnebaug River.

I met Henry Seymour, the father of Horatio, several times at Rochester in 1826 and 1827. He was a canal commissioner from 1819 to 1832, and for six years bore an active share in the construction of the Erie Canal. In 1826 and 1827 I was a clerk in the canal office at Rochester, whose chief was John Bowman, one of the so-called " Immortal Seventeen" Senators (the Clintonians denounced them as the " Infamous Seventeen") that defeated the bill for giving to the people the right of choosing presidential electors. Bowman's office was the rendezvous of famous Democratic politicians. I recall the visits of Comptroller Marcy, Secretary of State Flagg, Senators Mallory and Heman J. Redfield, two of the " Seventeen," and William C. Bouck and Henry Seymour, Canal Commissioners. My young ears were wide open, and I learned something about New York and national politics which I have not yet forgotten. Mr. Seymour had been in the State Senate before he was commissioner. He was the coadjutor — indeed, he was a member of the Albany Regency, that so long bore sway in the Democratic party. It will be readily believed that the unflinching politics of the son, and his devotion to the canal system of New York, were hereditary gifts from the father. In figure and face the late governor, when in his prime, bore a striking resemblance to his sire, but in manners and social intercourse he was far more spirited and entertaining.

In February, 1828, De Witt Clinton died, without a moment's warning, at Albany. The profound impression which his decease produced in New York has never been equalled by any similar event. The contest for the Presidency between John Quincy Adams and Andrew Jackson had just opened. Clinton had declared in favor of Jackson, and was bringing over to his standard as rapidly as possible his great following. The personal party which Clinton had built up was never surpassed in the state. Martin Van Buren, Senator in Congress, head of the Albany Regency, and an opponent of Clinton, was the Jackson leader in New York. It was understood that Jackson's partialities for Clinton were so strong that, in case of his election, he would have made him Secretary of State, and Van Buren would have had to wait. At a meeting of the New York delegation in Congress, held at Washington, in regard to the death of Clinton, Stephen Van Rensselaer, the Albany Patroon, presided, and Van Buren made the memorial speech. He closed with these words: "I, who never envied him anything while living, am now tempted to envy him his grave with its honors."

In the winter of 1828 Benjamin F. Butler, who had been the law partner of Mr. Van Buren, was in the Assembly from Albany. He was one of the revisers of the Statutes, and was sent to the Legislature mainly to look after the passage of the new code, John C. Spencer, another of the revisers, being in the Senate chiefly for the same purpose. The morning after the death of the illustrious governor, Mr. Butler, an ardent Democrat, announced the event to the Assembly in a eulogium on Clinton of rare eloquence. Mr. Van Buren followed this line of encomium in his speech at Washington; and then was commenced the concerted effort to bring Clinton's Jacksonian friends in New York to the support of the Kinderhook magician, as well as to the aid of the Hero of the Hermitage.

Van Buren was in due time nominated for governor for the ensuing election, to help Jackson carry New York. His first mission was to conciliate the friends of Clinton. In the summer of 1828 he made a tour for that purpose. He came to Rochester. The next day was the Sabbath. He attended the First Presbyterian Church, the wealthy and aristocratic church of the town, and occupied the pew of General Gould, one of the elders, who had been a life-long Federalist and supporter of Clinton. All eyes were fixed upon the man who held Jackson's fate in his hands. Mr. Van Buren was rather an exquisite in personal appearance. His complexion was a bright blonde, and he dressed accordingly. On this occasion he wore an elegant snuff-colored broadcloth coat with velvet collar; his cravat was orange with modest lace tips; his vest was of a pearl hue; his trousers were white duck; his silk hose corresponded to the vest; his shoes were morocco; his nicely-fitting gloves were yellow kid; his long-furred beaver hat, with broad brim, was of Quaker color. Roscoe Conkling, his distinguished successor in the Senate, never excelled that.

My idol, Mr. Clay, then Secretary of State, was involved in the struggle between Adams and Jackson, and I was, therefore, for Adams. Early in the spring I made a speech in favor of Adams at Rochester. In the summer I attended a Young Men's Adams State Convention at Utica, whereof William H. Seward was President. Here commenced an acquaintance between us which lasted till the death of that great statesman, in 1872. I delivered several addresses in Monroe County during this campaign, and wrote some articles in Mr. Weed's *Telegraph*, and in November cast my first presidential vote. The Adams nominee for governor, an old Bucktail, and then on the Supreme bench at Washington, was Smith Thompson, after whom Van Buren had named one of his sons. The day went against us in New York, owing to votes thrown away on Solomon Southwick, the Anti-masonic candidate for governor. Van Buren was chosen, and in March he resigned, and took the office of Secretary of State under Jackson.

The Convention at Utica was the first assemblage of the kind in any state of the Union. The fact, doubtless, seems exquisitely absurd to the few delegates that yet live, when they remember that for several years they were pointed out as "the Boys who attended the Young Men's State Convention." Our early celebrity was easily won.

I relate the following anecdote as I recall it when falling from Mr. Seward's lips, soon after the event. He had won distinction by his presidency over the Young Men's State Convention, and there was a general desire in the Adams party for his advancement. A member of Congress was to be chosen in the Cayu-

2*

ga district, but Seward did not aspire to the position. He was then twenty-seven years old. The party in Cayuga relied on his facile pen to draft the addresses of their conventions, which then filled the place of the long strings of resolutions of a later period. The Adams leaders in Auburn had fixed on the nomination of an old and popular citizen, not dreaming that the approaching convention would fail to accept him. Taking it for granted that he would be the candidate, young Seward wrote an address describing the nominee as an aged inhabitant of Cayuga, who had long dwelt in the county, had filled important offices during an honorable career, and was revered for his years, solid attainments, and many virtues. Having prepared the address, Mr. Seward left Auburn for a distant county to try a case in court.

The convention got into a snarl, and, after a long contest, rejected the foreshadowed candidate, and, as a last resort, compromised on Seward. In the dusk of the evening they adopted Seward's address without having read it, and sent the record of their proceedings to the printer of the weekly newspaper, with verbal directions to insert Seward's name in the address. It was put in type, and soon appeared. Judge of Seward's surprise and chagrin when he arrived home to find himself not only nominated for Congress, but presented to the voters of Cayuga as an aged inhabitant, who had long dwelt in the county, and was revered for his years and virtues, and so on, in the glowing phrases of his own address. He emerged from the ridiculous position in which the convention had placed him by peremptorily declining the nomination.

CHAPTER V.

Courts and Counsellors at Rochester in 1827–1830.—Daniel D. Barnard.—Addison Gardiner.—Samuel L. Selden.—Occasional Visitors.—Elisha Williams.—John C. Spencer.—Daniel Cady.—Henry R. Storrs.—Millard Fillmore.—William H. Seward and others.—Thurlow Weed Chosen to the Assembly in 1829.—"A good enough Morgan till after the Election."—Weed Founds the Albany *Evening Journal* in April, 1830.—The State Mends William L. Marcy's "Pantaloons."—The Patch a Campaign Issue when he Ran for Governor.—John W. Taylor, of Saratoga, and the Missouri Compromise.—Marcy and Silas Wright on its Repeal.—The Wilmot Proviso.—Marcy and Wright Compared.—The Rochester Clergy in 1830.—Charles G. Finney, the Famous Evangelist.—His Pulpit Oratory.

In January, 1829, I became Deputy Clerk of Monroe County. The clerk lived many miles out of town, and the responsibilities of the office fell entirely upon me. I officiated as clerk for nearly three years in all the Courts of Record. In witnessing conflicts of lawyers—and some of them were the heads of the profession—I learned a great deal of law, and especially in the matter of evidence. Indeed, I was studying law all these years. Among the leaders of the profession in Monroe were Daniel D. Barnard, Addison Gardiner, and Samuel L. Selden, names that will be instantly recognized by the Bar throughout the state. We had occasional visits from such men as Elisha Williams, John C. Spencer, Daniel Cady, Dudley Marvin, B. Davis Noxen, and Henry R. Storrs; while among the young lawyers who tried causes in our county were Millard Fillmore and William H. Seward. It was under such auspices that I took my first lessons in legal lore.

In 1829 it was resolved to run Thurlow Weed for the Assembly. The campaign was to the last degree acrimonious. Weed's leadership in the Anti-masonic excitement had raised up against him an army of enemies. The famous cry of "A good enough Morgan till after the election" was worked for all it was worth. Weed was a tremendous power at the polls. With one hand full of ballots and the other on the shoulder of a hesitating voter, it was impossible for his prisoner to escape the influence of his magnetic eye. Weed's opponent was a prominent member of the First Presbyterian congregation. It was deemed important that Weed should attend service there on the Sabbath previous to the election. He borrowed some garments, came in on time, wearing a wretched cravat and a shocking bad hat. He abstained from the polls, but could not help taking a seat in a loft which overlooked the principal voting-place of Rochester, and for three days during which the contest lasted he walked the room like a caged lion. I now and then repaired to the room, and, as Weed would look out upon the sidewalk, and see a doubtful voter approaching the polls, he would wring his hands and say, "Oh, what would I give if I could see that man for one moment!" Weed was triumphant, and went to the Assembly, and in April, 1830, he issued the first number of the *Albany Evening Journal*.

Anecdotes of the living paint truer likenesses than

funeral orations. The phrase "A good enough Morgan till after the election" grew out of the charge that Mr. Weed had clipped off with shears the whiskers of the dead Timothy Monro to make him pass for William Morgan, then not known to be dead, who had no whiskers. At Rochester, in the Presidential election of 1828, Mr. Weed, for three days, was waving his magic wand over the ballot-boxes. A rough fellow kept all the while close to his heels, clipping at him with shears three feet long, bearing the words "A good enough Morgan till after the election" engraved on each blade. Mr. Weed endured the insult with becoming equanimity.

Who has not heard of William L. Marcy's charge against the state " For mending my pantaloons, 50 cents"? In 1830 he was sent into western New York while Judge of the Supreme Court, under a special law, to try the Anti-masonic cases, the act providing for the payment of his travelling expenses. When auditing accounts as comptroller he always demanded itemized bills, and as special judge he adhered to this proper rule, and therefore put the fifty cents in with the other items. While running for governor, in 1832, this item literally cut a figure all over the state. At Rochester the Anti-masons erected a pole fifty feet high on the main street, and suspended at its top a huge pair of black trousers, with a white patch on the seat, bearing the figure 50 in red paint, where it flapped through three gusty days. The grand old governor always enjoyed this fifty-cent episode in his political career. So he did the prank of the stage-driver in whose coach he was riding in western New York in the summer after he was chosen governor. The road was horribly muddy and rough. As they were wallowing through a bad slough the driver shouted, "Now, ladies and gentlemen, hold on tight, for this is the very hole where Governor Marcy tore his breeches." The governor paid for the dinners at the next tavern.

Governor Marcy relished jokes on himself. Mr. Weed did not.

In the summer of 1830 I was dining with a friend at the Mansion House in Albany. On the opposite side of the table sat two gentlemen, one of whom I recognized as Silas Wright. The other was John W. Taylor, who had then been eighteen years in Congress, and twice speaker. My friend slightly knew Mr. Taylor, and introduced me to him, and he introduced us to Mr. Wright, the state comptroller. These three gentlemen represented the leading parties of New York, the politics whereof were then in a transition condition. Mr. Taylor followed Clay; Wright was a disciple of Van Buren, and my friend, who had been chosen to the State Senate the previous fall, was an Anti-mason. Mr. Taylor, being the eldest of the company, did most of the talking, and I, being the youngest, did most of the listening. Taylor told interesting anecdotes of public men he had met at Washington, and the genial comptroller contributed a few racy stories. One of Taylor's heroes was a Southern Congressman, who had been conspicuous in the contest over the admission of Missouri to the Union. This emboldened me to say that I had read, as soon as it appeared, Mr. Taylor's famous argument in that memorable controversy. The ex-speaker seemed pleased that so young a man remembered this crowning act in his long and distinguished Congressional career.

One of the ablest men that New York has sent to the Senate was Silas Wright, where he sat twelve years, till chosen governor of the state. His modesty would have kept him in the background among associates many of whom were eminent in the national councils, if his talents for deliberation and debate had not borne him to their front rank. A man's status in the Senate is determined by the calibre and skill of the opponents who are selected to cross weapons with him in the forum. Wright was unostentatious, studious, thoughtful, grave. He was, therefore, liable to be underrated by pushing, flippant, shallow, noisy members. Whenever he delivered an elaborate speech the Whigs set Clay, Webster, Ewing, or some other of their leaders to reply to him.

William L. Marcy was the immediate predecessor of Mr. Wright in the New York comptrollership and the United States Senate. Each possessed rare talents, but they were totally dissimilar in mental traits and political methods. Both were statesmen of scrupulous honesty, who despised jobbery. Marcy was wily, and loved intrigue. Wright was proverbially open and frank. Marcy never trained himself to be a public speaker, and did not shine in the hand-to-hand conflicts of a body that was lustrous with forensic talents. Few, however, have excelled him in the administration of executive offices, as was shown by his twelve years' service as comptroller and governor of New York, and his eight years' management of the War and State departments at Washington.

On the great question that loomed threateningly on the horizon while they were Democratic leaders Wright and Marcy took opposite sides. Wright moved calmly along with the advancing liberal sentiment of the period, and died a firm advocate of the policy of the Wilmot Proviso. On this test-measure Marcy took no step forward. Ten years after the grave had closed over his rival he descended to the tomb a mild apologist for the repeal of the Missouri Compromise.

The clergy of Rochester in 1830 were very able. The minister of the First Presbyterian Church was Dr. Penny; the pastor of the second was Mr. James, son of the Albany millionaire, familiarly called " Billy " James; the pulpit of the third was vacant; the Episcopal clergyman was Mr. Whitehouse, subsequently the distinguished Bishop of Illinois; Dr. Comstock, of the Baptist Church, had served six years in Congress; the Methodist preacher was a brother of Millard Fillmore. In October, 1830, Charles G. Finney, the famous evangelist, came to Rochester to supply the pulpit of the Third Presbyterian Church. I had been absent a few days, and on my return was asked to hear him. It was in the afternoon. A tall, grave-looking man, dressed in an unclerical suit of gray, ascended the pulpit. Light hair covered his forehead; his eyes were of a sparkling blue, and his pose and movement dignified. I listened. It did not sound like preaching, but like a lawyer arguing a case before a court and jury. This was not singular, perhaps, for the speaker had been a lawyer before he became a clergyman. The discourse was a chain of logic, brightened by felicity of illustration and enforced by urgent appeals from a voice of great compass and melody. Mr. Finney was then in the fulness of his powers. He had won distinction elsewhere, but was little known in Rochester. He preached there six months, usually speaking three times on the Sabbath, and three or four times during the week. His style was particularly attractive for lawyers. He illustrated his points frequently and happily by references to legal principles. The first effect was produced among the higher classes. It began with the judges, the lawyers, the physicians, the bankers, and the merchants, and worked its way down to the bottom of society, till nearly everybody had joined one or the other of the churches controlled by the different denominations. I have heard many celebrated pulpit orators in various parts of the world. Taken all in all, I never knew the superior of Charles G. Finney. His sway over an audience was wonderful. Do not infer that there was a trace of rant or fustian in him. You might as well apply these terms to heavy artillery on a field of battle. His sermons were usually an hour long, but on some occasions I have known an audience which packed every part of the house and filled the aisles listen to him without the movement of a foot for two hours and a half. In his loftiest moods, and in the higher passages of a discourse on a theme of transcendent importance, he was the impersonation of majesty and power. While depicting the glories or the terrors of the world to come, he trod the pulpit like a giant. His action was dramatic. He painted in vivid colors. He gave his imagination full play. His voice, wide in scope and mellow in pathos, now rung in tones of warning and expostulation, and anon melted in sympathetic accents of entreaty and encouragement. He was a fine singer, and, when a lawyer, used to lead the choir and play the bass-viol in his town. In singing the Doxology he alone could fill the largest edifices. His gestures were appropriate, forcible, and graceful. As he would stand with his face towards the side gallery, and then involuntarily wheel around, the audience in that part of the house towards which he threw his arm would dodge as if he were hurling something at them. In describing the sliding of a sinner to perdition, he would lift his long finger towards the ceiling and slowly bring it down till it pointed to the area in front of the pulpit, when half his hearers in the rear of the house would rise unconsciously to their feet to see him descend into the pit below. Bear in mind that this was without the slightest approach to rhodomontade or exuberant excitement on the part of the orator. Mr. Finney regarded his success at Rochester as among the greatest of his remarkable career. In theology he was a New-School Presbyterian.

CHAPTER VI.

The Author Goes to Lane Seminary in 1831.—President Lyman Beecher Tried for Heresy at Cincinnati.—Henry Ward Beecher Says his Father is "Plagued Good at Twisting."—New and Old School Theological Magnates.—"In Adam's Fall we Sinned all."—Dr. Beman's Parody.—Dr. Beecher's Eccentricities.—First Anti-slavery Speech.—James G. Birney, and General Birney, his Son.—"Boys, Keep your Eye on that Flag."—First Mob.—Anti-slavery Debate at Lane in 1834.—Its Consequences.—Early Anti-slavery Career.—The Author Addresses the Massachusetts Legislature on Freedom, in 1837.—The Epoch of Mobs.—East Greenwich.—Utica.—Boston.—Newport.—Providence.—Bishop Clark of Rhode Island.—Methodist Church Burned.—Pennsylvania Hall Burned.—Quaker Meeting-house Sacked in Portland.—John Neal, the Poet, Puts the Mob down.—Senator William Pitt Fessenden.—"I am that Person."—Mob in Norwich, Connecticut.—Mobbed in many States.—Never in Vermont.

I DESIRED to supply deficiencies in an imperfect education. After studying the classics a year or more in and around Rochester, during which time one of my instructors was Rev. Ferdinand D. W. Ward, father of the now notorious Ferdinand Ward, of Grant & Ward (the Wards were a distinguished Rochester family), I went in the spring of 1832 to Lane Seminary, near Cincinnati, over which Rev. Dr. Lyman Beecher was to preside. Having to support younger brothers in their educational aspirations, I would fain save a little by going to Cincinnati part way on a raft of lumber. I helped to load a raft at Olean, N. Y., and then aided to guide it down the whirling currents of the Alleghany River to Pittsburgh. There I took a deck passage on a steamboat to Cincinnati. I believe I did my full share of the work of managing an oar on the raft, and preventing it from following the bad example of several other rafts, which lost their heads and scattered their bones along the banks of the turbulent river.

Dr. Beecher was tried for heresy by the Presbytery of Cincinnati for certain utterances of his in New England. The case had reached the synod, which met in Cincinnati in 1834. The testimony was all in. One forenoon Dr. Beecher commenced summing up in his defence. As usual, he was able and ingenious while addressing his distinguished auditory. On the adjournment at noon he took a select party to his house for dinner, among whom were some of his antagonists. As was the doctor's wont in enthusiastic hours, he kept right on making his speech at the dinner-table. He was vivid, elastic, and facetious. He seemed particularly desirous of favorably impressing his moderate opponents. Suddenly there piped up from the lower end of the table a voice which uttered these words: "Father, I listened to your speech in the synod this morning, and I know you are plagued good at twisting, but if you can twist your creed on to the Westminster Confession of Faith, you can twist better than I think you can." The doctor's countenance fell, but only for a moment. He suddenly rallied, and said, "All my boys are smart, and some of them are impudent." Then, of course, rose a laugh. The voice that piped up from the lower end of the table belonged to Henry Ward Beecher. Whether he can twist his creed on to the Confession of Faith it does not become me to decide. The doctor's case went up to the General Assembly, and was yet undecided when the Presbyterian Church was rent in two in 1838.

Doctor Beecher was one of the magnates of the New School, in whose ranks shone Dr. Nathaniel W. Taylor, of New Haven; Albert Barnes, of Philadelphia; Dr. N. S. S. Beman, of Troy; and Charles G. Finney. Mr. Beman was the debater of his faction. The leader of the Old-School side was Dr. Ashbel Green, President of Princeton College. The combatants fought just like the world's people, and kept the Church in turmoil for years. Dr. Beman was often sarcastic. It will be remembered that in the fly-leaf of the old catechism were poetic couplets, arranged under the letters of the alphabet, and set to horrible rhymes. The one under A read:

> "In Adam's fall,
> We sinned all."

Dr. Beman used to repeat this, and then add to it:

> "In Adam's fall,
> We sinned all;
> In Cain's murder
> We sinned furder;
> By Doctor Green,
> Our sin is seen."

I could give many anecdotes illustrating the peculiar characteristics of Dr. Beecher; but I forbear except to tell one, to show his chronic absent-mindedness. He preached in the Third Presbyterian Church, the aristocratic, rich church of Cincinnati. He was always doing some odd thing. One Sunday he came in late; the house was packed; he walked rapidly up the aisle with a roll of blotted manuscript in his hand; ascended the pulpit; opened the Bible; spread his manuscript, took his text, and was about to begin his sermon without any preliminary exercises. One of the elders rose from his pew, and stood. The elder looked at the doctor; the doctor looked at the elder. The elder came out of his pew, the doctor came down the stairs, and they met. The elder whispered a few words in the doctor's ear, the doctor reascended, closed his Bible, and said, "Let us pray." This was a specimen of many such performances. I don't know of any better way of accounting for it than to tell what the doctor said to us at the seminary when giving a lecture on oratory. "Young gentlemen," said he, "don't stand before a looking-glass and make gestures. Pump yourselves brimful of your subject till you can't hold another drop, and then knock out the bung and let nature caper." In the instance of the sermon the doctor had pumped himself full in his library, and when he reached the church was too eager to knock out the bung.

In the summer of 1832, I was passing through the hall of the seminary, and saw on the bulletin-board of my club that the question for debate that evening was this: "If the slaves of the South were to rise in insurrection, would it be the duty of the North to aid in putting it down?" I glanced at the board, and never dreamed there would be more than one side to the question, and that in the negative. When the hot evening came, to my surprise everybody arranged themselves in the affirmative part of the room except myself. As it afterwards came to pass that this was the beginning of my life-work, and lent color to my whole future existence, I shall be pardoned for a few personal details. This was in the midst of the Southampton insurrection in Virginia, when Nat Turner, a deluded negro, had raised an insurrection which made the cheek of the ancient dominion turn pale and its knees smite together in terror. As the only person on my side of the pending debate, I had the privilege of waiting till all my opponents were through before I spoke. I first divested myself of my cravat, then of my coat, then of my vest. As the debate went on, and the perspiration started from me in unwonted streams, I repaired to my room, took off my boots, put on my slippers, and returned to the club. When I arose to speak, I might be regarded as standing in the regular ball costume in Arkansas, viz., a shirt collar and a pair of spurs; but I never spoke with more fervor and satisfaction for three quarters of an hour than on that occasion. This was my first anti-slavery speech. For nearly forty years I "fought it out on that line," till I saw the Thirteenth, Fourteenth, and Fifteenth Amendments incorporated into the Constitution, and Horace Greeley the regular Democratic candidate for president, when I was ready to say with one of old, " Now lettest Thou thy servant depart in peace, . . . for mine eyes have seen thy salvation."

In 1834 I went to Danville, Ky., to obtain a letter from Mr. Birney, giving his reasons for joining the Anti-slavery Society. It was a remarkably able document, and had a large circulation. He had been a slaveholder, belonged to one of the first Kentucky families, and was a profound lawyer. He was corresponding secretary, with Elizur Wright and me, of the American Anti-slavery Society. I will disregard the chronological order of events by adding that, in the London Convention of 1840, he, by his solid and varied attainments, rich fund of information, courtesy, candor, and fine debating powers, inspired confidence in his statements and reflected credit upon his country. He was a wise and patriotic man. The Liberty party honored itself by making him its first candidate for the presidency. His son, David B. Birney, sacrificed a lucrative law-practice in Philadelphia to become a defender of liberty and the constitution on the battle-field. While commanding a corps in front of Richmond, in 1864, he was stricken with fever and took to his couch at home, where he became delirious. One night, his cheeks all ablaze, he suddenly sprang up in the bed and shouted, in tones that made the house ring, "Boys! keep your eye on that flag!" and fell back dead.

I attended the anniversary of the American Anti-slavery Society in New York in 1834, and there encountered the first of my two hundred mobs. We had a great Anti-slavery debate at Lane Seminary, and formed a society during that fall. Pro-slavery trustees required that we should dissolve it. We refused to do so. They then passed arbitrary rules in respect to discussion, and even conversation, on the subject of slavery at the seminary. A goodly portion of us, who were not to be thus throttled, left. It was a heavy blow to the seminary, which hardly regained its feet for the next six years. I was on the committee that issued an address in vindication of our course. It produced a deep impression. In the early spring of 1835 Mr. Birney and myself went east on an Anti-slavery mission. We spoke at Philadelphia and New York. I then held meetings at Providence, R. I., Boston, Mass., and Concord, N. H., intending to return west and pursue my studies. On reaching New York I received a commission as general agent of the American Anti-slavery Society. I immediately entered upon the work which occupied so large a share of my life.

When I entered this field slavery had the State and Church by the throat; and though the Abolitionists advocated peaceful measures for the emancipation of the bondmen, they were everywhere at the mercy of mobs. For the dozen years following the fall of 1834 I was engaged in this conflict. I was several years on the executive committee and secretary of the American Anti-slavery Society, and as such I addressed millions of men and women in every northern state, from Indiana to Maine, and in Kentucky, Maryland, and Delaware, and in England, Scotland, Ireland, and France. I appeared before ten legislative committees in seven states, and addressed the first committee of that kind in the country—that of the Senate and House of Massachusetts, in February, 1837, in support of John Quincy Adams's heroic struggle in Congress. The Hon. S. G. Goodrich—better known as Peter Parley—was a member of that committee. I spoke for two days in the Hall of Representatives in Boston; and at the close joint resolutions were passed by the legislature in favor of the abolition of slavery in the District of Columbia, and John Quincy Adams's course in Congress was approved. Three hundred thousand copies of my speech on that occasion were distributed.

The early Anti-slavery men doubtless made hard hits. But, in the language of Webster in his reply to Hayne, we recognized the fact that there were blows to take as well as blows to give. Indeed, it was my habit to covet questioning while on the platform, and to invite replies when I was through. And what was the usual response—*mobs*. Vice-president Wilson, in the "Rise and Fall of the Slave Power," is my authority for saying that I was mobbed at least two hundred times. I always spoke strongly in favor of the Constitution, the Union, and the Church; and yet, in ten free states, through a series of years, I advocated the claims of the slaves to their liberty at the hazard of my life. I have a right to say this, because, in this turbulent epoch, I was voluntarily pleading for a humble race which, by no possibility, could reward me, or ever hear of my existence.

In 1835 I went into the town of East Greenwich, R. I., and was the guest of Judge Brown, a gentleman of high standing. My Anti-slavery meeting was advertised. A constable arrived at Judge Brown's, and I was served with a warrant warning me out of town as a vagrant without visible means of support, and therefore liable to become a town charge. Judge Brown gave bail for me, and I held the meeting, and invited the constable to hear me. In those days it was the practice to get signatures to the Anti-slavery roll. The first name signed was that of the constable who had served the warrant. I viewed the capture of that constable as a great achievement.

We resorted to odd expedients to get in Anti-slavery speeches. The temperance cause was popular. In 1835, in Rhode Island, I agreed to address an audience an hour and a half on temperance if they would then let me speak an hour and a half on slavery. On the next Sabbath the compact was faithfully fulfilled on both sides, in the presence of a large concourse.

The year 1835 was an epoch of mobs. In the forenoon of October 21, 1835, a large convention met at Utica to form a State Anti-slavery Society. Judge Henry Brewster, of Monroe County, my uncle, presided. Leaders like Lewis Tappan, Alvan Stewart, Beriah Green, and Gerrit Smith were present. A mob, headed by the Utica member of Congress, and afterwards chief-justice of the state, entered the church where the convention was sitting, and dispersed it by violence. To avoid mistakes, I will add that this man's name was Samuel Beardsley. No bodily harm was done to any one in particular, except the tearing of a few garments and the shaking of cowardly canes over the heads of some aged Abolitionists.

In the afternoon of the same day the Boston Female Anti-slavery Society, in which Mary S. Parker and Maria W. Chapman were conspicuous members, held a meeting. William Lloyd Garrison was present. A violent mob, which some of the Boston newspapers called an assemblage of "gentlemen of property and standing," compelled the ladies to abandon the hall wherein their society was sitting. They pursued Mr. Garrison into an adjoining building, where he had retired to avoid these peculiar "gentlemen." They seized him, put a rope around his body, and led him through the streets. Pretty much all that was really accomplished by these "respectable" rioters may be summed up by saying that they thoroughly frightened the women and covered themselves with infamy.

In the evening of the same day I was honored with a little mob while addressing a small meeting at Newport, R. I. The Anti-slavery advocates in that town were "a feeble folk." The mob was of respectable size in comparison with the dimensions of the assembly. It was led by an ex-lieutenant or midshipman of the navy. They stoned the building, smashed the windows, and drove us into the street.

Soon afterwards I met Lewis Tappan. He facetiously said that he had ascertained the distance from Utica to Boston, and thence to Newport, and the precise time when the mobs broke out, so as to see how many miles an hour the devil had to travel to take charge of all three of them.

In 1836 I was outrageously treated while attempting to speak to a meeting in a Methodist church at Providence. The mills of the gods ground slowly, but they did not stop. I addressed an immense Fremont out-door meeting at Providence in 1856. In respect to slavery, I dealt with it far more severely than in 1836. There were plenty of governors on the platform, and Bishop Thomas M. Clark, of that diocese, was at my right hand. A man on the platform, bedecked with orders, was chief marshal. His enthusiasm, in repeatedly calling for cheers, bothered me while speaking. After I had finished I asked who that chief marshal was, and the bishop said, "Don't you remember that, in 1836, when you were delivering an Anti-slavery address in the Methodist church here, a mob came rushing up the aisles, shaking their fists at you and yelling, and finally broke up the meeting? Well, he was the leader of that mob, and now he is making amends."

The respectable individuals who encouraged these crimes against society had no regard for the kind of edifices their vulgar tools assailed. I delivered one evening an address in a beautiful little church in Livingston county, N. Y. I cannot now recall the name of the town where I spoke. The next morning the building was a heap of ashes. Pro-slavery incendiaries had set it on fire during the night.

This calls to mind the burning of Pennsylvania Hall, in Philadelphia, a large, costly structure, erected by the friends of free speech. It was dedicated in May, 1838, with imposing ceremonies, wherein I bore a humble part. The principal oration was by Alvan Stewart. Whittier contributed a noble poem. On May 21 the women were holding an Anti-slavery meeting in the hall, when a brutal mob, which some newspapers called indignant citizens, burned it down. For many years the charred ruins frowned on the city founded by William Penn, and which witnessed the birth of American independence.

In Portland, in 1838, an Anti-slavery convention sat for four days in the old Quaker meeting-house. General Samuel Fessenden, the leading member of the bar of Maine, presided, but not all his influence could deter the mob. The meeting-house was utterly riddled. At length the best men of Portland said, "This won't do." The poet John Neal organized about a hundred special constables, and, leading them himself, put the mob down. Years afterwards, meeting General Fessenden's son, Senator William Pitt Fessenden, in Washington city, I eulogized his father's steady courage in 1838. He asked, "Do you recollect that on one of those evenings a young man took your arm as you walked out of the meeting to go through the outside mob, and said, 'I will accompany you to your lodgings, and share the peril with you'?" I told him I well recollected it, and had often wished I knew who the young gentleman was. "I am that person," said the senator.

To close the subject of mobs, and make room for other matters, I will refer, quite out of the order of time, to one that occurred in my native county when I was practising law at Boston. In 1845, I went to Norwich to deliver an Anti-slavery address in the town-hall. The hall was stoned, and all the windows broken, and we adjourned until evening. In the intermission, three-inch planks were spiked on the inside of the window near which I had to stand, to shield me from the missiles of the mob. In that same town-hall I addressed a crowded meeting in the Fremont canvass—a meeting presided over by William A. Buckingham, subsequently governor and senator—and I was introduced to the audience by Governor Chauncey F. Cleveland. I remembered the mob.

and freed my mind for two hours. A throng came over from Griswold and Preston, and I received enthusiastic plaudits instead of whizzing brickbats.

In remote days it was fashionable for everybody to read the Waverley novels. An English gentleman, who had long been in foreign countries, returned home. Wherever he went, he was pointed out as the man who had not read the Waverley novels. He liked the distinction so well that he resolutely abstained from those fascinating volumes. By a queer sort of analogy, this reminds me of the course of Vermont during the mob period, where I delivered from time to time some Anti-slavery addresses. I was mobbed in every state from Indiana to Maine, except Vermont. I never heard of an Anti-slavery mob within its borders. The land of Stark abstained from that fascinating recreation.

I shall say no more about mobs, though I "assisted" at a few after the one in Norwich.

CHAPTER VII.

John G. Whittier and the Author Visit Gettysburg for Anti-slavery Lecturers.—Whittier's Services to Liberty.—Caleb Cushing a Candidate for Congress in 1840.—Whittier Gets a Letter that Averts Cushing's Defeat.—Origin of the Republican Party.—Peculiar Honors paid to John Quincy Adams in 1837.—Author at Washington in 1838.—Adams and the Right of Petition.—Speaker Polk.—Latimer's Case.—The Reel on Mr. Adams's Desk.—Vice-President Dick Johnson Compared with Van Buren as a Presiding Officer.—The Lions in the Senate in 1838.—Foreshadowing the Methods for Overthrowing Slavery.—The Author's Early Newspaper Productions.—Sylvester Graham, the Dietetic Reformer; his System.

Wishing to enlarge its lecturing corps, the Anti-slavery Society deputed me, in 1836, to go through the country and employ seventy public speakers. I travelled far on this errand, paying special attention to colleges, theological schools, and young lawyers. I visited Gettysburg on my tour. I was at the Lutheran Theological Institution on Seminary Ridge, which loomed high above the village on the west. The view was beautiful. It swept over Cemetery Ridge, Culps Hill, and the Round Top, lying easterly of the town. The intervening fields smiled with fruit trees and waving grain. Little dreamed I then that twenty-seven years later these landmarks would win world-wide celebrity by listening to the roar of one of the bloodiest battles of modern times, waged to defend and destroy the cause I was there to promote.

John G. Whittier accompanied me during a portion of this tour in search of lecturers, cheering me with his genial presence and wise counsel.

I am not so beside myself as to imagine that any encomium from me could add to Whittier's literary fame. But having toiled by his side for several years, and spent many a delightful hour in his cottage at Amesbury, it may become me to record that he rendered valuable aid to the Anti-slavery cause by his brave example, while his pen sent ringing words of encouragement and shed unfading lustre over the field where the battle raged.

After the expiration of a week or two the picked men whom we had selected assembled in New York, and were instructed in the usual Anti-slavery arguments by a series of discourses in which Theodore D. Weld took a prominent part. Thus equipped, they reaped where the harvest was abundant and the laborers few.

In 1838 the Abolitionists began to put test questions to candidates for Congress, and then cast their votes for or against them as their answers were satisfactory or otherwise. Caleb Cushing was one of those who replied unsatisfactorily. We held a convention at Salem, Mass., to take measures to defeat him. I handled him severely in a speech in a church in the evening. I was not then aware that he was a listener in a dark corner of the gallery. Mr. Whittier, a friend of Cushing, visited him early the next morning at his hotel, and told him that he must instantly write another letter to appease the Abolition convention, which was about to adjourn, or he would be ruined at the polls. His night robe was very thin, and the chair was very cold. But the epistle was penned, and the writer was re-elected. Caleb Cushing was a man of extraordinary talents, but an unscrupulous politician. The exposure of his duplicity in regard to Secession finally brought him to grief when he was nominated for Chief-justice of the United States Supreme Court.

The Republican party grew out of this practice of putting questions to candidates. This plan proving to be unsatisfactory, the Liberty party was organized in the spring of 1840, with James G. Birney as its presidential nominee. This ripened into the Freesoil party of 1848, when Martin Van Buren led its attack on the slavery propagandists. This ultimately widened into the Republican party of 1855–56.

John Quincy Adams received extraordinary honors in the year 1837. He encountered unusual abuse in the early weeks of the session of Congress in that year, because of his fearless defence of the right of petition. He was threatened with expulsion from the House, and assassination on its floor. But there came a recoil of the wave. I have already stated that the Massachusetts Legislature, in February, 1837, by the unanimous vote of both Houses, approved his course at Washington.

I participated in a scene at Quincy, in the following summer, which showed the reverential regard felt for him by his constituents. A great throng of gentlemen of both political parties met in the town-hall of the ancient home of the Adamses, to present him with a cane made of the wood of the dismantled frigate *Constitution*, that had won fame in the war of 1812-15, by capturing the British frigates *Guerrière* and *Java*. The sage delivered a characteristic speech on receiving this historic memorial. Near the close of his address his hand and voice quivered with emotion as he illustrated his own position by relating a story of a scarred Russian soldier who was ushered into the presence of the emperor, and received a medal for an extraordinary feat of valor in a recent battle. Suddenly mounting the top step of the rostrum in the hall, Mr. Adams exclaimed, in shrill tones, "The old soldier shook from head to foot as he took the medal, and was only able to stammer out his thanks by saying, 'Though I tremble in the presence of your majesty, I never trembled in the presence of your majesty's enemies.'" The hit was so happy that I thought the cheers would bring the roof down.

I witnessed the crowning honor bestowed upon the veteran in this memorable year. He was then under the ban of the pro-slavery party of the country. Nevertheless, the *élite* of the commercial metropolis invited him to deliver the semi-centennial address commemorating the formation of the Federal Constitution. In September he pronounced an appropriate and instructive oration before a learned and brilliant assembly that filled to repletion the Middle Dutch Church, then the largest audience-room in the City of New York.

The services of Mr. Adams during his seventeen years in Congress eclipsed his previous civil career, long, varied, and lustrous though it had been. He became the ablest and most dreaded debater in a legislative hall that displayed rare oratorical talents. In many close, protracted, and almost savage collisions with trained, bold, and bitter antagonists, like Wise, Rhett, Marshall, and their coadjutors, he showed his superiority in learning, courage, sarcasm, and every element of dialectic skill in one of the famous deliberative bodies of the world.

I went to Washington, in 1838, to look after the imperilled right of petition. Mr. Adams, who was fighting our battle in Congress, received me with marked courtesy, partly, perhaps, because I had defended him so warmly in my speech before the committee of the Massachusetts Legislature. I saw him on a field-day in the House. He coolly presented his pile of Anti-slavery petitions one by one, and scarified the Southern members who interrupted him. Mr. Polk, the speaker, was annoyed, but could not help himself. Indeed, he was evidently afraid of Mr. Adams, the old man eloquent. In youth he had exhibited the wisdom of age; in age he was displaying the vigor of youth.

At a later day I witnessed the spectacle when Mr. Adams presented the petition in the famous Latimer case, the fugitive slave that sought shelter in Boston, and whose beleaguered master was finally persuaded, by stress of circumstances and a few dollars, to abandon the attempt to recover his human chattel. The petition was of such an immense length that, for convenient handling, it was wound on a great reel, which, on the morning of presentation, stood on Mr. Adams's desk in the House. This unique object was the observed of all observers in the hall, which was crowded to repletion, as the old patriot shook its rustling folds in the face of the frowning speaker.

A word about speakers of the House. I have seen nine in the chair. As presiding officers I think Mr. Banks was the best and Mr. Pennington the worst.

While at Washington, in 1838, I spent a few hours in the Senate. The lions were there—Clay, Webster, Calhoun, Wright, and Benton. I had previously heard Mr. Clay on a platform in New York, Mr. Webster before a jury in Boston, and Mr. Wright in the New York Senate. I now listened to a ten-minute speech each from Mr. Benton and Mr. Calhoun, and had to be therewith content. Vice-president Richard M. Johnson was in the chair. He was shabbily dressed, and to the last degree clumsy. What a contrast between him and Martin Van Buren, his urbane, elegant predecessor. Colonel Johnson owed his promotion largely to two acts, neither of which he performed. He was as guiltless of the killing of Tecumseh at the battle of the Thames, in the war of 1812, as was William Tecumseh Sherman, and he did not write a line of the famous Sunday-mail report.

In 1838 I made a speech before the American Antislavery Society, wherein I predicted that slavery would ultimately fall by means of an amendment of the Constitution, and that this would result from the preponderance of free states in the West. My prediction came to pass nearly thirty years afterwards. The speech is on record.

From 1832 onward I wrote much for the Antislavery press, and for such religious and political newspapers as would give us a hearing. My contributions would fill volumes, for which, as a general rule, I received no pay.

In 1839 I contributed a series of articles to the *New York American*, conducted by Charles King, subsequently President of Columbia College. The title of the series was "Glances at Men and Things." The signature was "Rambler." The topics were miscellaneous. Some of the numbers were widely copied. The author was not then known.

Dr. Sylvester Graham was one of the early Anti-slavery men, but will be longest remembered as the most radical dietetic reformer in the country. He began to be generally known in New England and New York about the year 1830, and elicited attention in rather a narrow circle as a writer and lecturer for twenty years. He was well educated, and, though ultra in his opinions on food and regimen, was a logical and eloquent speaker. The salient feature of his system was a rigid adherence to a vegetable diet; or, rather, entire abstinence from meat, fish, and oleaginous substances of whatever kind, butter included. He waged exterminating war not only on intoxicating drinks, but on coffee, tea, pepper, and stimulating condiments of every description. Like all reformers, he overshot the true mark, but we are indebted to him for many improvements in the field he assiduously cultivated. Those that drink chocolate or milk, or only water, at their meals, and eat oatmeal or cracked wheat at breakfast, and prefer bread made of unbolted flour, and cut short their fat meats and crisp pastry, and substitute therefor ripe vegetables and fruits, and believe in fresh air, frequent baths, and long walks, should remember their patron saint, Sylvester Graham.

There was a dash of amusing egotism in Graham. One day he had partaken very freely of cucumbers, green corn, and watermelon (as substitutes for the savory meats on the table) at the house of a friend. The mixture was too much for an internal organism enervated by close application to study in the previous three months. While expounding his dietetic system to the dinner-party with his usual fervor, he was seized with intense pains in the stomach and colon. He threw himself on the carpet, and, while rolling around and writhing in agony, would now and then ejaculate, " Yes, gentlemen! Posterity will do me justice! (Oh, my bowels!) Yes, gentlemen! Posterity will build monuments to my memory! (Oh, these gripes!) Yes, gentlemen, my system will flourish and ultimately spread through the world."

Among Graham's early disciples were William Cullen Bryant, Horace Greeley, and Charles G. Finney.

CHAPTER VIII.

Abolitionists and the Constitution.—Anti-slavery Leaders: Garrison and others in Boston; Tappan and others in New York; Smith and others in Central New York, Lovejoy and others in the Western States.—Celebrated Women: Prudence Crandall; Mrs. Child; The Grimkes; Mrs. Mott; Lucy Stone; Harriet Beecher Stowe; Elizabeth Cady Stanton; Susan B. Anthony.— Leading Colored Men: Frederick Douglass; Robert Purvis.— Eccentricities of Abolitionists.—A Motley Group in Boston.— Father Lampson and his Scythe-snath.—Crazy George Washington Mellen. — Disturbing Religious Meetings. — Stephen S. Foster Imitates George Fox. — Charles C. Burleigh's Vile Garments Torn off and Carried away.—Rev. Dr. Channing Eulogizes Burleigh's Oratory.—Controversy between Garrison and Wendell Phillips.—Lord Timothy Dexter.

THE Abolitionists were compelled not only to study the science of mobs, but also to familiarize themselves with the Federal Constitution. That instrument had no more diligent students than those who conducted the Anti-slavery argument, for, from the outset, they were opposed on constitutional grounds by the great leaders in State and Church. The ignorance of its text and spirit by persons well informed on other subjects was both amazing and amusing. I was riding in a stage-coach, in New England, when slavery became the topic of discussion. My antagonist, opulent in flesh and pomposity, was called Judge, and had been in the Legislature. For ready reference, the Anti-slavery Society had caused to be published a copy of the Constitution so small that it could be put in one's vest-pocket. During the warm debate the Judge purported to quote from the Constitution something that was not in it. I pulled out the small brochure, and, tendering it to him, said, quietly, "Sir, will you turn to the clause you have cited?" Drawing himself up, he replied, with mingled dignity and contempt, "That little primer the Constitution? Why, the Constitution of the United States is as big as a family Bible!"

In and around Boston clustered a constellation of leaders in the Anti-slavery cause whose central figures were William Lloyd Garrison, Francis Jackson, John G. Whittier, Samuel J. May, John Pierpont, Wendell Phillips, and Amos A. Phelps. Its equal in importance appeared in and near New York, whose most conspicuous members were Arthur Tappan, Lewis Tappan, James G. Birney, Elizur Wright, William Jay, Joshua Leavitt, and Theodore D. Weld. These two cities were the fountains whence arose currents that flowed to the remotest parts of the country—in heavy volumes at the East and North, in trickling and fitful streams at the West and South.

For many years an influence in behalf of the slave radiated from the central counties of New York which was felt beyond the borders of the state. It was largely due to four men quite unlike in salient characteristics, though each was remarkable in his sphere. They were acute reasoners, ready writers, and never quailed before mobs. Those who witnessed the majestic eloquence of Gerrit Smith, the quaint humor and pathetic appeals of Alvan Stewart, the luminous logic and merciless sarcasm of Beriah Green, and the instructive disquisitions and pointed periods of William Goodell will regard this as a faint tribute to their abilities and services.

The most rapid glance over this locality could not fail to see Wesley Bailey, long the able editor of the *Liberty Press*, and subsequently elected a State-Prison Inspector. He was the father of E. Prentiss Bailey, now the editor of the *Utica Observer*. In 1838 Rev. Mr. Hawley, a Methodist clergyman, removed from North Carolina to central New York. Having witnessed the evils of slavery, he was of great value to the Emancipation party. He was the father of General Joseph R. Hawley, who served with honor in the war of the rebellion, and is now the editor of the Hartford *Courant* and Senator in Congress from Connecticut.

Turning westwardly, no one beyond the Alleghanies would overlook Elijah Parrish Lovejoy, the Alton martyr; Cassius M. Clay, the brave Kentuckian; Joshua R. Giddings, Salmon P. Chase, and Gamaliel Bailey, subsequently editor of the *National Era*.

Emancipation in this country and Great Britain owes much to women. In 1824 Elizabeth Heyrick issued in England a pamphlet advocating immediate, as contrasted with the prevailing doctrine of gradual, abolition. It struck the keynote of the contest which resulted ten years later in the overthrow of slavery in the British West Indies.

In 1833 Prudence Crandall changed her boarding-school for white girls at Canterbury, Conn., into a school for colored girls. Miss Crandall was a semi-

Quaker, of benevolent disposition, mild manners, and the highest respectability. I took unusual interest in her enterprise (though far away at Lane Seminary), because Canterbury adjoined the town where I was born. Immediately there commenced a persecution of Miss Crandall and her scholars that would have disgraced barbarians in the dark ages. Its ferocity was excelled only by its meanness. The citizens dragged her school-house into a swamp, grossly insulted the preceptress, and pelted the timid pupils with stones and offensive filth. Of course the school was broken up. The leader of Miss Crandall's defenders was the eloquent divine, Samuel J. May, who then preached in Brooklyn, near Canterbury. The leader of her infamous assailants was Andrew T. Judson, afterwards United States District Judge for Connecticut.

Lydia Maria Child had won distinction in literature when, in 1834, she issued her "Appeal in behalf of that class of Americans called Africans." This admirable production, replete with apposite facts, graphic sketches, and pathetic exhortations for justice and mercy to a proscribed race, at once became the text-book of the advocates of the slave.

Early in the struggle Angelina and Sarah Grimke, cultivated women of Southern birth, delivered Anti-slavery addresses in the Eastern States that elicited high encomiums, while the beautiful life of Lucretia Mott, even to its golden sunset, was adorned by her good works for the negro race.

One of the early Anti-slavery orators was Lucy Stone. She is now the principal editor of the *Wom-*

an's Journal, in Boston. Miss Stone was born in West Brookfield, in 1818, was educated at Oberlin College, and ultimately became a lecturer in the Antislavery cause. She was an eloquent speaker, and charmed her audiences. One evening, in western New York, I took a democratic lawyer to hear her. As we were leaving the hall at the close of the meeting my friend turned towards the platform where Miss Stone was still standing and said, in a dazed sort of way: "Little lady, I do not believe in your doctrines, but God made you an orator."

I merely glance at Mrs. Stowe's "Uncle Tom's Cabin." It gave the Anti-slavery cause an impulse that never subsided until the Thirteenth Amendment was engrafted upon the Constitution. One of my cherished memories is the occasional glimpses I caught at Walnut Hills of Harriet Beecher, ere she was the wife of my learned, witty, and rather sarcastic teacher, the Reverend Dr. Calvin E. Stowe.

The celebrity in this country and Europe of two women in another department has thrown somewhat into the shade the distinguished service they rendered to the slave in the four stormy years preceding the war and in the four years while the sanguinary conflict was waged in the field. I refer to Elizabeth Cady Stanton and Susan B. Anthony.

The negro himself was an important element in the struggle for emancipation. The representative man of the race in this country, their most eloquent orator and distinguished leader was, and is, Frederick Douglass. Born in slavery, he was indebted for personal freedom to his own stern purpose, clear eye, fleet foot, and brave heart; and he reached his high position among his fellow-citizens mainly by his own exertions. Looking down the long vista of the past, I recognize the fine presence of Robert Purvis, of Philadelphia, a colored gentleman of rare excellence, who during the third of a century previous to emancipation was the wise champion of his brethren in bondage.

As reformers in all ages, when fighting their battles against desperate odds, have been wont to be indiscriminate in their censures, so was it with the early Abolitionists (especially those of the Boston type). Ultimately the Anti-slavery men were divided into two classes, known as the Boston school and the New York school; the former very radical, the latter rather conservative. In a few years the Bostonian platform broadened till it covered many evils besides slavery; and in the opinion of the New York leaders their brethren of the Trimountain City became somewhat loose in their doctrines and fanatical in their operations. I pass no judgment upon the merits of this feud.

I would not disparage Abolitionists of any type. The ultras of the Bostonian school were charged with fanaticism in the stages of the contest previous to the formation of the Republican party. One of the last of their conventions that I saw was in Boston before the war. There was a representative array on the front seat, near the platform. First was Garrison, his countenance calling to mind the pictures of the prophet Isaiah in a rapt mood; next was the fine Roman head of Wendell Phillips; at his right was

Father Lampson, so called, a crazy loon—his hair and flowing beard as white as the driven snow. Lampson always dressed in pure white, from head to foot, even including the shoes. He was the inventor of a valuable scythe-snath, and invariably carried a snath in his hand. His forte was selling his wares on secular days and disturbing religious meetings on Sundays. Next to Lampson sat Edmund Quincy, high born and wealthy, the son of the famous President Quincy. Next to Quincy was Abigail Folsom, another lunatic, with a shock of unkempt hair reaching down to her waist. At her right was George W. Mellen, clad in the military costume of the Revolution, and fancying himself to be General Washington, because he was named after him. Poor Mellen died in an asylum for the insane. Well, it is no wonder. The terrible strain put upon the human intellect in those old Anti-slavery days turned some light-headed persons' brains. I must add that high over these motley assemblages rose the inspiring strains of the celebrated Hutchinson family.

Parker Pillsbury, an Anti-slavery leader, pungent on the platform and in the press, with a rich vein of humor in his composition, told me that he made a stumping tour in New Hampshire with Stephen S. Foster, and that pretty much all his time was consumed in getting Foster bailed out of jail for interfering in religious meetings in his peculiar style. Foster would sometimes advance up the aisle during the sermon and call the minister a wolf in sheep's clothing, whereupon the deacons would carry him out, Foster emerging from the scuffle minus one or two of his coat-tails. He thought he was a second George Fox.

Charles C. Burleigh, brother of William H., the poet and journalist, was a vehement orator of rare logical gifts. He traversed the country delivering Anti-slavery lectures. He dressed like a tramp. In the Anti-slavery office at New York we once tore a shabby coat off his shoulders, vowing that he should not represent the society in such a vile garb. John G. Whittier took a hand in this performance. At a later day we were to celebrate at Fall River, in the month of August, the anniversary of West India Emancipation. Burleigh was to be one of the speakers, the member of Congress for that district was to preside, and Rev. Dr. William Ellery Channing and a distinguished company from Newport were to attend. Burleigh came the day previous, wearing white duck trousers, that looked as if they had not dropped in at a laundry during the summer, and an out-at-the-elbows coat, and other abominable garments to match. We arranged with a tailor to carry off Burleigh's clothes in the night while he slept, and to leave a new suit in his bedroom. The following day Burleigh appeared in fresh pepper-and-salt habiliments, and delivered a speech that elicited encomiums from Dr. Channing.

During the war and the early stage of reconstruction Mr. Garrison took a more sensible and practical view of the situation than Mr. Phillips did. While a million and a half of armed men were fighting on a hundred battle-fields about slavery, and especially after the adoption of the Thirteenth Constitutional

Amendment, Garrison did not see the utility of keeping up the old American Anti-slavery society. So sharp was the collision between these two leaders on this and cognate points that they did not speak to each other for many months.

While describing eccentric men, mostly of Massachusetts, this may be a suitable place to dispose of Lord Timothy Dexter. About fifty years ago I was riding with Whittier in the westerly suburbs of Newburyport, when we came upon the old mansion once occupied by that eccentric shipping merchant known as Lord Timothy Dexter. Though he had then been dead thirty years, his celebrity, as one of the oddest of Yankees, still lingered in New England. The former lordly dwelling had, I think, degenerated into an inn, but it yet bore the Dexter impress. A wide piazza ran along the front, whose roof bore up life-size statues of Washington, Franklin, Adams, Hancock, and other revolutionary heroes, arrayed in gaudy and fantastic costumes. In his youth Dexter was very poor; in later years he became quite rich. In my boyhood I heard many queer stories about this strange person, whom some called a dupe and some a devil. He was about to send a vessel to the West Indies, and was searching for freight. A practical joker advised him to load her with warming-pans. He did, and when the cargo reached the tropics, it sold for an enormous price. The sugar-planters took off the perforated lids of the warming-pans and used them to skim the caldrons where the cane was boiling, and they employed the pans themselves, with their long handles, to ladle out the contents of the caldrons.

This successful venture gave Dexter his first start towards wealth. This peculiar mortal erected a tomb in his garden. A coffin was within the mausoleum. At fixed hours in the day he would lie in the coffin, when a servant would knock at the portal of the tomb and say, "Lord Timothy Dexter! Lord Timothy Dexter! arise and come to judgment!" Dexter would then get out of the coffin, repair to the house, and gravely eat his dinner. He published a sarcastic book, which he entitled, "A Pickle for the Knowing Ones." I have seen it, but do not remember precisely its contents. The peculiar feature of the production was that from end to end there was not a punctuation point of any kind; but in an appendix he printed several pages made up exclusively of points of every sort, telling his readers to sift them into the text of the book to suit themselves. But enough of this eccentric Lord Timothy.

4

CHAPTER IX.

Tour in Europe in 1840.—Current Description of Author's Travels.—The Main Object of the Tour.—World's Anti-slavery Convention in London.—Leading Members.—Distinguished Women.—Haydon's Large Painting of the Convention; his Anecdote of the Iron Duke.—House of Peers.—Scotch Church Debate.—Brougham Speaks.—Melbourne, the Premier.—Lord Lyndhurst, a Boston-born Boy.—Wellington Speaks on an Irish Question.—Earl Grey Enters.—The Reform Bill of 1832.—Grey's Warning to the Peers to Set their Houses in Order.—Sydney Smith and Dame Partington.—Gorgeous Pageant at the Funeral of Earl Durham, Son-in-law of Grey, and the Persecuted Ex-Governor of Canada.

I took ship for Europe on May 12, 1840. I was united in marriage, on May 1, 1840, with Elizabeth Cady, of Johnstown, N. Y., daughter of Daniel Cady, then a leader of the New York Bar. The main object of my trip was to attend a convention in London for the promotion of the Anti-slavery cause throughout the world.

On June 3, 1840, we first approached London from the west, striking the Thames at Reading. To see old Father Thames had been my day-dream in life's morning march, when my bosom was young. And here it dazzled my eyes! As we neared the metropolis, we discovered a lofty object that floated on a sea of fog and smoke. It was the dome of St. Paul's, lifting its gilded cross high above the dark canopy that hovers over London so much of the year.

I shall say little in this book of my travels. While in Europe, I wrote letters to the *New York American*, describing my tour, under the caption of "Foreign Rambles," signed "Rambler." Towards the close a few bore the signature of "Manhattan." They extended from July, 1840, to Feburary, 1841. Portions of them were widely copied. In the winter of 1848-49 I published a long series of numbers in the *National Era*, of Washington, a Free-soil paper, edited by Dr. Gamaliel Bailey, an accomplished scholar, whose press had been thrown years before into the river at Cincinnati. They were entitled, "Sketches of Reforms and Reformers in Great Britain and Ireland." After retrenchments and additions they were issued, in 1849, in a volume of four hundred pages, bearing the same title, in New York and London, by John Wiley. Portions were translated and printed in Paris. At a later date a second edition was issued by Charles Scribner. Every reform that has since been carried through Parliament for Great Britain and Ireland was foreshadowed in those numbers of the *Era* and in that volume.

The Anti-slavery Convention met in London in June, 1840. Thomas Clarkson, the Abolition patriarch, was president. James G. Birney was one of the vice-presidents, and I was honored with a seat among the secretaries. Many nations were represented. I will name a few of the most distinguished who took part in the proceedings, viz.: The Duke of Sussex, uncle to the queen; Lord Brougham; Lord Morpeth, then Chief-secretary for Ireland; Daniel O'Connell; Guizot, the French Minister at the Court of St. James;

Dr. Lushington; Dr. Bowring; Thomas Campbell, the poet; Samuel Gurney, the great Quaker banker; Joseph Sturge; Sir Thomas Fowell Buxton; Sir Eardley Wilmot; Sir C. Buller; the Rt. Hon. C. P. Villiers, Edward Baines, and many other Parliamentary leaders; Rev. John Angell James, Rev. Dr. Cox, Rev. Thomas Binney, Rev. Dr. Wardlaw, and a long list of clergymen of various denominations; and two young men then little known—John Bright and William E. Forster. The cause of Abolition wore gold slippers in England. The Duchess of Sutherland, Mistress of the Robes; the Duchess of Brunswick; Lady Byron, widow of the poet; Elizabeth Fry, Mary Howitt, Amelia Opie, Lady Lovelace, Elizabeth Pease, and several other female celebrities smiled upon the convention. The proceedings were reported in a volume of six hundred pages.

While Thomas Clarkson was delivering the opening address of the Anti-slavery Convention, I noticed at my elbow a gentleman with pale cheeks and keen eyes, wearing a silk capote cut short in the skirts, and a brigand cap that towered high over the cranium, who seemed to be sketching the outlines of the convention. This was Benjamin R. Haydon, the famous painter. Why artists affect this fantastic style of costume when at work, I never could understand. I have seen newspaper reporters who wore the brigand cap, but they were usually too "short" to sport a long silk capote. Haydon executed a large painting of the prominent members of the convention, which now hangs in the National Portrait Gallery. While employed on this picture he told me many anecdotes of Wellington, Grey, Brougham, Russell, and other eminent statesmen who had adorned his historic canvas. I recall this of the Iron Duke. Wellington said he had sat about two hundred times for his portrait since Waterloo, and probably as many for miniatures and busts. He told Haydon he had rather storm a fort than sit to an artist. Haydon had painted him just previous to this interview. One day, during a sitting, the old soldier fell asleep in his chair, and continued so a long time. The artist employed the occasion to bestow some touches of the pencil on the dress of his illustrious subject. Time being precious, however, and wishing to resume the coloring of his features, he cried out in a loud tone, "I hope the light don't hurt your grace's eyes?" Wellington roused up as suddenly as if he had been caught napping on the field of battle, and replied, "Oh, no! I have faced too much fire for that!" and, as the painter expressed it, "the old fellow stared at the light with the eye of an eagle."

Poor Haydon! he had the infirmities of genius. He died by his own hand in 1846.

A debate on the famous Scotch Presbyterian question (then in a critical condition, and which ultimately rent that powerful Church asunder) was to occur in the House of Peers. I went to the House in company with a Birmingham lawyer, and asked the doorkeeper for admission to the gallery. He said it was full. The offer of a silver crown did not reverse his decision. My Birmingham companion counselled a retreat. I took my card and addressed it to Lord Brougham, writing thereon that I was Secretary of the World's Anti-slavery Convention, from New York, and would be happy if he would admit me and a friend to the gallery to hear the pending debate. The lawyer and the doorkeeper were astounded at my audacity. "I think I know my man," was my response. The card was taken in, and in a minute the flunky returned, bowing nearly to the floor. We were ushered into the space allotted to the Commons when summoned to the bar of the Peers. We were the sole occupants. Lordly eyes were turned upon us, and a buzzing bevy of peeresses from behind a curtain craned their necks, wondering probably who on earth we were. Earl Dalhousie, an elder in the Scotch Church, was closing a speech. Brougham arose. For twenty minutes the lawyer, statesman, and orator whose name and fame were the property of mankind rolled off sonorous periods on the subject under debate. He then crossed the chamber in front of where we were sitting, and made a bow, as much as to say, "What do you think of that?" He was, perhaps, the vainest man in England. The premier, Lord Melbourne, delivered the last speech. He was majestic in personal appearance, elegantly dressed, and had the fatherly aspect which fitted him to act as a sort of a guardian to the youthful queen. But what an orator! His speech was clumsy and slipshod in the extreme.

I will recall a few famous figures in the scarlet chamber. The homely Yankee face of Lord Lyndhurst, with a "calculating" shrewdness in his eye, and lips firmly set under an aquiline nose, a heavy brow, and a slouched hat that a Bowery boy would hardly have picked up, was pointed out side by side with the snowy locks, long, narrow head, and crescent-like visage of the illustrious chief of Waterloo. Crouching in his seat Wellington looked short, but when he stood up he seemed tall. The Iron Duke ran much to legs. Ex-chancellor Lyndhurst was a Boston-born lad. When his father, John Copley, was painting in London the famous picture of the death of Chatham, now hanging in the National Gallery, he could not have imagined that his New England boy would rise to be one of the leading lawyers and debaters in the House where the great William Pitt fell. I heard Wellington deliver a short speech one night, if it could be called a speech. Several hours had been spent in discussing an Irish question. The duke rose up. He occupied ten minutes in stating the conclusions he had reached on the thorny subject. He made no gestures, he argued nothing, but stood as straight and stiff as a musket, and talked in a low voice. But everybody in the chamber, peers and spectators, listened carefully to each word uttered by the soldier who overthrew the first Napoleon.

Suddenly all eyes are turned towards a tall, slender man, his brow silvered by age, who is just entering the chamber leaning on the arm of one much younger. As he approaches the ministerial bench several lords rise and pay him marked deference. Even Brougham, who is at cross-purposes with Melbourne, the premier, comes trippingly forward from the corner where he is scowling, and greets him warmly; while Lyndhurst, Wellington, and two or three other Tory noblemen lift their hats and bow. This is Charles Earl Grey, now in his seventy-seventh year, who, as premier, with the aid of Brougham, carried the Reform Bill of 1832 through the House of Peers; or rather, as might be more fittingly said, drove it over the House of Peers. Seating himself, the venerable patrician looked around with the lofty bearing of one accustomed to take the lead among great minds. More than half a century before this Charles Grey, then in the Commons, was the youngest member of the famous committee that managed the impeachment of Warren Hastings. The sparkling eulogium of Grey in Macaulay's brilliant description of that event in the *Edinburgh Review* of October, 1841, will occur to the reader.

Earl Grey's solemn admonition to the House of Lords in 1832, not to reject the Reform Bill that had twice passed the Commons and been thrown out by the Lords, was a model of eloquence worthy of the best days of Greece or Rome. Coming from an old nobleman like him, it was more influential than Brougham's argument and closing appeal to the Peers "on his bended knees" to pass the measure, and more effective than the ridicule poured on the hostile lords by Sydney Smith in his story of Dame Partington's unsuccessful conflict with the Atlantic Ocean in the terrible storm at Sidmouth. In his last speech on that gloomy night when the fate of the British empire hung on his lips, Grey said to the Peers: "Though I am proud of the ancient rank to which we in common belong, and would peril much to save it from ruin, yet if your lordships are determined to reject this bill, and throw it scornfully back in the face of an aroused and indignant people, then

I warn you to set your houses in order, for your hour has come!" The threat of Grey was more potent than the logic of Brougham or the sarcasm of Smith. The bill was passed. The serf rose up a man, and the man stepped forth an elector.

In August, 1840, I met Earl Grey at the funeral of his son-in-law, Earl Durham, who had recently returned from Canada and died of mortification because of his unsuccessful management of the affairs of that then turbulent colony. The sad spectacle was at the country-seat of the deceased nobleman, near the city that bore his name. The scene was unusually grand. Being the guest of the Mayor of Durham, and an American, I had a good opportunity for contemplating the ceremonies. I was conducted by "His Worship," who glistened in a scarlet robe and gold chain, through the stately edifice of the earl to the little room, dimly lighted by wax candles five feet long, where lay the body, guarded by four mutes, from whose shoulders drooped black cloaks of the mediæval period. One hundred of the tenantry of the rich peer were boisterously feasting in the kitchen on solids and liquids of refreshing varieties. A numerous assemblage of Whig noblemen, members of Parliament, and untitled people assisted in the solemn pageant, for Durham was a leader of the Liberals and the hope of the rising Radicals. From the window of the chamber where lay his stricken daughter Earl Grey watched the long procession that bore the remains of his persecuted son-in-law through the adjacent groves to the place of interment.

4*

CHAPTER X.

The House of Commons.—Debate on Canada.—Macaulay's Speech.
—Lord John Russell.—The Lions of the House.—O'Connell
Aims a Stinging Arrow at Disraeli, the Future Beaconsfield.—
Stanley, the Inchoate Earl Derby, Collides with Howick, Son and
Heir of Earl Grey.—Sir Robert Peel Compared with Clay, Calhoun, and Webster.—Gladstone, "The Rising Hope of the
Stern and Unbending Tories."—Talfourd.—Bulwer's Dandy
Dress.—Anecdote of Brougham and Buxton.—Clarkson's Description of Wilberforce's Oratory.—Manners in the English
Commons and the American Congress Compared.—The Englishman's H.—Oratory in America and Great Britain.—American
Snobbery.—Joseph H. Choate and William E. Forster before
the Union League Club.—Dean Stanley, Canon Farrar, Sergeant
Ballantyne, and Matthew Arnold Facing American Audiences.—
How they Appeared.

In dealing with the House of Commons I shall glance only at a few of the celebrated members, who are best known in America.

I entered the Commons to hear a discussion concerning Canada, just then on the verge of a rebellion. I was just seated when from under the gallery there poured a stream of words, pitched in a monotonous key, sparkling with metaphors. The House had been rather thin, when instantly the doors began to slam, tidings having passed out that Macaulay was up. His address reminded me of his essays in the *Edinburgh Review*. Lord John Russell, colonial secretary, and Whig leader in the Commons, closed the debate. He was a better orator than Melbourne, but our House of Representatives would have listened to him impatiently.

One of the lions of the House was Daniel O'Connell. In heated controversy he was as much dreaded by opponents as was John Quincy Adams in our Congress. I speak more particularly of the Irish orator in another place. Directly across the floor from O'Connell we recognized the curly locks and flashing eyes of Benjamin Disraeli, the undeveloped Beaconsfield. He was then inclined to be ashamed of his Hebrew origin. Hence the keenness of the sting of O'Connell's arrow, who, in a recent exchange of epithets during a violent quarrel, declared that Disraeli was the lineal descendant of the impenitent thief that reviled Jesus on the Cross.

Lord Stanley, known in later times as Earl Derby, the Premier, was the most rapid speaker I ever heard. Dashing, bold, sarcastic, he was the Joachim Murat of debate. As secretary of the colonies, in 1834, he carried through the Commons the bill for the abolition of slavery in the West Indies. Previous to 1840 he had turned to be a Tory, and followed Sir Robert Peel. I witnessed a sharp collision between Stanley and Lord Howick, better known in America as the second Earl Grey. The conflict was personal and bitter. The fiery and ill-tempered attack of Stanley was admirably foiled by the cool, caustic reply of Howick.

Sir Robert Peel was then at the summit of his reputation as a Parliamentary leader. I heard him on the Irish registration bill, a measure that evoked hot blood and fervid oratory. Though Sir Robert had not the glowing rhetoric of our Clay, nor the nervous logic of Calhoun, nor the overshadowing majesty of Webster, his speech was cogent, lucid, dignified, remarkably courteous towards opponents, and displayed that rare tact which enabled him to hold together what, at that juncture, was an incongruous and factious party. Near him sat William Ewart Gladstone, a cold, serene, haughty, and intensely ambitious scholar and orator, whom Macaulay had described, in the *Edinburgh Review* of the previous year, as "a young man of unblemished character and distinguished parliamentary talents, the rising hope of those stern and unbending Tories who follow, reluctantly and mutinously, a leader (Peel) whose experience and eloquence are indispensable to them, but whose cautious temper and moderate opinions they abhor." This was a faithful portrait of the author of a bigoted book in favor of the extremest doctrines of the advocates of a union of Church and State, which Macaulay was caustically criticising in the *Whig Quarterly*. Who could then have dreamed that this "rising hope of the stern and unbending Tories" would turn with the tide and aid in repealing the Corn Laws, and, as premier, disestablish the Irish Church and carry the right of suffrage almost up to the American standard, and denounce in acrimonious terms old Liberals who had often served in his cabinets, because they would not accept without question a personal scheme, which even he could not clearly explain, for bestowing an independent parliament on the land of Emmet and O'Connell?

There were then in the Commons four authors

whose writings were popular in America, viz., Macaulay, Disraeli, Thomas Noon Talfourd, and Edward Lytton Bulwer. Having read their works at home, I took pains to hear them in the national forum. I have touched upon the three first named, and will briefly refer to Bulwer, a Liberal member, then famous as a novelist and dramatist, and in subsequent years as a conservative peer, bearing the title of Lord Lytton. When I saw him he appeared to be something of a dandy. Tall, with an Israelitish curve to a long nose, he was dressed at the very height of the fashion. There was a dash of dudism in his manners, his cut-away brown coat, white-duck trousers, and green-silk cravat. I was rather surprised to hear such extreme radicalism from such aristocratic lips. But though nothing else could have been logically expected from the author of "Paul Clifford," "Eugene Aram," and the "Lady of Lyons," the hue of Bulwer's politics, whether he shone as a liberal Commoner or a Tory lord, was as easily changed as the color of his cravats.

Sir Thomas Fowell Buxton was made a baronet in 1840, in return for services in Parliament in the cause of West India emancipation. This anecdote was told to me by one of his family: In the year 1824, when Buxton and Brougham were in the Commons, some petitions were confided to them for the abolition of slavery in the West India Colonies. On consultation they agreed to submit a motion for the amelioration of slavery. Buxton was to make the motion and Brougham to support him. Due notice was given, and the West India interest was on the *qui vive* for opposition. A tempest was anticipated. Buxton was apprehensive he should be unceremoniously coughed and scraped down. The day came. Just as Buxton was about to lift his majestic form—he was six feet six inches high—Brougham whispered to him, "I will cheer *you* while you are speaking, and you must do the same for *me*." "Agreed," responded the agitated brewer, as he rose and commenced speaking amid evident signs of impatience on the part of many Commoners. A storm was brewing, but Brougham cried, "Hear! Hear!! Hear!!!" with all his might, and clapped and stamped so lustily that the House was struck with amazement, thought he was crazy, and permitted Buxton to conclude his speech without much interruption. In an instant Brougham was on his feet, his eye flashing fire, and his hair erect with excitement. Members cried, "Divide! Divide!" in stentorian tones. "Harry the Commoner" stood unmoved as a rock. When silence was restored he went forward, kindling with his theme, rolling out splendid thoughts and glowing illustrations, which held the House in awe. The shouts of "Hear! Hear!! Hear!!!" from Buxton became contagious, and at the close of his speech Brougham sat down amid rounds of applause.

Thomas Clarkson's unique mansion, near Ipswich, was erected in the same year that Columbus discovered America. It had its moat and drawbridge, the water in the former fragrant with pond-lilies, and the railing of the latter entwined with creeping-roses. With pride glistening in his eye he showed me the original records of the first society—formed by him and William Wilberforce and their associates, in 1786, for the abolition of the African slave-trade. He gave racy anecdotes and sketches of illustrious men whom he had known and wrought with in that cause, and spoke particularly of Wilberforce, the younger Pitt, Fox, Burke, Sharpe, Windham, Bishop Porteus, and others of the great dead among his coadjutors, and of Brougham, Buxton, and O'Connell, with whom he had toiled in the later struggles to overthrow slavery in the West Indies. I asked him about the oratory of Fox, and if Mr. Wilberforce was a good speaker in Parliament, telling him that in America it was generally believed that Wilberforce was not a commanding figure in the Commons. The cheek of the patriarch glowed with enthusiasm as he replied that Fox was terrible in debate, attacking his enemies in a style that sometimes bordered on ferocity. He feared nothing; but, though a lion on the floor, was as mild as a lamb in private intercourse. In response to my inquiry concerning Wilberforce, he drew himself up to full height, and exclaimed, "Mr. Wilberforce not an orator! He was one of the most eloquent men in Parliament. His voice was as musical as a flute, and his choice words followed each other with a regularity and beauty that fell on the ear like the swells of an organ." I asked if he was not rather diminutive in person. "Yes," said Mr. Clarkson, "but his earnestness and pathos, and the magnitude of his theme when exposing the evils of the slave-trade made him look large in debate."

When I was in England the manners of the House of Commons were often rude and boisterous. Two or three times I witnessed scenes that would have befitted the spectators at a prize-ring better than the members of a legislative assembly. Such cheers, yells, hisses, groans! Such vituperation and personal abuse, for which representatives in Congress would have been required to promptly apologize on pain of expulsion! I have seen some of the most angry collisions that ever occurred in our Senate and House. They were perilous, and came near to bloodshed; but they were less coarse and noisy than those I beheld in Parliament. Ours were the quarrels of inflamed gentlemen. Theirs were the conflicts of heated bullies. Perhaps the House of Commons has improved in late years, but those rude outbreaks during the recent debates on Home Rule do not tend to prove it. American congressmen do not scrape an opponent down by shuffling their feet, nor silence him by concerted coughing, nor drown his voice by cries of "Divide! Divide!" "Oh! Ah!" nor drive him to his seat by ironical cheers, nor jeer him by affected yells of "Hear! Hear!" A congressman might kill a colleague in a duel for words spoken in debate, or even shoot him, or plunge a knife into his abdomen in an encounter in the lobby, but he would scorn to bellow him down like a bull. He prefers to leave that style of argument to the members of a body which has been called "An Assembly of the First Gentlemen in Europe."

The American who would thoroughly master the utterance of the English nation, whether in Parliament, at the bar, in the pulpit, on the platform, or in the streets, must pause and consider the letter *h*. It modifies their language, and is to them the key of the alphabet. He who supposes that the peculiarity in this regard relates only to the common people is quite mistaken; it crops out not infrequently in persons of the higher types, and especially the middle class.

The facility of the average Englishman in dropping out and picking up the *h* was brought vividly before me on the second day I was in the kingdom. I present it as a sparkling drop from "the well of English undefiled." I was on the coach between Exeter and Bath, with a seat by the driver's side. I caught sight of a great edifice in ruins on a distant hill. It was my first ruin in the Old World, and I wished to make as much of it as possible. I eagerly asked the coachman what it was. "Sir," said he, "that is Glastonbury habbey. In the reign of King 'Enry the Heighth, the hold habbot rebelled, and the king 'ung 'im hon a gallows, hand then cut hoff 'is 'ead, and confiscated 'is lands." Telling the coachman that I had just landed from America, he kindly gave me an extra stop of fifteen minutes to glance at the ruins of the famous abbey, which cover many acres, and where moulder the bones of renowned bishops and princes, whose history I had read in Hume, or 'Ume, as John Bull would call him.

While in England, Scotland, and Ireland, I heard much public speaking in Parliament, at the bar, in the pulpit, and on the platform from persons of all types. It is only echoing the general opinion to say that this foreign oratory was far inferior to ours. The English specimens could hardly have been worse. Such hesitating, hemming, hawing, stammering, stuttering, stumbling! They cultivate this style, and think it aristocratic. While they seem to reverence their sleezy diction and slipshod utterance as if it were a part of the British Constitution, to other nations it appears not merely contemptible, but makes their orators a laughing-stock. Of course, I met a great many exceptions to this sweeping rule.

On the other hand, not only in the matter of oratory, but in everything else, the British turn up their noses at us. It is no wonder. The snobbery and servility of our tourists in that country, and of some of our ministers to the Court of St. James, have confirmed them in their fancied superiority over the Americans. Indeed, our toadyism has reached a point where it is deemed unfashionable to give American names even to our hotels, and therefore we call them after some of the most infamous characters in British history.

Some of our citizens can recall a scene that enabled them to compare American with English orators. I refer to the reception given by the Union League Club, of New York, to the Right Honorable W. E. Forster, for his steady advocacy of the Union cause in the House of Commons during the Civil War. Arrayed in a dress coat and white cravat which Beau Brummel or George IV. would have envied, Joseph H. Choate, the president of the club, rained down for half an hour upon Mr. Forster a brilliant shower of encomiums that made the plainly dressed semi-Quaker quail. In matter and manner it was one of Choate's happy efforts, while Forster's response was thoroughly English in style and sentiment. The contrast between the two performances was striking and instructive.

Even fresher illustrations of the superiority herein asserted will occur to those who listened in this country to Dean Stanley, Canon Farrar, Sergeant Ballantyne, and Matthew Arnold. The two distinguished divines utterly failed to sustain the reputation as pulpit orators which they brought here; the learned lawyer hopelessly broke down when confronting his first American audience; and the famous essayist, who lectured for years with great *éclat* in his native land, had to take lessons in elocution after reaching our shores before, on his own admission, he felt competent to face a trans-Atlantic assembly.

CHAPTER XI.

Westminster Hall.—The Courts: Lords Cottenham, Denman, and Abinger, Sir Frederick Pollock, and other Members of the Bench and Bar.—In France.—Deputy Isambert and Advocate Cremieux.—The Great Napoleon's Mausoleum in Preparation on the Banks of the Seine.—Napoleon, "the Pretender," Seized while Raising a Rebellion at Boulogne.—Return to England.—London in a Fog.—William the Conqueror and Battle Abbey.—Runnymede and Magna Charta.—Bosworth Field and Richard III.—Cromwell's Schoolhouse, Mansion, and Farm.—Judge Jeffreys and the Bloody Assizes.—William III. and the Battle of the Boyne.—Old Sarum, the Model Rotten Borough.—The Chartists and their Creed.—Main Cause of their Failure.

I ENTERED the great Hall of William Rufus, in Westminster, whose old oaken arches had witnessed the crowning of many kings, the trial of Charles I., the expulsion of the Rump Parliament by Cromwell, and the bursts of eloquence of Burke and Sheridan on the arraignment of Warren Hastings for high crimes and misdemeanors, and I was spellbound as I paced its stone floor, worn by the footsteps of centuries. I visited the apartments where the courts were in session. There sat Lord Chancellor Cottenham, Chief-Justice Denman, of the Queen's Bench, Lord Abinger, of the Exchequer, better known to the bar in America as Sir James Scarlett. Of course I was deeply interested in witnessing the proceedings of tribunals that gave law to so large a part of Christendom, and whose decisions are daily cited in the courts of the

United States. I had heard a speech from Lord Cottenham in the Peers. I now listened to arguments in the courts from Sir Frederick Pollock, Sergeant Talfourd, and Sir William Follett, leaders of the bar. In matter they were able; in manner bad.

I was abroad till January, 1841. I delivered thirty or forty speeches in Great Britain and Ireland, and attended two conferences in France. I had come from the land of mobs, where the press, with few exceptions, delighted to misrepresent Abolitionists. It seemed a pleasant change to find myself introduced to audiences by members of Parliament, fellows of the universities, lord mayors of cities, peers of the realm, bishops of the Establishment, and the manager of the *Edinburgh Review*, and then to see my speeches fully and fairly reported in the newspapers. I took courage, and dared to say in the words of a Radical rhymer:

> "There's a good time coming,
> A good time coming;
> We may not live to see the day,
> But Earth will glisten in the ray
> Of the good time coming;
> Wait a little longer."

I lived to see the day.

While in France, in the summer of 1840, I attended two important Anti-slavery conferences in Paris. This was a part of my object in going to Europe. These conferences were participated in by M. Isambert, a prominent member of the Chamber of Deputies, and M. Cremieux, subsequently minister of justice in the government of Lamartine, and other leaders of opinion. I cannot even allude to the many famous places I visited on the Continent, but I will except two or three. It was in a memorable Napoleonic year that I saw France. In Paris, under the dome of the Hôtel des Invalides, they were preparing a magnificent mausoleum for the great emperor, whose remains were to be received from St. Helena in the autumn. The old soldiers on the banks of the Seine, who had fought under the Little Corporal in many battles, were aglow with enthusiasm at the approach of the pageant. I stopped in July in the public square of Boulogne and noted its points of interest. Two weeks later the young pretender, known afterwards as Napoleon III., dashed into the square with fifty armed followers, posted a proclamation on the walls, and called upon the people to rise and drive Louis Philippe from France. The wild adventurer was sentenced to the citadel of Ham for life, but he contrived to escape from his grim prison in May, 1846. Other historic mile-stones dwelt in my memory, and furnished the keys whereby I subsequently interpreted the downfall of Louis Philippe, in 1848, and the extinguishment of the Napoleonic dynasty, in the Franco-German war of 1870.

On returning from the Continent we had a night ride on a coach from Dover to London. We reached Shooter's Hill just as the orb of day was breaking through a bank of clouds. The basin wherein the great metropolis reposes seemed a vast lake, whose bosom was rippled by the wind. The dome of the Cathedral loomed above the surface and glistened in the morning sunbeams, while Highgate stood sentry over the scene on the north. The illusion was perfect.

I shall run through the country at random, merely pointing to a few landmarks, which stand as blazed trees along the track where history has hewed its path. I am not writing a sketch of my travels. The letters to the *New York American*, above mentioned, give glimpses of my wanderings, and show that I did not attend solely to Anti-slavery matters, but for six months went the beaten track of a tourist. In what I jot down I shall generally have some reference to human progress.

I went down to Hastings to see the harbor and the pier where William anchored the seven hundred vessels and landed the sixty thousand men for the great conquest. Six miles inland is the field where the grim invader, in October, 1066, fought the battle that placed the kingdom of Alfred the Saxon under the heel of William the Norman. Poor Harold, the English monarch, pierced in the eye by an arrow, lost his crown and his life in the struggle. Here the Conqueror, " of pious memory," erected Battle Abbey as a memorial of the victory that gave England the feudal system and the Domesday Book. The abbey is a frowning edifice, partially in ruins, a crumbling landmark of British history.

On the south bank of the Thames, a few miles from London, I saw a beautiful meadow. At the west I caught sight of the towers of Windsor Castle, while my eyes scanned the dense smoke that canopied the metropolis on the east. In 1215 there transpired on this little meadow one of the most important events in the history of England. Gloomy King John came over from Windsor to Runnymede to confer with his rebellious barons. On the 19th of June, at their dictation, he affixed the royal seal (perhaps he could not write his name) to Magna Charta.

Thousands of Englishmen daily sail up and down the Thames, past this sedgy spot, without being aware that their Declaration of Independence was issued here six hundred years ago. There is nothing strange in this. Crowds of Americans daily beat their surges against a little brick edifice in Philadelphia without remembering that within its walls, on July 4, 1776, a few feeble colonies issued the immortal document that hurled defiance (to quote Webster) at a power whose morning drum-beat, starting with the sun and keeping company with the hours, encircled the earth with one continuous and unbroken strain of the martial airs of England.

The wars of the Roses changed the line of descent of the English crown from the Plantagenets to the Tudors. In 1485 the White Rose of York was blasted by the Red Rose of Lancaster, on Bosworth field. I had seen the battle fought so often on the stage by Booth, Forrest, and Macready, that, after viewing the old schoolhouse at Leicester, wherein Dr. Sam Johnson was once usher, I rode a little way out of town to the plain where the genuine crook-backed Richard was slain, and the coronet placed on the brow of Henry VII. by Lord Stanley. The guide was loquacious, as became his calling. I swallowed his stories without a grimace, till he told me my feet at that moment rested on the very sod where

Richard cried aloud, "A horse! A horse! my kingdom for a horse!" Then I was tempted to bolt the track, because no historian informs us that "White Surrey" had been killed or had fled; and while that renowned steed lived what need had Richard of another horse?

However, I early learned to accept such tales as true, and get as much enjoyment out of the delusion as possible. When, for example, they exhibited the block in the Tower of London whereon Lady Jane Grey is said to have been beheaded, I admitted that some sharp instrument had made a cleft in it. They pointed me to the schoolroom at Huntingdon where Cromwell learned his A B C's, and to the identical wooden desk at which he sat. I conceded that the latter had been thoroughly whittled, and the only wonder was that it had stood the jack-knives so well for two hundred and fifty years. When gazing at certain suspicious-looking scratches on the window-sill of Whitehall, and on being assured that these were the prints of the spikes that helped to hold up the scaffold whereon Charles I. was put to death in 1649, I did not for a moment dispute that that unfortunate monarch lost his head in that vicinity about that time. So when in the Highlands of Scotland an ancient dame charged only a crown for letting me handle Rob Roy's alleged musket, I drew an approving smile from the old crone by the remark that the barrel was uncommonly long and the lock very rusty. Is not this the best way to deal with this kind of so-called information? Tourists must not be too crit-

Oliver Cromwell prepared the way for the expulsion of the Stuarts. I walked through the brick house and over the fair fields of Huntingdon where the Puritan spent his youth. The mansion resembled a large Pennsylvania farmhouse of the higher class. Here, in mature years, he trained his Ironsides, who marched to the tune of Old Hundred, but in many an encounter met undismayed the legions of the court and hierarchy, oft sweeping them like chaff before the wind. His well-planned battle at Naseby ruined Charles. I traversed the hillock over which the lion-hearted general, sword in hand, led the decisive charge. When he became Protector of the Commonwealth he took up the despised name of Kingless England, and bore it aloft on the eagle-wings of a far-sighted policy, and made it respected and feared at every court in Europe. He was a great soldier and a greater ruler, and stood among the foremost men of his time.

I skirted the fatal field of Sedgemoor, where the unfortunate followers of Monmouth sought to dethrone James II. before his hour had fully come. I sat in the old Court-house at Taunton, where the monster Jeffreys held the Bloody Assizes, which condemned to death three hundred and twenty-six men, women, and boys for participating in this uprising, and sent eight hundred and forty-one victims into perpetual slavery. The vials of retribution were poured upon the head of this infamous judge when his master fell. He cowered in a tap-room at Greenwich, disguised as a servant, and, on discovery, begged to be lodged in the Tower as a protection from the populace, who threatened to tear him limb from limb. There he howled like a maniac, haunted by the ghosts of those whom he had condemned to the gallows and the galleys at Taunton. The blackest villain that ever stained the bench was George Jeffreys.

Torbay is one of the most beautiful ocean inlets my eyes ever beheld. It lies in the lap of luxuriant Devonshire. I saw it in the high noon of summer exuberance. In this bay, on the 5th of November, 1688, William, the Stadtholder of Holland, anchored the great fleet, and landed the grand army he brought over to drive James II. from the British throne. The credulous king was slow to believe that his nephew had been invited to invade England by eminent leaders of public opinion. It was an easier conquest than that of the other William, who landed at Hastings six hundred and twenty-two years before. James fled to France. In July, 1690, he made a last feeble rally for his throne at the battle of the Boyne. In early youth I read a pictorial history of England. Among its illustrations was a vivid sketch of William crossing the Boyne and shouting to his soldiers, "To glory! My lads, to glory!" It has been the rule of my life to deepen the good impressions of my youth. Of course I saw the Boyne, and sat down on the northern bank, where William was wounded, and fancied I saw the cowardly James fleeing over the hills on the opposite side, the first one to run away. William III. was the greatest monarch who ever sat on the British throne.

The rotten borough called Old Sarum was the laughing-stock of the Whigs in the day of the first Reform

Bill of 1832. I visited its site, getting glimpses of Salisbury Plain, a locality which had nestled in my memory since I read the religious tract entitled "The Shepherd of Salisbury Plain." I could scarcely believe my eyes as I looked upon Old Sarum. For centuries previous to the Reform Bill it had sent two members to Parliament, though not a soul had lived there since the Tudors mounted the throne. It was a mere sand-hill, without showing even the ruins of a dwelling, though once it had a small population. Yet this utter waste, down to 1832, had as large a representation in the Commons as Lancashire, with its million and a half of people. The voting at elections used to be done by the owner of Old Sarum, who sent himself and a favorite, or two of the latter stripe, to Parliament.

Though the Reform Bill of 1832 abolished absurdities like Old Sarum, it left the representation in the House of Commons in a very unsatisfactory state. This led to Chartism, a well-meaning but rather turbulent faction, whose five foundation-principles were universal suffrage, voting by ballot, equal parliamentary districts, no property qualification for representatives, and the payment of salaries to members. This platform will seem familiar to the people of the United States, but the announcement of the Chartist creed threw England into convulsions. I happened to speak at a large Chartist meeting. Some English friends warned me not to attend, but I said I had rode out many mobs in America, and rather liked it. The organization was already drifting upon the shoals of violence. I cautioned them against disorder. But in a few years they destroyed themselves and their party by outbreaks and bloodshed. In later times, and under the guidance of Gladstone, Bright, William E. Forster, and their associates, the cause of free suffrage and parliamentary reform has recovered some of the ground which the Chartists proved incompetent to occupy.

CHAPTER XII.

Some British Poets.—Thomas Campbell.—In the London Convention he Ridicules American Poets.—He is Answered.—Ebenezer Elliott.—James Montgomery.—Lord Byron's Widow.—His Daughter, Ada Augusta.—Thomas Carlyle.—He Calls Victor Hugo a Humbug, and Criticises Emerson.—In Scotland.—Rev. Doctors Chalmers and Wardlaw as Pulpit Orators.—The Manager of the *Edinburgh Review* Presides over an Anti-Slavery Meeting.—Sydney Smith Preaches a Sermon.—Lord Francis Jeffrey on Law Reform, the New York Revised Statutes, and Jeremy Bentham, the Codifier.—The Field of Culloden.—Charles Edward Stuart.—Clarkson's Opinion of the Four Stuarts and the Four Georges.—In Ireland.—O'Connell on the Repeal of the Union.—John Randolph Said he was the First Orator in Europe.—Other Famous Men and Places.—Return to America.—Admitted to the Boston Bar.

An amusing scene occurred in the London Antislavery Convention that may be worth mentioning. I was on the platform reading a report when Thomas Campbell entered. He was greeted with applause. I stopped reading. Mr. O'Connell, with a flourish, reminded the American delegates that the author of "Gertrude of Wyoming" stood before them, and there were loud calls for a speech. The poet, in a muddled style, began to compliment American institutions, and then plunged, in a zigzag way, into a contemptuous criticism of our poetry. His manner was peculiar, his pose unsteady, his tongue thick. I replied, eulogizing his productions, and warmly vindicating the authors he had assailed. He kept jumping up and interjecting responses, and our colloquy kept the audience in a roar. All this was taken down by the stenographer, but it was omitted from the published report by the English managers on their excuse that Campbell was intoxicated. But I was not disposed to sit still and hear Bryant, Whittier, and Longfellow abused by any British bard, whether sober or drunk.

A glance at two or three other poets must suffice. A letter of introduction brought me in front of "Elliott & Co.'s Iron and Steel Warehouse," at Sheffield. I went to his house, where I was greeted with a hearty "Walk in!" from the Corn-law Rhymer, who was standing on the threshold in his stocking-feet. He made no apology for his rough appearance, drew on his shoes, and opened a racy dialogue about America. He was enthusiastic in his admiration of General Jackson, and dilated on his heroism in the battle with "Biddle and the Bank." Elliott, like Burns, was the poet of the poor, and his songs were the lays of labor. Unlike the Ayrshire ploughman, the Yorkshire ironmonger did not draw his inspiration from open, breezy fields, but from the stifling air of hot furnaces. Burns was the bard of yeomen, Elliott was the bard of artisans. Presenting me with a copy of his works, and slightly changing his dress, we ascended the hill to the embowered cottage of James Montgomery. The contrast could hardly have been greater than that between the rugged rhymester and the sacred singer. Polished in manner, neat in dress, calm in conversation, Montgomery inquired about the Pro-slavery mobs in the United States, especially the destruction of newspapers, his voice rising to indignation as he spoke of his own imprisonment in York Castle in early days for the publication, in the *Sheffield Iris*, of liberal doctrines, offensive to the administration of the younger Pitt.

In London I met Lady Byron, in company with her daughter, Lady Lovelace, Lord Byron's Ada Augusta, the "gentle Ada," sole heiress of her father's fame. The mother took a deep interest in emancipation and common-school education in America, but evaded all reference to her late husband. The eyes of the daughter sparkled when I told her that not only in the mansions of the rich in the cities, but in log-huts beyond the Alleghany Mountains, his poems were familiar as household words. Her countenance seemed to me to reflect more closely the brilliant features of the father than the plain face of the mother.

I met Thomas Carlyle. He was dressed in a shabby suit of gray. I was not delighted with this "writer of books," as he called himself. We talked about America, and he betrayed great ignorance of a people at whom he sneered. He conversed rapidly, walked the room nervously, and shot out porcupine quills indiscriminately at good and evil. As a specimen of his talk I will say that he called Victor Hugo "a glittering humbug." His vicious style of writing caused him to go by crooked ways up to an idea instead of advancing towards it by a straight path. Much of his assumed profundity sprang from this source. In later times his execrable style grew more and more misleading. Take, for instance, some of his lauded writings, and disentangle and analyze paragraphs that appear to hide in their meshes ideas too deep and awful to be expressed in plain Anglo-Saxon, and you will discover that the matter is either quite meaningless or very commonplace. But, notwithstanding his crabbed sentences, rooted prejudices, and sour temper, Carlyle's war on "Shams" was beneficial to mankind, while his pen, at lucid intervals, shed valuable light along the track of history and biography. Americans must not be too severe on the unique Scotchman, though he is reported to have said of our Emerson that his few ideas would be more clearly and beautifully clothed if he used half as many words to cover them. Transcendental writers do indeed need translators to put their productions into idiomatic English. It is mere affectation to go into raptures over chapters one third of which nobody really understands. Life is too short to be wasted in sifting a few kernels of wheat out of bushels of chaff.

I might describe many persons whom I met abroad, men and women, celebrities, oddities, famous, infamous, but I have no room for them. Several are noticed in my volume of "Sketches of Reforms and Reformers."

We must give England a rest, and repair to Scotland. I went the grand rounds of the Lowlands and the Highlands, and sketched outlines of my tour in letters to the *New York American*. Repetitions will be avoided. I jot only here and there. I listened to a sermon by Dr. Chalmers, then in the fulness of his prime, and the leader in the movement that ultimated in the disruption of the Church of John Knox. His discourse was a chain of close reasoning, glittering imagery, and glowing with fervor. Its drawback to me was the strong Scotch accent of the orator. His delivery lacked the mellow cadence of Dr. Ralph Wardlaw of Glasgow, who, to Dr. Chalmers, was as Apollos to Paul.

Our large Anti-slavery meeting in the Scotch capital was presided over by the manager of the *Edinburgh Review*. With what dash, audacity, and brilliancy did that celebrated periodical leap into the arena of journalism in the dark, troubled, and despotic epoch of 1802. The cause of freedom in both hemispheres is its debtor. Perhaps at the head of the long list of writers who imparted lustre to its pages and gathered fame by their contributions during the first forty years of its existence stand Sydney Smith, Francis Jeffrey, Henry Brougham, and Thomas Babington Macaulay. It made them all lords except Smith, who would have been a lord-bishop if he had not cracked so many jokes over the head of the Established Church. I had heard Brougham and Macaulay in Parliament. In a country parish I rode ten miles in the rain to listen to a sermon by Smith, the Canon of St. Paul's, who was visiting a rural rector. It was a plain discourse, though two or three paragraphs reminded me that Peter Plymley was in the desk. In Edinburgh I had an interview with Lord Jeffrey, then at the head of the Scotch judiciary. He took an interest in law reform, and asked me a good many questions about the New York Revised Statutes and their authors, which I reciprocated by inquiring into the habits and studies of the strange codifier Jeremy Bentham, then deceased, who always seemed to me to be in law what Dr. Franklin was in science, Dr. Johnson in literature, and Dr. Greeley in journalism. I deemed it fortunate that I had seen and heard the four greatest of the Edinburgh reviewers.

The last Stuart made a gallant stand at Preston-Pans in 1845, just below Edinburgh, for the crown of his grandfather. His Scotch claymores "hewed deep their gory way" into the ranks of the English, and they fled. But the tide turned against the young prince the next year. On a bleak ridge near Inverness he fought the fatal battle of Culloden in April, 1746. In spite of his winning manners and indomitable courage his cause was ruined. Having again and again declaimed at school Campbell's "Lochiel! Lochiel! beware of the day," I saw Culloden on a blustering October afternoon, and almost wished that the chivalrous Charles Edward had fared better. At Playford Hall, the residence of Thomas Clarkson, the conversation turned upon the Stuarts. "The four Stuarts," said the companion of Granville Sharp and William Wilberforce, "were a bad lot." Then, as if in parenthesis, he added, "And so were the four Georges." Time will never reverse this verdict.

When in London Mr. O'Connell invited me to Dublin, and laughingly said he would induct me into the mysteries of his agitation for the repeal of the union between England and Ireland. His son John, then in the Commons, presided at our Anti-slavery assembly in Dublin. He was a faint copy of his sire. The father gave me a special ticket to a Repeal meeting. He delivered an elaborate address of two hours' length, intended, as he said, to inform me of the ends he had in view. Mr. O'Connell was foremost among the eloquent public speakers of his era. John Randolph said he was the greatest orator he heard in Europe. He won the title of " Liberator of Ireland." In the address I have referred to he said that no political reform was worth the shedding of one drop of blood. His repeal agitation brought him to prison, and came to naught. Though something of a demagogue, he was the friend of man, irrespective of clime, color, creed, or condition. Wherever humanity sank under the blow of the tyrant there were found the genial heart and clarion voice of Daniel O'Connell sympathizing with the fallen and rebuking the oppressor.

Other scenes rise before me, but I must stop and hie to America. It would be pleasant to sketch a visit to Boston, where William Brewster, my Puritan ancestor, was long imprisoned for nonconformity; and to the gloomy jail at Bedford, where John Bunyan wrote the " Pilgrim's Progress;" but there is no space for them. Nor is there for descriptions of other famous places I saw, as, for example, Flodden Field, immortalized by Scott in " Marmion;" and the site of the Rye House, whose plot sent Algernon Sydney and William Russell to the scaffold; and Moor Park, where William III. was wont to consult Temple, and where Swift captivated and ruined " Stella;" and Blenheim Castle, whose stately halls saw streams of dotage flow from Marlborough's eyes; and Daylesford, rebuilt by Warren Hastings, and to which he retreated when pursued by Burke, Fox, and Sheridan in the great impeachment trial; and Birnam Wood, where I cut two memorial canes and took them to

Dunsinane, and could then have assured Macbeth (if there ever were such a king, and he had been present) that Birnam Wood had come to Dunsinane; and the sanguinary field of Bannockburn, where a minstrel, accompanying his melodious voice on a harp, sang the immortal ballad of Burns:

> "Scots, wha hae wi' Wallace bled,
> Scots, wham Bruce has aften led."

I dismiss all these scenes, and gladly hie to America, where I arrived in 1841. On my return I completed my law studies, and, in 1842, went into practice at Boston. But I still performed much work in the Anti-slavery cause, both on the platform and in the press. To make way for other matters, I shall say little of my labors in this latter field.

CHAPTER XIII.

The Law.—Boston Bench and Bar.—Judges Story, Sprague, and Shaw.—Jeremiah Mason.—Daniel Webster.—Rufus Choate.—Their Triumphs in the Criminal Cases of Avery, the Knapps, and Tirrell.—Samuel Hoar.—He is Sent to South Carolina to Test the Constitutionality of Laws Imprisoning Free Colored Seamen.—Expelled from the State by Force.—Mr. Hoar's Fee as a Referee.—Choate before Juries.—Shaw on the Bench.—Choate's Stimulants, Hot Coffee and Hot Water.—Tirrell's Two Celebrated Trials for Murder and Arson.—Parker, the Prosecuting Attorney.—Somnambulism the Defence.—George Head's Manufactured Testimony, and Rufus Choate's Marvellous Oratory, Twice Save Tirrell's Life.

In disposing of judges, lawyers, and courts at one sitting, I shall illustrate the rule that adherence to the order of topics is more important than regard for the order of dates. I shall begin at Boston, where I was first admitted to practice. As a general rule (though there will be many exceptions), when I take up a lawyer or a case, I shall get through with them before the man or the subject is laid down.

At the time of which I am speaking, the bench and bar at Boston were exceptionally distinguished. Joseph Story was in the zenith of his fame; Judge Sprague, of the United States District Court, who won a high reputation as Senator in Congress, was his worthy associate. Chief-justice Shaw, of the State Supreme Court, was one of the ablest lawyers in New England. The leader of the bar was, of course, Mr.

Webster, though Jeremiah Mason stood close to him. But, viewed in some lights, the most brilliant figure was Rufus Choate. He was appreciated by the five great men just mentioned, and was the admiration of his junior brethren of the profession, who were accustomed to pack the courts to witness his wonderful displays of logic, learning, and eloquence.

While I dwelt in Boston, Jeremiah Mason was one of its greatest lawyers. For half a century he was a commanding figure at the New England bar. Born and educated in my native county, he spent his best years in New Hampshire, whence he removed to Boston in 1832. I recall his tall form, six feet seven inches high, as he passed along the streets, or towered above his brethren in the courts. I heard him once before the full bench. Deliberate, methodical, luminous, compact, with little rhetoric and few gestures, his argument was a masterly performance of steel-linked logic.

Daniel Webster in his autobiography, written in 1838, gives a graphic sketch of his great rival. I quote a paragraph: " For the nine years I lived in Portsmouth, Mr. Mason and myself, in the counties where we practised, were on opposite sides of each case pretty much as a matter of course. . . . If there be in this country a stronger intellect, if there be a mind of more native resources, if there be a vision that sees quicker or sees deeper into whatever is intricate or whatsoever is profound, I confess I have not known it. I have not written this paragraph without considering what it implies. I look to that individual who, if it belong to anybody, is entitled to be an exception. But I deliberately let the judgment stand." The individual referred to was Chief-justice Marshall. This opinion of Mason was recorded after Webster had been thirty-four years at the bar and twenty years in Congress.

One of Mr. Mason's greatest achievements while in Boston was his successful defence, under the most adverse circumstances, at Newport, R. I., of the Rev. Ephraim K. Avery, on an indictment for the killing of his mistress, a Miss Cornell, while trying to produce an abortion by his own unskilled hand. The trial was replete with dramatic incidents, and famous in its day. Mr. Mason cleared another sort of prisoner by quite a different method. After he had become distinguished in New Hampshire, he went into a rural county to try a civil suit. A pompous little judge was on the bench. He assigned Mason to defend a negro on an indictment for petty larceny. With surprise, tinged with indignation, Mason declined the task. "Sir, you must obey the order of the court," said the little judge. "All you need do is to take your client into the adjoining room and give him the best advice you can." This struck Mason in a funny light, and he arose, beckoned to the negro, and stalked into an empty room with his "client" at his heels. "Are you guilty?" asked Mason. "Yes, sir," responded the negro. "Can they prove it?" "Yes, sir; all the witnesses are here." Mason put his head out of the open window and said, "It is about fifteen feet to the ground. Do you see those woods?" The negro leaped, and Mason returned into the court. By and by the case was called, but the negro did not respond. "Where is your client?" asked the little judge. "I do not know," replied Mason. "Your honor directed me to give him the best advice I could, and the last I saw of him he was running for those woods over there." Everybody laughed except the little judge, and the curtain fell on the scene.

The acquittal of Avery by Mr. Mason, the conviction of the Knapps by Mr. Webster for the murder of Joseph White of Salem, and the acquittal of Albert J. Tirrell by Rufus Choate for the murder of Maria Bickford, were the greatest triumphs in criminal cases ever won by Boston lawyers.

It was a rare privilege to listen, as I did, to Mr. Webster's eulogium on Joseph Story and Jeremiah Mason when announcing their death before the bench and bar of Boston.

Samuel Hoar was for a long time one of the leaders of the Massachusetts bar, to which he was admitted in 1805. The first time I saw him was in 1836 or 1837, in the trial of a celebrated will case before a jury at Boston. Mr. Webster was his chief opponent. Rufus Choate was one of the junior counsel. I heard both Webster and Hoar address the jury in this case on two successive days, Mr. Webster speaking first. It was apparent that "the Great Expounder" stood a little in fear of the calm, cool, incisive logic of the wary advocate that was to follow him, whose pose and style reminded the spectator of Jeremiah Mason.

In the turbulent days South Carolina was accustomed to seize free negro seamen who came into her ports from the Northern States, and lodge them in jail until the vessels whereon they served sailed away. If any of these negroes happened to be left behind, the commonwealth of John C. Calhoun would sell them into perpetual slavery to pay the jail fees. In 1844 the Legislature of Massachusetts (some of the colored sailors of that state had been thus imprisoned) sent Mr. Hoar to Charleston to test the constitutionality of these statutes in the courts sitting in that state. He arrived there in November, when the Legislature of South Carolina passed a law directing the governor to expel him from the state by force. On December 5 he was collared and put on shipboard, and might have been killed by a "chivalrous" mob that pursued him to the wharf, had it not been for the presence of his daughter. It was a long line of deeds of this kind that almost reconciled us to seeing South Carolina ravaged by Union troops during the war, and subsequently trodden down by a negro legislature sitting in the capitol that passed the law for the expulsion of Mr. Hoar, and subjected for a while to the robber rule of that infamous rogue, Governor Franklin J. Moses.

In Boston some Connecticut clients employed me to sue the owners of the woollen mill at Lowell, whereof Abbott Lawrence and his brothers were the principal proprietors, for an alleged violation of a contract for the purchase of a quantity of wool. Other wool-growers in Connecticut had commenced similar suits against the same defendants. The amount involved was large, and it was agreed that there should be only one trial, and that the result in all the cases should hinge on that trial. It was further agreed that the whole matter should be sent to Mr. Hoar to hear and determine as referee. He resided in Concord, and took the testimony in Boston, where there were several sittings. The controversy was decidedly sharp, and the swearing pretty hard. One of the Lawrences sold his shares in the Lowell mill, and thus qualified himself to be a witness, thereby gaining an advantage over my clients, who, under the law of evidence as it then stood, could not testify. On the turning-point in the case Lawrence contradicted my witnesses explicitly. Mr. Hoar was on intimate social and political relations with the Lawrences.

I have told this commonplace anecdote for the single purpose of stating the fee of the referee. Mr. Hoar decided the case in my favor. When he handed me his report as referee I asked him how much his charge was. "Twenty dollars," was the quiet reply. Shades of Tweed, and the long procession of departed referees of our epoch (not to speak of those who survive), how times and prices have changed since the days of honest and inflexible Samuel Hoar!

Mr. Hoar married a daughter of Roger Sherman, who was on the committee that drafted the Declaration of Independence. He was the father of E. Rockwood and George Frisbie Hoar. The mother of William M. Evarts was also a daughter of Roger Sherman.

What spectator that beheld Rufus Choate in a great cause could ever forget that tall figure, that sallow complexion, that piercing dark eye, those black locks, which hung in curls over an expansive forehead, those dramatic gestures that gave point and emphasis to pungent sentences, that majestic tread, which shook the room till the windows shivered, that voice whose notes now swelled like a trumpet, and anon sank into a wail as if a gentle breeze were sighing in the tree-tops, and all this without the slightest affectation, and with a clearness of vision that saw the pinch of his case, and a sincerity of manner which proved that victory, and not display, was the end he kept steadily in view? Mr. Choate argued a case in the Supreme Court at Washington. A distinguished Southern Senator heard him, and speaking to Mr. Webster the next day said: " I listened to your Mr. Choate yesterday. He is an extraordinary man." " An extraordinary man!" replied Webster. " Sir, he is a marvel."

Like Edmund Burke, whom he studied and admired, Mr. Choate drove " a substantive and six." Chief-justice Lemuel Shaw was a man of few words. He looked like a rough fragment of the feudal system. Short, thick, with a head covered with coarse, frowzy hair, which appeared never to have been combed, he had a habit of resting his elbows while in court on the shelf before him, and holding up his chin by his hands, and glaring at counsel through spectacles trimmed with tortoise-shell instead of silver or gold, a rather striking resemblance to a grizzly bear sitting on his haunches. But his head was clear as sunshine, and his rhetoric a model in style, though his growling voice made the short opinions he delivered on side issues during the trial of a cause seem like nectar gurgling from a tar-barrel. The Old Chief, as he was familiarly called, had a gentle heart, and there was a soft place in it for Choate, of whom he was really proud, though apt to jerk him up with a short rein when too wordy. One afternoon I stepped into court when Choate was flashing his lightnings around the Chief-justice, who kept interrupting him. Walking with Mr. Choate to our lodgings an hour later, I remarked that the Old Chief was unusually restive and annoying during his argument. "Yes," said Choate, "he is an old barbarian!" Then taking a few long strides, he added in slow, solemn style, "But life, liberty, and property are safe in his hands." He was arguing on another occasion a novel point of law before the full bench. He was on the crest of the wave. He expressed his gratification at the opportunity of discussing this new question at the bar of a tribunal whose reputation for learning and integrity had long since overflowed the boundaries of the commonwealth of Massachusetts, and reached the uttermost limits of the Union. The Old Chief broke in: "Mr. Choate, do you present that as a serious argument to this court?" "Oh, no, your honor," replied Mr. Choate, in his humorous style, "it was only a rhetorical flourish." Then, stooping down, he said to his associate in a tone loud enough to be heard all around, "The Chief-justice is an urbane gentleman. It is a pity he don't know any law." But there is no end to stories of this sort about Mr. Choate, and I forbear.

It has been my fortune to hear many of the foremost lawyers in this country and in Great Britain. As an advocate before a jury, especially in a difficult case, I never saw the superior of Rufus Choate.

The habits of such consummate orators are worthy of study. Immediately before he was to address a jury Mr. Choate would step across the street to the Boston Delmonico's and drink two or three cups of strong, piping-hot coffee. A jug of smoking-hot water would stand by his side in the court-room. The coffee stimulated the brain. Sips of the water kept up the stimulus and lubricated the throat. And now came the cyclone. The man knows little about physiology who resorts to brandy before making a speech, and imbibes cold water during its delivery.

The interval between Mason and Choate was very wide. The happy mean was hit by Mr. Webster when addressing either the court or the jury.

I hesitate about relating the following instance of manufactured testimony. What I shall state is true, but I remember the adage that "even the truth is not to be spoken at all times." However, this occurred so long ago that the principal parties passed from earth many years since, and the recital may serve a valuable purpose as an illustration of what I believe occurs oftener than the outside public suppose, *i. e.*, the manufacturing of testimony to meet an emergency in judicial proceedings.

One of the celebrated criminal cases in New England was that of Albert J. Tirrell, who was tried at Boston in 1846, on two indictments, for the double crime of murdering his mistress, Maria Bickford (I think I give these names correctly), and then setting fire to the assignation-house in which he concealed her. Tirrell's family was respectable and wealthy. He was a wild fellow, had a wife, was infatuated with the Bickford girl, feared he was about to lose her, and this was supposed to be his reason for cutting her throat with a razor, and firing the house to cover the deed. Each of these offences was punishable with death. The leading counsel for Tirrell was Rufus Choate, and who that ever saw Samuel Dunn Parker could forget the long-headed, hard-working prosecuting attorney? His form, voice, manner, victories and defeats are among the interesting memories of the Boston bar.

The hinge-point in the defence in this case was somnambulism. It was selected by the junior counsel in preference to an *alibi* (which was tendered), because, as one of them remarked, the latter was liable to break down. Mr. Choate, who doubtless knew nothing of the circumstances of this selection, merely said that he liked the line of defence, for an *alibi* was stale, but there was a fresh flavor about somnambulism. It is proper to state that I was wholly unaware of these preliminary matters, and had no suspicion that any of the testimony had been manufactured until after Tirrell was acquitted on both indictments.

George Head (I draw on my memory for his first name) kept a livery stable in the heart of Boston. He slept over his stable, and in the night had a lantern burning in the hall below. The small house where Maria boarded was in an obscure street, and about eight minutes' walk from the stable. The murder and arson were committed just before daybreak, a waning moon still shining. Head and Tirrell for some years had been " hale fellows well met." They travelled together and drank and played cards together, and did many other things in partnership. Head had a clear brain, steady nerve, rare self-poise, and was a faithful confederate in a desperate straight. Before he was placed on the witness stand the extraordinary line of defence was fully explained by one of the junior counsel to the jury, which lifted the experienced prosecuting attorney quite off his feet with surprise. The way was prepared for Head by preliminary testimony from two or three members of the Tirrell family concerning the alleged sleep-walking habits of Albert in his youth, and how he would glare wildly and utter guttural sounds on such occasions. The path was still further cleared by showing the precise hour when Tirrell left the assignation-house on that morning, uttering guttural noises as he went stumbling down the steps.

Head now entered the witness-box, and fixed the precise time when he was awakened by guttural noises at the door of his stable, which was exactly ten minutes later than the guttural noises on the steps of the assignation-house. Amid much other matter Head testified, in substance, that he looked at the clock, thrust his head out of a window, and asked, "Who is there?" A man turned his face up, and the moonbeams showed that it was Tirrell. He opened the door and let him in. Albert glared at him with eyes that had no "speculation" in them, and in broken paragraphs said, "They are after me!" "They are trying to kill me!" "They want my blood!" "They are setting the house on fire!" Head said he knew of Tirrell's somnambulistic fits and was not much surprised, but could not imagine what he was talking about. He took him by the collar and walked him around the stable, called him a d———d fool, and wanted to know what ailed him. After exercising him in this style for some minutes Albert suddenly woke up and stared at Head and the lantern. His first inquiry was, "George, how came I here? Have I been in the stable all night?" still gazing with dazed eyeballs at Head and the lantern, and so and so forth, with much additional testimony from the calm and plausible Head on the direct examination. The protracted and severe cross-examination by crisp, sharp old Parker did not shake him a particle. His recital of the stable scene produced a profound impression on the jury, one of whom subsequently told his counsel that it was mainly on this testimony that they acquitted the prisoner.

Now for the real facts of the meeting of Head and Tirrell at the stable. The former was fully aware of the latter's relations with Maria. After perpetrating the murder and the arson, he walked over to Head's stable, arrived about the time stated by Head, knocked at the door, made himself known, was admitted, told Head the particulars of the murder and the arson (without a speck of somnambulism!), consulted him as to the best mode of escape, and was driven in the early dawn to his home at Weymouth in one of Head's close carriages.

The public know the rest. Tirrell immediately sailed clandestinely to New Orleans, was indicted for the double crime in Boston, was brought thither under an executive requisition, and on two trials for his life was acquitted by means of the manufactured testimony of George Head and the marvellous oratory of Rufus Choate.

6

CHAPTER XIV.

The Law.—Several Novel Cases.—Libel Suit at Taunton.—The Vivid "Dream."—Criminal Prosecution for Libel at New London.—John T. Wait and Lafayette S. Foster for the State.—The Daniels's Case at Boston.—Charles G. Loring and Benjamin R. Curtis Counsel for the Defendant.—Choate for Plaintiffs.—A Patent Suit.—Charles Sumner, Benjamin F. Hallett, and Horace E. Smith Counsel.—Joel Prentiss Bishop, the Law-writer.—John P. Hale as Lawyer and Senator.—Theodore Parker under Indictment.—Hale his Counsel.—Parker on Fish and Phosphorus.

In 1844-45, William Wilbar kept a large wholesale and retail liquor store in Taunton, Mass. Benjamin Williams printed a lively temperance newspaper in that town. Under the similitude of "A Dream" he published a scathing article about Wilbar's store. The dream painted the establishment in the most appalling colors. The devil, fire and brimstone, liquid death and distilled damnation figured conspicuously in the lurid sketch. From the heads of the casks there flamed out labels bearing such inscriptions as "murder," "suicide," "arson," "soul-destroyer;" and the devil and Wilbar were on high seats in the counting-room, selling the casks to drunken customers. The dream went so far as to say that Wilbar carried on a lucrative trade in the business of picking the pockets of the poor, and putting them to a lingering death, and consigning their wives and children to the alms-house; and it mentioned the names of two of his victims who had died sad deaths, and were remembered in Taunton. It need hardly be said that these serious charges enmeshed the case in embarrassing difficulties.

Wilbar sued Williams for libel, laying his damages at several thousand dollars. Williams retained me as his counsel. *The plaintiff was selling liquor without a license.* I set up in defence that the publication was an allegory, and not to be construed literally, and that, so far as it confined its descriptions and pictorials to Wilbar's business of liquor selling, he could not recover because, as he had no license, he was himself violating the law, and *therefore had no standing in court.* The case was tried in the Supreme Court before Judge Samuel Hubbard and a jury. After a close contest of four days, the court ruled with me on the law, and my client got a verdict. The case was reported, and several thousand copies of the trial were sold.

The next year I appeared for the defendant in a criminal prosecution for a similar libel, at New London, Conn. It bristled with difficult points, but I got a verdict for my client. The prosecution was ably conducted by District-attorney John T. Wait, the present representative in Congress, and La Fayette S. Foster, afterwards United States Senator, both of Norwich.

I could find no reported case in this country or England that covered the precise ground in controversy at Taunton and New London.

George Daniels, a slippery shoe manufacturer, had for a year or more been in the habit of making notes payable to the order of Alfred Daniels, his wealthy brother, and then forging Alfred's name on the back of the notes, and passing them in Boston. George absconded, leaving notes to the amount of some $25,000 unpaid in the hands of his victims. I brought suit against Alfred Daniels in a single action on all these notes, simply declaring against him as endorser in the usual form. Rufus Choate was counsel with me. The defence was conducted by Charles G. Loring and Benjamin R. Curtis. The latter was subsequently appointed a justice of the Supreme Court of the United States. We tried our case before Justice Wilde and a jury at Boston. We proved that from time to time some of the notes in suit and others just like them had been presented to Alfred Daniels, and he was asked if they were "all right," and that his replies were either evasive or that the notes would probably be looked after when they became due. We took the ground that if Alfred Daniels's name was forged, and he knew it, and our clients did not, Alfred should then and there have exposed the forgery, and that from his failure to do this the jury might infer that Alfred had made George his agent for passing such notes. We could find no case in the books like the one at bar. But Judge Wilde ruled for us. It had devolved on me to put in the testimony during the contest of four days. Mr. Choate argued the case to the jury with his usual power and splendor. The jury gave the plaintiffs a verdict.

I have said that my early acquaintance with machinery aided me in the trial of patent suits. About 1847, one Hovey and one Stevens, of Massachusetts, were rival manufacturers of a machine for cutting straw by spiral blades or knives. The blades revolved on their axis, and the straw passed between them and a cylinder. The blades had to be ground so that when in motion they would describe a perfect circle. There was no patent on the straw-cutter, but Hovey had obtained a patent for a machine for grinding the knives or blades. Impelled by sharp competition, Stevens "pirated" Hovey's grinding-machine. He sued Stevens, who applied to me to defend him. There was no escape from heavy damages except to invalidate Hovey's patent by showing that he was not the first inventor of the grinding-machine. I remembered that thirty-three years before, in my father's woollen factory at Jewett City, they sheared broadcloth with spiral knives or blades that operated like those in the straw-cutter, and I inferred that there must have been a machine for grinding them. I sent Stevens to Jewett City, where he learned that such a machine was formerly used there, but some twenty years since it had been bought by two men and taken to a factory at Hoosick Falls, N. Y. I sent Stevens there, where he found the two men, who hunted up in an outbuilding the dilapidated and abandoned grinding-machine, with the dried grit of the stone still adhering to it. It was exactly like Hovey's alleged invention. Stevens brought the antique to Boston, and at the trial the two men appeared as witnesses. Under appropriate pleadings the old machine cut a great figure in the contest. The counsel for the plaintiff were Benjamin F. Hallett and Charles Sumner. The defence was conducted by Horace E.

Smith and myself. Of course we whipped them out of their boots.

Mr. Smith was for some time my partner at Boston. For several years past he has been the accomplished dean of the Albany Law-school. Joel Prentiss Bishop, of Boston, the widely-known author of valuable treatises on the law, was admitted to the bar while a student in my office. He was at home in a library of rare old law-books.

Mr. Sumner had read many volumes of law, and written some learned annotations thereon. But he seemed to have little taste for the sharp conflicts of the forum, where the enduring laurels of an exacting profession are won. If he tendered "sage counsel in cumber," he carried not the "red hand in the foray." Though he studied patent law at the feet of Judge Story, he was not expert in comprehending and applying those mechanical principles which are so frequently involved in cases that arise in that department. He acted wisely, therefore, when he retired from the bar, and devoted himself to the delivery of orations on the platform and speeches in the Senate.

Mr. Hallet, who led for the plaintiff in the trial above mentioned, was a wiry, pertinacious advocate. He was not familiar with the intricacies of patent law, and handled mechanical principles very clumsily; but he was a sturdy opponent to grapple with even when he was on the weaker side. This was partly due to the fact that his cuticle was unusually thick. For a while he conducted a newspaper in Boston, and championed some valuable reforms. He subsequently became an active Democrat, and President Pierce appointed him United States Attorney for the District of Massachusetts.

John P. Hale is not so well known as a lawyer as a Free-soil Senator. In his younger days, however, he was prominent at the New Hampshire bar, and in later years occasionally led in the trial of important causes at Boston.

One of the boldest of the early blows against the slave power from a public man was struck by Hale in New Hampshire in 1844. He was in Congress, and was the regular Democratic candidate for re-election. The pending issue was the annexation of Texas. First in a pungent letter, and then in a powerful speech, he declared against annexation. The leaders of the Democracy rose upon him, and the state was soon all aflame. I went up from Boston to help the robust rebel. After a long struggle Hale was defeated for Congress, but Dover sent him to the Legislature, and his services in the Free-soil cause were soon rewarded by his election to the United States Senate.

Hale was a novice in Anti-slavery literature, and I assisted in preparing two or three of his early speeches in the Senate. He was indolent, a brilliant declaimer, but an indifferent reasoner. Surrounded by foes, it was his proverbial jollity that protected him from assault. He bubbled over with wit and humor. I entered his room at Washington one warm evening, where an inextinguishable coal fire, fed by a stupid servant, had run the thermometer up to about one hundred degrees. He was stripped to his skin; the perspiration was dripping from his chin; a great pile of documents was before him, which he was industriously franking. Putting out his hand, he said, "This is the penalty paid for greatness."

He told me this fact, which illustrates a peculiarity of that extraordinary man, Theodore Parker. In a trial in the Federal Court at Boston which grew out of the famous attempt to rescue by force a fugitive slave from the clutches of the law, Hale was counsel for Mr. Parker, and for two weeks his guest. Twice each day Parker had baked fish served (with no meat), because this diet furnished, as he said, phosphorus for the brain. It was his ordinary custom to have baked fish only once daily, but, to meet the strain of the trial, Hale, who hated fish in any form, was required to lay in a supply of phosphorus at every breakfast and dinner while the legal conflict lasted.

CHAPTER XV.

The Law.—Bench and Bar of the Empire State.—Kent, Spencer, and other Eminent Jurists.—Four Great Lawyers of Columbia County.—The Power of Elisha Williams over a Jury.—Henry R. Storrs.—Lawyers and Trials at Rochester.—Selleck Boughton.—Jesse Hawley, the Land Surveyor, Foreshadowing the Erie Canal.—Charles M. Lee.—General "Mad" Anthony Wayne's Storming of Stony Point Saves a Counterfeiter from the State Prison.—John Griffin, the Rough Judge of Allegheny County, Sits down on a Dandy Attorney.—Alvan Stewart.—Some Albany Lawyers.—The Famous Firm of Hill, Porter, & Caggar.—Quirk, Gammon, & Snap.—Eseek Cowan's Rare Law Library.—Marcus T. Reynolds.—Samuel Stevens.—Daniel Cady.—Joshua A. Spencer.

I HAVE always felt at home with the judges and lawyers of the state of New York, for it was with them that I first began to be acquainted sixty years ago.

The old Supreme Court, the Court of Errors, and the Court of Appeals, in the opinions pronounced by Kent, Spencer, Thompson, Nelson, Cowen, Sutherland, Bronson, Denio, and their associates, illuminated all branches of the law in a style worthy of the best efforts of Mansfield and Marshall. The decisions of the courts of New York have, from the first volume of Johnson downward, held superior rank in the judicial tribunals of the Union, and have been quoted with approbation at London, Paris, and Berlin. In 1814, James Kent, the new chancellor, took his seat in one of the small rooms of the capitol. Throwing its doors wide open, he caused the proceedings of the court to be regularly reported, and thus poured a flood of light along the track of equity jurisprudence in this country. It would be in vain to attempt to give the names of the great lawyers of New York who have aided the bench in erecting its judicial system on solid foundations. The bench, of course, has been selected from the bar. Besides this, the profession in New York has furnished one chief-justice and five associate justices in the Supreme Court of the United States, and five attorney-generals.

I have before me a rapidly prepared and imperfectly presented article on this subject, which appeared in the appendix to the eighteenth volume of Barbour's New York Supreme Court Reports. Perhaps it will repay perusal.

Columbia County was the birthplace of four distinguished lawyers—Elisha Williams, Daniel Cady, William W. Van Ness, and Martin Van Buren. I listened to them all except Judge Van Ness, who had a great reputation for a peculiar style of attractive eloquence, though Williams was his superior before a jury. This scene was described to me by Mr. Cady, but so long ago that it has somewhat faded in my memory. He was junior counsel with Williams, who led for the plaintiff in a trial which involved a large tract of land bordering on the Hudson River. The plaintiff's recovery depended on sustaining the correctness of a line run by two surveyors, just after the Revolutionary War, in which they had won honor as officers. At the time of the trial they had been dead about twenty years, but their memory was revered in the counties along the Hudson.

In addressing the jury, the defendant's counsel vehemently denounced the two officers, attacking at great length their capacity as surveyors and their characters as men. And now came Williams's turn to reply. The court-room was so densely packed, especially near the door, that the audience reached down the stairs into the street. Williams vindicated the two surveyors and scathed their traducer in glowing terms, or, as Mr. Cady called it, in "thunder-clap eloquence." He referred to their unblemished reputation, their services in the struggle for independence, and described their personal appearance and the military uniform they had worn in the field. He wished they could be there, and take the stand, and confound their assailant. The audience had been wrought up to the highest pitch, when Williams, assuming a slow, solemn air, said, amid breathless silence: "The imposing figures of the revered patriots rise before me; I feel the approach of their awful presence." Lowering his voice and bowing his head as if listening, he continued, "I hear their footsteps on the stairs. They will take the witness-box and speak for themselves." Then suddenly turning towards the stairs, and waving his hand, he exclaimed, in a thrilling tone, "Make way for them! They come! They come!" The crowd around the door opened to the right and left, and the twelve jurors rose and stood on tiptoe to see two men enter the court-room who had been in their graves twenty years.

I heard this great advocate try an important cause

at Rochester as early as about 1828. The opposing counsel was Henry R. Storrs of Oneida, who was rapidly advancing to the front rank of the profession. It was a contest between giants. Each possessed rare oratorical gifts. Storrs was the more wary and argumentative; Williams, the more extravagant and impassioned.

Anecdotes of minor lawyers illustrate the vicissitudes of the profession quite as well as elaborate sketches of its eminent members. When I was clerk of the courts in Rochester, Selleck Boughton was one of the queerest practitioners at the Monroe bar. He had been a constable, was turning gray, dressed like a scullion, weighed about one hundred pounds, chewed a whole paper of tobacco at once, had studied law in a narrow sphere, wielded a sharp metaphysical mind, and would stand and split hairs from morning till night. A fellow was indicted for trespassing on lands, and Boughton defended him. Of course the title to the lands was in question. Jesse Hawley, an old citizen of Rochester, was a surveyor of high repute, and had run the lines of most of the tracts in that region. Even before De Witt Clinton had fully conceived the idea, Mr. Hawley wrote a series of articles in a Canandaigua newspaper in support of the feasibility of constructing a canal from Lake Erie to the Hudson River. He was a witness for the prosecution on the trial I have mentioned, and his testimony pressed hard on the defendant. Boughton objected to every question put to Hawley by the district attorney, and argued each objection at an interminable length, Hawley meanwhile resting. There was plenty of quaint humor in Hawley's mental composition. During one of Boughton's speeches the badgered witness slid into a seat by me. "At the Day of Judgment," said he, "I intend to get my case put on the calendar right below Selleck Boughton's. I shall never be placed in peril, for when he is on trial he will stand and object to all eternity."

Charles M. Lee, who figured at the Rochester bar at the same time with Boughton, exhibited a vociferous style of oratory that made a deep impression upon bucolic jurors from the rural towns. A revolutionary soldier was indicted for passing counterfeit money. He had followed General "Mad" Anthony Wayne up the craggy steep of Stony Point, on the Hudson, in the dark night of July 16, 1779, when that fortress was carried by storm. Lee defended the silver-haired veteran on his trial. The evidence against him was clear, and there was not a shadow of doubt of his guilt. Lee summed up the case with rare vehemence, graphically described the bloody attack on Stony Point, and with tears dripping down his cheeks implored the jury to acquit the old soldier. So plain was the case for the people that the district attorney spoke barely ten minutes. It was not then known that the father of the foreman of the jury had stood shoulder to shoulder with the defendant in the perilous night when Wayne captured the British stronghold. The jury were out an hour. When they returned the clerk said, "Gentlemen of the jury, have you agreed upon a verdict?" "We have," replied the foreman. "Do you find the prisoner at the bar guilty, or not guilty?" "Not guilty, because he helped to storm Stony Point!" shouted the foreman.

In those early days justice in that portion of the country was sometimes administered with a rough hand. John Griffin was First Judge of the Court of Common Pleas in Allegheny County, then a rude frontier settlement. In size and manner he was a prototype of Abraham Lincoln. He dressed shabbily, was a good lawyer, and carried a clear head on his shoulders. I was summoned to Judge Griffin's court as a witness, with some records from the Monroe Clerk's Office, in a case where certified copies would not answer the purpose. One of the counsel was a loquacious young limb of the law, of small stature, from another county, who dressed like a dude of the present era. He raised objections at every step in the trial, which the grim judge invariably overruled, whereupon the pert attorney would keep on arguing, and wind up by expressing his regret for feeling compelled to differ with his honor. The judge endured this for about the tenth time, when, at the close of an unusually ridiculous episode, Griffin asked the dandy if he was through talking on that point. He said he was. "Sit down, then, and shut your mouth, you little d——d fool!" responded the judge, in a loud voice, and with a blow on the bench that made the lawyer's head swim.

I hardly dare lift my pen in an attempt to outline the commanding figure of Alvan Stewart as a lawyer, for my personal knowledge of his marvellous victories in a field where he shone conspicuously as a leader for a quarter of a century, was quite limited. Moreover, his participation in the Anti-slavery conflict, when I was fighting by his side, naturally tended to eclipse in my eye his earlier fame at the bar. I knew enough of him, however, to say that he was an unusually well-read lawyer, had studied the profession as a science, and in some lines of the practice, especially before juries, he had no superior in central New York. His quaint humor was equal to his profound learning. He was skilled in a peculiar and indescribable kind of argumentation, wit, and sarcasm that made him remarkably successful in "laughing a case out of court;" and lucky would it be for the opposing counsel if he did not have to go out with his case. Even to the present day the dozen counties around Otsego and Oneida are fertile in traditions of the forensic triumphs of Mr. Stewart in every department of the law. I never saw this extraordinary man try an action in court, but before Anti-slavery conventions in several states I heard him argue grave and intricate constitutional questions with consummate ability.

Though Albany has always been the judicial centre of the state, it was more exclusively such prior to the Constitution of 1846 than it has since been. Even for a considerable time after the adoption of that instrument it continued to be the chief seat of this department of the government. This kept in practice at Albany, during the first sixty years of the present century, a body of lawyers who had no superiors at the New York bar. Whoever looks through the reports of Johnson, Cowen, Wendell, Hill, Denio, and some of the later authors, will find them liberally sprinkled with the names of Albany lawyers that appeared as counsel in the cases. For the latter half of this period I knew many of these lawyers, and some of them intimately. I heard before courts and juries the foremost in this long procession of learned and eloquent advocates, from Abraham Van Vechten to Nicholas Hill. There is space to refer to only a few of them.

In the later stages of this cycle one of the ablest law firms in Albany was composed of Nicholas Hill, John K. Porter, and Peter Cagger. They did a business so extensive that it brought them in contact with the profession all over the state. Hill had been trained in the office of Eseck Cowen, at Saratoga Springs. Cowen certainly had the largest law library in the state, and probably in the Union. I think it was Hill who told me that Cowen possessed a copy of every law book issued by an American author (Statutes not included) except one, and that he had ransacked the country to find the missing work. After Judge Cowen left the Supreme Bench Hill brought a liberal selection of his books to Albany.

Nicholas Hill was one of the most profound and successful counsellors that ever appeared before the court in *banco* in New York. The members of its highest tribunal had entire respect for his opinions. He was the embodiment of lucid logic, though perhaps rather too refined in his methods of reasoning for the comprehension of minds of ordinary mould. Mr. Porter was an ornate orator, as smooth as oil in his diction, picturesque and dramatic at times, and wielded great sway over juries, whether summoned from the Capitoline precincts or the Helderberg hills. Mr. Cagger, his veins pulsating with the warmest

Celtic blood, went off in the court-room like a hair-trigger on the duelling-ground. An attorney who hoped to circumvent Cagger's moving affidavits on a motion at Chambers needed a keen eye, a sharp pen, and a facile client.

Everybody in Albany knew Hill, Porter, and Cagger, at least by sight. At the time of the occurrence which I am now to describe their offices were on the second floor of a building in State Street. In the room above was a photographer's establishment. Specimens of the artist's work were displayed at the foot of the wide stairs by the sidewalk—the stairs that led up to the law-offices. As a captivating advertisement of his vocation (then quite new) the photographer hung up a large plate in the vestibule containing admirable likenesses of Hill, Porter, and Cagger, the two former sitting in chairs, and the latter standing behind them with a hand on the shoulder of each. The picture was so perfect, and the countenances of the three so characteristic, that their friends laughed to look at it. The famous novel of Warren, the English barrister, entitled "Ten Thousand a Year," wherein are depicted the arts, the loquacities, and the rascalities of the law-firm of "Quirk, Gammon, & Snap," was then in the hands of everybody that read novels. Many American lawyers that rarely looked into works of fiction were laughing and crying over "Ten Thousand a Year," alternately sneering at the metaphysical blockhead Quirk, detesting the oily hypocrite Gammon, and despising the sharp rogue Snap. One night a wag procured a printed label containing the words "Quirk, Gammon, & Snap," and slipped it into the picture that bore the familiar likenesses of Hill, Porter, and Cagger. The next morning the three lawyers (taking an old friend along) reached the entrance to their offices in company. An amused crowd cumbered the sidewalk. The lawyers pushed through. Cagger's eye fell on the label. He exploded with anger. "It was an outrage! A detective should ferret out the perpetrator, and he should be criminally prosecuted for libel! The photographer must instantly throw the thing into the street!" Porter seemed to be meditating points in the eloquent speech he could make to a jury in a civil action for damages. Meanwhile the philosophic Hill stood, with folded arms, looking at the picture. Soon he burst into a laugh that shook him from head to foot. "No!" said he, "not a bit of it! It shall remain as it is. It is the most capital hit I ever heard of. It describes us exactly. It is the best advertisement we shall have in years. Let it stand."

I cannot do justice to that wittiest and most sarcastic of advocates, Marcus T. Reynolds, nor to Samuel Stevens, who had few equals as a special pleader under the old practice, and at a later period excelled as a patent lawyer. I witnessed an amusing scene between Reynolds and Stevens before Chief-justice Samuel Nelson. They were arguing a motion. The papers had come to each from remote country attorneys. Reynolds possessed an extraordinary measure of imperturbable self-possession. In the hurry of the moment he had scarcely glanced at his papers, and he caught a wrong idea as to the side on which he was retained. He opened, and in his terse and pointed style was arguing effectively against his own client. Stevens stared at him, looked at his papers to make sure that he himself had not made a mistake, and then listened, and again stared at Reynolds. The strange manner of his antagonist arrested the attention of Reynolds just as he was about to close his opening, and he took a steady look at his papers, and saw that he was speaking on the wrong side. Without the slightest change of countenance, and with perfect coolness of manner, he said, "Your honor, I have been tracing in the clearest language I can command the line of argument that my learned opponent will no doubt pursue, and I shall now proceed to show how utterly futile and untenable it is." He then delivered an unusually powerful address in behalf of his own client, and left Stevens to take care of his side of the case as he pleased.

Daniel Cady appeared so often in the courts at the state capital that he might fairly be called an Albany lawyer. He went to the roots of every case he tried or argued. He dealt little in rhetorical embellishments, but wielded a ponderous logic that ground adversaries to powder. Unless his case were utterly hopeless he always came off victor in the hand-to-hand conflicts at *Nisi Prius*. Joshua A. Spencer, of Utica, an accomplished advocate, whose name is sprinkled all through the reports, told me he had tried two hundred jury cases against Mr. Cady, and that whenever he succeeded in winning a verdict from his secretive, wary adversary, he never felt sure that a mine was not to be sprung under him and engulf him, until he had obtained from the clerk a certified copy of the verdict, and the court had adjourned for the day. Mr. Stevens, of whom I have spoken, argued appeals *in banco* with an amplitude of learning and logic second only to Nicholas Hill. A suit for libel between two surgeons, wherein Cady and Stevens were counsel for the bitter belligerents, had at last reached the Court of Errors, after passing through a long series of circumlocutions in the lower tribunals that covered several years. Mr. Stevens argued for the appellants, consuming a day. Mr. Cady replied, and, as my informant said, he took Stevens up by the collar in the first sentence, and never let his feet touch the carpet for four hours.

CHAPTER XVI.

The Law. — The Corning and Burden Spike Case. — Seward, Blatchford, and Stevens Counsel. — Reuben H. Walworth, Referee. — Jarndyce *vs.* Jarndyce. — Clients Erect Federal Buildings at Buffalo and Oswego, and Sue the Government. — Speaker Grow, R. E. Fenton, and William Steele Holman Intervene. — Captain Cornelius Vanderbilt and the Fist Fight. — His Son, Cornelius Jeremiah, is Sued, and Blows his Brains out. — The Controversy over the Commodore's Will. — The Spencers. — John C. Spencer. — His Acute Legal Mind. — Interview with his Son, who was Executed for Alleged Mutiny on Board *The Somers*. — Chief-justice Ambrose Spencer. — John C. Spencer Concocts the Canal Bill of 1851.

AFTER I removed from Boston to Seneca Falls, in 1847, I became associated in the famous suit of the Burden Company against the Corning Company of Troy and Albany, brought for an alleged violation of the patent of the former by the latter for the manufacture of hook-headed spikes, used for fastening T rails to ties on railroad tracks. The case had been carried on appeal to the Supreme Court at Washington, which had given a decision in favor of the plaintiffs, and had issued the usual order to the Circuit Court in New York to enter final judgment for the plaintiffs, and then send it to a master, to take an account of the damages and fix the amount thereof. Lawyers will understand this line of proceedings.

The case had been a long time reaching this point. Samuel Stevens, my associate, was leading counsel for the plaintiffs, and Governor Seward for the defendants, with whom was Samuel Blatchford. We tried in vain for a good while to agree upon some one to take the account. Judge Samuel Nelson, of the Supreme Court, finally referred the matter to ex-Chancellor Walworth. And now commenced a series of interminable delays, which threw Jarndyce *vs.* Jarndyce, of Bleak House fame, quite into the shade. Burden, an ardent man, believed the proceedings would be closed in three months, and that, as the defendants had made an enormous amount of spikes, the plaintiffs would be awarded at least $250,000 damages. Alas! Burden had not carefully studied Jarndyce or Walworth.

The case went on, it stood still, it went on, it stood still, till all the original counsel were frozen out of it or had died. But the tough ex-chancellor, who was drawing heavy fees as he went along, was like Jefferson's Federalist office-holders—he neither died nor resigned. And so the years rolled away till the constantly accumulating testimony reached tens of thousands of folios, and being put in print from time to time filled many great volumes. An incident or two will illustrate the mode of taking evidence. The ex-chancellor held the reference in his office in Saratoga, where all the witnesses appeared. One witness came from Troy, and was sworn. At Saratoga he became acquainted with a young lady, married her, and was a father before he left the stand. Another witness was sworn. Burden saw him well under way, and then sailed for Europe to take out certain patents in foreign countries. He travelled extensively for this purpose in Great Britain and on the Continent, and after an absence of several months he returned and found the same witness still testifying. These facts will serve as specimens. After wasting years on the case, Walworth decided that the plaintiffs were not entitled to recover any damages whatever. An appeal was taken from this decision, and what then became of the matter I do not know.

Walworth for nineteen years occupied the seat which James Kent had adorned. He was a nightmare on the jurisprudence of New York. One of the moving causes for the adoption of the Constitution of 1846 was to rid the state of the Court of Chancery and of Reuben Hyde Walworth as Chancellor.

Clients of mine erected for the federal government at Buffalo and Oswego buildings for post-offices, custom-houses, and other purposes. In 1855-56 I brought suit for damages in the Court of Claims for violation of our contracts. The government fought desperately, and the conflict was long and weary. The court awarded my clients $36,000. I took the case to Congress, which increased the award to about $80,000. *This was the only case in which Congress ever increased an award of that court.* The amount we obtained was fair and just. The government, without the slightest regard to the merits of the case, first threw the weight of its influence against us in the court, and then in both the Senate and the House. My success in Congress was mainly owing to Reuben E. Fenton, William S. Holman, and Speaker Galusha A. Grow, while I received valuable aid from Senator Daniel Clark, of New Hampshire.

In the summer of 1838 or 1839 I took passage at New York on a Vanderbilt steamboat plying through Long Island Sound. A Southern gentleman with a colored chattel and a large trunk in his train violated the rules by putting the trunk in his stateroom. Soon after passing Hell Gate the deckmaster pulled the trunk out. A scuffle ensued, and the Southerner seized the deckmaster by the collar, the negro lowering darkly in a corner as a reserved corps. A crowd of passengers were spectators of this sharp tussle, in which the Vanderbilt forces were getting worsted. Suddenly a well-knit man dashed into the ring with a battle-cry that sounded exactly like swearing. In an instant his coat was off and his fists doubled. Just at this point the colored contingent wheeled into line. The new-comer dealt a blow that set the negro spinning, and then moved at double-quick on the Southerner's works. The affair was rapidly approaching the precincts of a rough-and-tumble fight between the four combatants when the passengers intervened and proposed an adjournment. The motion was carried. The trunk remained outside the stateroom, and the other chattel retired to repair his nose. This was the first time I ever saw Captain Cornelius Vanderbilt.

About forty years after this I was retained to collect for a client a just debt of $10,000 from Cornelius Jeremiah Vanderbilt, a son of the commodore, which had somehow become mixed in the contest over the commodore's estate. Patient negotiations having failed to secure a settlement, I brought suit against C. J. Vanderbilt to recover the debt. The summons was served in the morning, and in the evening of the same day he blew his brains out. Poor Cornelius! He had generous qualities, and in mien and manners was a closer copy of his father than were any of the other children. The effort to collect this debt brought me unwillingly into the possession of a mass of so-called facts concerning the famous controversy about the commodore's will, some of which were true and some of which were false. They abounded in the dramatic, and contained materials for more than one tragedy, comedy, and novel. I shall not soil these pages with any of this scandalous matter. The family fight of these coarse-grained people over the old commodore's dead body was one of the most unsavory in the annals of American litigation. Four of the conspicuous characters in that conflict have since gone to that undiscovered country from whose bourne no traveller returns. It required all the learning, skill, and forbearance of Mr. Surrogate Calvin to hold the scales of justice with an even hand among the fierce combatants.

In January, 1841, on my return from Europe, I was on the way to Rochester. One of my chance travelling companions was a son of John C. Spencer. We stopped overnight at Geneva, and Spencer brought down from Hobart College his younger brother for an evening call. He was a student at Hobart. His manner was easy, and his conversation unusually interesting for one so young. This was the youth who was put to death by Captain Alexander Slidell Mackenzie, in December, 1842, for an alleged mutiny at sea on board *The Somers*. I have always thought

7

that his fate was cruel and unjust. Mackenzie was the brother of the notorious Senator, John Slidell. The elder of the Spencer brothers told cock-and-bull stories of a recent trip to England as bearer of Federal despatches, and his possession of the law library of his grandfather, Ambrose Spencer, with notes on the margins of the volumes by the famous chief-justice, all of which I subsequently learned was a draft on the imagination.

John C. Spencer was for a long period one of the heads of the bar in western New York. I first heard him at Rochester, in 1829-30, when he was special counsel for the state in the prosecution of the Antimasonic cases. He was a wary and dangerous adversary in the trial of actions that involved nice legal distinctions, and where falsehood was curiously intertwined with truth. His clear head and plastic hand had much to do in the revision of the New York Statutes. Gerrit Smith told me that pretty much all he learned when a wild young man, during the short time he was in Spencer's office as a law student, was a method of blotting out writing so skilfully that what was obliterated could by no possibility be ascertained.

It was the acute mind of Mr. Spencer which devised that cunning evasion of the Constitution of New York known as the Canal Bill of 1851. The long struggle over this measure in the legislature and the courts will be referred to in another place. Mr. Spencer's versatile talents were always in request by his party. He held more offices than any citizen of New York, except perhaps Martin Van Buren and John A. Dix.

I close the chapters on Law and Lawyers by remarking that I have shown my regard for the profession by inducting four of my sons into its intricacies. Daniel Cady Stanton was for one year a supervisor of registration, and for two years a member of the legislature of Louisiana, in the turbulent era of reconstruction. Henry Stanton, a graduate of the law school of Columbia College, is now the official attorney of the Northern Pacific Railway Company. Gerrit Smith Stanton and Robert Livingston Stanton are also graduates of the Columbia School. The former cultivates the soil, and dispenses the law in Iowa. The latter practises his profession in the city of New York. The reader who peruses the miscellaneous matter that is to follow will discover that much of it relates to lawyers.

CHAPTER XVII.

Dr. Samuel B. Woodward and Senator Albert H. Tracy.—Close Resemblance to Washington and Jefferson.—Webster and the Conscience Whigs in Faneuil Hall in 1846.—Crittenden on Clay and Webster.—Clay before the Supreme Court.—Mrs. James Madison.—John Sargeant.—Chief-justice Taney.—Clay in the Senate.—A Galaxy of Talents.—"Biddle and the Bank." —The Sub-Treasury Question.—Clay's Speech in New York.— His Personal Magnetism.—His Funeral Pageant.—A Cluster of Political Rivals.—George P. Barker.—Sanford E. Church.— Church in the New York Assembly in 1842.—Hoffman, Dix, Seymour, and other Members.—Church makes Barker Attorney-General.—Anecdote of Church and James W. Nye at the Buffalo Convention in 1848.

It is natural to desire to see distinguished persons; and next to seeing the very individuals is the privilege of conversing with their doubles. Who does not wish that he could behold two men who look and talk as Washington and Jefferson did? I boarded for some months in Boston at the United States Hotel. Whenever he visited the city, Dr. Samuel B. Woodward, Principal of the Insane Asylum at Worcester, dined at that hotel. As he walked erect and majestic through the long room to the head of the table, every knife and fork rested, and all eyes centred on him. He received similar notice when appearing as an expert witness in the courts. The reason was this: Young men who saw George Washington after he passed middle life traced the very close resemblance between him and Dr. Woodward. Aware of the cause, the doctor was flattered by these attentions. Forty-five years ago, I spent a long evening at Buffalo in the company of Albert H. Tracey, who had previously been prominent in Congress and the State Senate. In the latter body he often pronounced the guiding decision of the old Court of Errors. In mien, size, bearing, visage, and conversation, he was the counterpart of Thomas Jefferson when about the same age. Mr. Tracy was fully conscious of this likeness between him and the author of the Declaration of Independence.

The Whig State Convention of Massachusetts met in the fall of 1846, at Faneuil Hall. It was during the Mexican war. The Whig party in that state had long been seconding the Presidential aspirations of Mr. Webster. An element known as "Conscience Whigs" elected several delegates to the convention, among whom were Stephen C. Phillips, Horace Mann, Charles Allen, and Charles Francis Adams, all good debaters and full of courage. They offered resolutions about the war and slavery that did not run in the Websterian grooves. In the afternoon the discussion waxed warm, and the revolting faction (the counterpart of the New York Barnburners) were getting the best of it in their encounter with the Conservatives. Charles Francis Adams (I think it was) was on the platform, throwing out short, pungent sentences that flew like arrows through the hall. I was a close observer of the scene from the gallery, which looked down upon the rostrum, but had not noticed that two prominent Whig leaders had left an hour before. The convention sat with its back to the great door of the hall, around which was a crowd of spectators. While Adams was speaking, a clapping of hands suddenly broke out near the door, and instantly there emerged from the excited throng the grand form of Webster leaning on the arms of Abbott Lawrence and Robert C. Winthrop. A shout of "Webster!" went up from the floor, and three cheers bounded to the roof. The two messengers found the Great Expounder (so it was reported) at dinner. His cheek was a little flushed. Adams subsided, and Webster ascended the platform. His first sentence was, "I like to meet the Whigs of Massachusetts in State Convention assembled, because their proceedings always breathe the spirit of Liberty." He hesitated a second or two before pronouncing the word "liberty," but when it came out it seemed to weigh ten pounds. It was a shot right between wind and water. He spoke briefly, closing substantially as follows: "In the dark and troubled night that surrounds us, I see no light by which to guide our course except in the united action of the united Whig party of the United States."

The resolutions of the Conscience Whigs were laid on the table; but in due time the recoil came, and six years later Daniel Webster turned his face to the wall at Marshfield, and died, because he could not obtain a nomination to the Presidency, while these Whigs marched onward with the procession that ultimately saved the Union and destroyed slavery.

A dozen years or more after this event in Faneuil Hall, I happened to be one of a dinner-party in Washington where John J. Crittenden and Thomas Corwin were the shining lights. The conversation turned on Clay and Webster, both of whom were then in their graves. Mr. Crittenden said: "We all (*i. e.*, the Clay Whigs) desired to see Clay and Webster elected to the Presidency, and we felt that to accomplish this object it was necessary that Mr. Clay should come first, but we were never able to make Webster and his personal friends see this, and therefore neither of them won the prize." The following anecdote was vouched for by competent authority. In the stormy days of John Tyler, while Webster was Secretary of State, and Rufus Choate was in the Senate, and Congress was in extra session in the fall of 1841, the question of chartering a United States bank was shaking the country. Mr. Clay, as chairman of the Finance Committee in the Senate, was pressing the measure, and Tyler was resisting it. A conference of leading Whig Senators was held. Clay, with lofty mien, was for waging relentless war on the accidental president, who had stepped into the White House over the dead body of General Harrison. Choate again and again told what Webster thought ought to be done. Clay was restive, and exclaimed, "Who cares a d—n about what Webster thinks?" In 1844, Clay was the Whig candidate for President. The tariff and the annexation of Texas, wherein he had conspicuously figured, were the leading issues of the canvass. On a memorable occasion in the campaign, Webster made an elaborate speech, but never once mentioned Clay's name. It must have severely taxed his ingenuity to avoid it.

These are fair illustrations of the relations in which these eminent statesmen stood towards each other during the last ten years of their lives.

I went to Washington in February, 1848, to attend to business in the Supreme Court. I heard Mr. Clay argue a case. For two hours his sonorous voice pealed through the corridors, and delighted a great throng. Mrs. James Madison sat by his side. The venerable lady, who was dressed quite young for her years, was gallantly complimented by Mr. Clay, and seemed as proud of the orator as she was thirty-six years before, when he championed the administration of her eminent husband in Congress during the war with England. The counsel that argued the other side of the case was John Sergeant of Philadelphia, who had confronted Clay in Congress in the Missouri controversy, but had been on the ticket with him as Whig candidate for the Vice-Presidency in 1832. It was an interesting group of celebrated historical characters, especially when we include Chief-justice Taney, the Secretary of the Treasury that removed the deposits, whom Clay had denounced in the Senate as one of the great scoundrels of the century.

The first time I saw Mr. Clay was in the Senate in the winter of 1838, when he spoke for a few minutes. His manner was easy and graceful, but imperious and commanding. The Senate then shone with exceptional lustre. In the front rank towered Clay, Webster, Calhoun, Benton, Buchanan, and Wright. Next to them stood such statesmen and orators as Crittenden, Southard, Tallmadge, Rives, Preston, and Clayton. Even distinguished men like King of Alabama,

Frank Pierce, Grundy, Robert J. Walker, Allen of Ohio, and Hugh L. White felt honored by being assigned to the third class. The conflict between rechartering the United States Bank and establishing the Sub-treasury was then at its height, and Clay and Webster predicted a revolution if the latter prevailed over the former. But they lived years after the marble building in Philadelphia, where the bank so long kept watch and ward, was quietly converted into a sub-treasury. If the ghost of Nick Biddle ever revisits the glimpses of the moon, it must be shocked as it glides up Chestnut Street, and sees "the base uses" to which the fine old Grecian edifice is put.

In the summer of 1839 I heard Mr. Clay deliver an elaborate speech on the Bank and Sub-treasury question from an open barouche, at the steps of the New York City Hall. He had been conducted by a long cavalcade of horsemen from the banks of the Hudson, and he was now surrounded by an immense concourse. I stood at the junction of Broadway and Park Row. His voice rang out so loud and clear that his words were distinctly reverberated from the wall of the Astor House. He was then putting in his bid for the next Presidential nomination. But, though their greatest leader, the Whigs declined to run him in the campaigns of 1840 and then in 1848, when he could certainly have been successful. Soon after the disastrous contest of 1844, in a short, humorous speech he accounted for his failure. He said some of his opponents were like those of Tom Brown's Doctor Fell:

> "I do not love you, Dr. Fell,
> The reason why I cannot tell;
> But this alone I know full well—
> I do not love you, Doctor Fell."

He was looking forward to a nomination in 1848. I watched him with interest as he lingered in the Senate Chamber and Supreme Court, surrounded by admirers over whom the sway of his personal magnetism was as irresistible as that of Napoleon over his Old Guard.

One summer evening, in 1852, I arrived at the Delevan House, in Albany, retired to rest, and was soon fast asleep. By and by the strains of martial music floating on the midnight air awoke me, and called me to the open window. It was a band playing the Dead March in Saul at the head of a procession that had just taken the remains of the great Kentuckian from a steamer on the Hudson, and was escorting them to the train that was to bear them to their final resting-place at the West.

Rivalries of the type displayed by Clay and Webster have been common among leaders of parties, and have often torn them in pieces, as, for instance, those of Jackson and Calhoun; Van Buren and Cass; Benton and Atchison; Marcy and Wright; Buchanan and Dickinson; Ritchie and Blair; Cass and Douglas; John Van Buren and Seymour; Seward and Chase; Weed and Greeley; Wade and Chase; Greeley and Raymond; Dix and Tilden; Conkling and Fenton; Hendricks and McDonald; Cameron and Grow; Thurman and Payne; Blaine and Conkling.

The glass shows many more. Let no one complain

that his name is omitted. If all were included, the line would stretch out till the crack of doom.

This class of politicians are wont to make chasms in parties through which they themselves often drop, and disappear forever.

In the fall of 1841 I was in Buffalo at a Democratic meeting addressed by George P. Barker, who had won a reputation for a style of oratory like that ascribed to John Van Buren. Tall, graceful, with a kindling eye and clarion voice, Barker's speech swept the audience along like an overflowing river. The annexation of Texas was beginning to loom threateningly upon the horizon. The Democracy generally were favoring the scheme. Barker was suspected of unsoundness on this question. A few Whigs had gone in with the throng. One of them, in the hope of annoying Barker, who was dashing forward in his usual brilliant manner, cried out, " Are you in favor of annexing Texas to strengthen the slave power of the country ?" Turning to his questioner, but not pausing in his speech, Barker threw in the reply, as if it were a parenthesis, " All the world for freedom; Salt River for the Whigs." This sally silenced the Whig, and drew cheers from the Democrats.

In the following January I was introduced to Sanford E. Church, then the youngest member of the Assembly of 1842, where appeared such leaders as John A. Dix, Horatio Seymour, Michael Hoffman, Arphaxad Loomis, and Peter B. Porter. I referred to the scene at Buffalo, and Church said he was going to make Barker attorney-general; and he did, and the worthy predecessor of John Van Buren he was.

Mr. Church was a member of the Buffalo Convention of 1848. Dean Richmond, James S. Wadsworth, James W. Nye, and I were taking a lunch, when Church came in, dripping with perspiration, and said there was a great clamor in the convention, some calling upon Charles Francis Adams for a speech, and others shouting for Frederick Douglass. "Nye," said Church, "it is a contest between a Whig and a negro, and they have agreed to compromise on you. Will you go over?" This tickled Nye's fancy, and he went to the tent under which the convention sat and made one of his witty speeches, that restored the sweltering assembly to good-humor. Mr. Church rose steadily in favor when twice lieutenant-governor and as comptroller and chief judge of the Court of Appeals. He was not a genius, knew little of general literature, but brimmed all over with sagacity and common-sense.

CHAPTER XVIII.

Democratic National Convention of 1844.—Van Buren, Polk, and Cass.—Polk Nominated for President.—Wright Nominated for Vice-President.—He Declines.—First Use of the Morse Telegraph.—Polk's Duplicity in Forming his Cabinet.—Marcy, Secretary of War.—The Barnburners Angry.—Death of John Quincy Adams.—The Barnburner Revolt of 1847-48.—"The Assassins of Silas Wright."—List of Barnburners and Hunkers.—Utica Convention of 1848.—Young, Cambreling, and Tilden Present.—Cass and Taylor Rival Candidates for President.—Convention at Buffalo in 1848.—B. F. Butler's Speech.—"D—n his Turnips!"—Van Buren Nominated for President, and Charles Francis Adams for Vice-President.—The Barnburner Revolt Defeats Cass and Elects Taylor.—Reunion of the New York Democracy in 1849.—The Election and its Results.

MR. VAN BUREN having been beaten in 1840 on the sub-treasury and cognate issues, the great body of the Democrats believed that he ought to be renominated in 1844. He had a majority of the delegates in the National Convention of the latter year; but an intrigue, in which General Cass was the central figure, sprung on him the two-thirds rule, and defeated his nomination. To prevent Cass or any of the other intriguers from getting it, the friends of Van Buren (who had previously conferred with James K. Polk about putting him on the ticket for Vice-President) now changed front in the convention, and nominated Polk for President. It is interesting to remember that Silas Wright was nominated for Vice-President, but instantly declined, and that the messages which passed between the convention at Baltimore and Wright at Washington on this subject were the first ever sent over the Morse telegraph. Polk owed his candidacy to the Barnburners, and expressed gratitude to them for it. To enable him to carry New York at the election, Wright, then a leader in the Senate, consented to run for governor. The prize having been won, and Henry Clay beaten by the loss of New York, Polk now turned traitor to the men who had made him President. Wright having been chosen Governor, was out of the question for a seat in the Cabinet, but Polk hypocritically offered him the Treasury. Wright declined it, and, with the concurrence of Mr. Van Buren and all the leading Barnburners, proposed that the representative of New York in the Cabinet be either Benjamin F. Butler for the State Department or Azariah C. Flagg for the Treasury. Polk whiffled, equivocated, fell into the hands of the Hunkers, and spurned the recommendation of those who had lifted him from obscurity into the Presidency. The Barnburners " nursed their wrath to keep it warm," and in 1848 emptied the vials on the head of General Cass, the Hunker candidate for President, and opened the breach in the party that was never closed till slavery was overthrown.

In the chilly morning of February 21. 1848, I met Mr. John Quincy Adams by the fireplace in the rear of the Speaker's chair in the House of Representatives. He had walked, as was his wont, to the Capitol. As he shook my hand, he trembled with cold. He took his usual seat. Some fulsome resolutions eulogizing General Taylor, who was looming as a possible Presidential candidate, were the first business. They created an uproar. Forty members were shouting to the Speaker. Mr. Speaker R. C. Winthrop was vigorously plying his gavel. My eye fell upon Mr. Adams. His hand was nervously creeping up his desk as if he were trying to rise. I thought he was about to take part in the din that filled the hall. But instantly I saw the pallor of death on his cheek. His hand dropped by his side, and he slowly inclined over the arm of his chair. I spoke to Washington Hunt, a member, and subsequently Governor of New York: "Look to Mr. Adams, he is falling in his chair." He rushed towards him. A call for help arrested the attention of the House. It became silent as the grave. The aged patriot was borne to the Speaker's room, never to leave it alive. Sage of Quincy! He had fought a good fight for the liberty of the Press, Freedom of Speech, and the Right of Petition. He fell in the plenitude of his fame, on the theatre of his grandest achievements, with the roar of battle sounding in his valiant ear.

In the fall of 1847 I was a spectator at the Democratic State Convention of that year, held in Syracuse. The convention tore itself asunder in a desperate struggle over the renomination of Azariah C. Flagg as comptroller, the defeat of Martin Van Buren at the Baltimore Convention of 1844, the political assassination of Silas Wright when running for governor the second time in 1846, and the attempt to incorporate the Wilmot Proviso into the platform of the party. The great chiefs of both factions were on the ground, and never was there a more fierce, bitter, and relentless conflict between the Narragansetts and the Pequods than this memorable contest between the Barnburners and the Hunkers. Mr. Wright was the idol of the Barnburners. He had died that summer. James S. Wadsworth voiced the sentiments of his followers. In the convention some one spoke of doing justice to Silas Wright. A Hunker sneeringly responded, "It is too late; he is dead." Springing upon a table, Wadsworth made the hall ring as he uttered the defiant reply: "Though it may be too late to do justice to Silas Wright, it is not too late to do justice to his assassins." The Hunkers laid the Wilmot Proviso on the table, but the Barnburners punished them at the election.

The Barnburners were the Girondists of the Democracy. Listen to a sample of names: Martin Van Buren, Silas Wright, B. F. Butler, Churchill C. Cambreling, Michael Hoffman, Dean Richmond, John Van Buren, Samuel J. Tilden, David Dudley Field, Addison Gardiner, A. C. Flagg, Samuel Young, G. P. Barker, Nicholas Hill, Sanford E. Church, John A. Dix, William Cullen Bryant, Preston King, James S. Wadsworth, Arphaxad Loomis, J. W. Nye, William Cassidy, Andrew H. Green, Abijah Mann, John Bigelow, Thomas B. Carroll, Reuben E. Fenton, and Charles J. Folger. A slight acquaintance with the politics of New York suffices to show that these were men of mark.

In the stormy epoch of 1847-48 the Hunkers were ably led by William L. Marcy, Daniel S. Dickinson, Edwin Croswell, Horatio Seymour, Charles O'Conor,

Reuben H. Walworth, Samuel Beardsley, and William C. Bouck.

The Syracuse Convention of 1847 had divided the New York Democrats into two bitter factions. The convention for nominating the national ticket was to meet at Baltimore in May, 1848. Each faction appointed full delegations, each claiming to be regular. In 1848 the Democratic legislative caucus, at Albany, issued an address to the country, defending the regularity of the Barnburner delegates, and presenting with consummate ability the Free-soil side of the slavery controversy. It is now known that this address was the joint production of Martin Van Buren, Samuel J. Tilden, and John Van Buren. After an acrimonious contest at Baltimore the convention refused to admit the Barnburners as the sole delegates, but would allow half of them and an equal number of Hunkers to represent the state; or, as I happened to put it in a speech at a meeting soon afterwards in Albany, which tickled Nicholas Hill, the chairman, "The regular delegates might occupy half a seat apiece, provided each of them would let a Hunker sit on his lap." The Barnburners declined to enter on these conditions. General Cass was then nominated for President, and the Free-soil Democracy resolved to defeat him.

The proceedings at Baltimore set the Free-soil ball a-rolling, and enthusiastic meetings were held all over New York. A tumultuous assemblage in the City Hall Park was addressed by John Van Buren and Churchill C. Cambreling, the latter declaring, in sonorous tones, that "slavery had received its death sentence." A Democratic state convention met at Utica in June. A large representation of the most distinguished Democrats of New York was present, and the veteran Samuel Young took the chair. He delivered a vehement speech, in which he said, "A clap of political thunder will be heard in this country next November that will make the propagandists of slavery shake like Belshazzar." Utterances like these from Democrats of such eminence as Cambreling and Young reverberated all over the Union, giving slavery a blow from which it never recovered. Mr. Tilden made an able report respecting the proceedings at Baltimore, and Martin Van Buren addressed a noble letter to the convention, vindicating the constitutionality and wisdom of the Wilmot Proviso. The convention nominated him for President. The Free-soil stream soon broke over the Barnburner dykes, and the result was the famous gathering in August at the Queen City of the Lakes.

The nomination of General Cass for the Presidency by the Democrats and General Taylor by the Whigs led to the Buffalo Convention of 1848. The Barnburners had opposed Cass in vain at the Baltimore Convention. They had made the Monumental City lurid with their wrath, frightening the delegates from the back states almost out of their wits. At Buffalo I was one of the committee that drafted its Free-soil platform. It was a motley assembly. Pro-slavery Democrats were there to avenge the wrongs of Martin Van Buren. Free-soil Democrats were there to punish the assassins of Silas Wright. Pro-slavery Whigs were there to strike down General Taylor because he had dethroned their idol, Henry Clay, in the Philadelphia Convention. Anti-slavery Whigs were there, breathing the spirit of the departed John Quincy Adams. Abolitionists of all shades of opinion were present, from the darkest type to those of a milder hue, who shared the views of Salmon P. Chase. An immense tent was raised on the court-house square for the accommodation of the convention, where the crowds were regaled with speeches and music. Its real business was conducted by delegates locked in a Baptist church close at hand. There was a rooted prejudice against Mr. Van Buren among the Whigs and Abolitionists. But the adroit eloquence of his former law partner, Benjamin F. Butler, of Albany, and an admirable Free-soil letter from the Sage of Lindenwald himself, carried him through, and he was nominated for President, with Charles Francis Adams for Vice-President.

A rather amusing illustration of this prejudice occurred while Mr. Butler was speaking. It will be remembered that, in his inaugural address as President, Mr. Van Buren pledged himself to veto any bill passed by Congress for the abolition of slavery in the District of Columbia unless the measure was sanctioned by the states of Virginia and Maryland. This pledge gave great umbrage to Anti-slavery men of all types, and, though eleven eventful years had since elapsed when the Buffalo Convention was held, the hostility to Van Buren on account of this old pledge remained unshaken in many minds. In his speech Butler was getting around thorny points in Van Buren's career very skilfully. While graphically describing a recent visit to the ex-President's Kinderhook farm, and telling how he was now absorbed in bucolic pursuits, like Cincinnatus, the model yeoman of his epoch. Butler spoke of the agility with which Van Buren leaped a fence to show his visitor a field of sprouting turnips. A Whig in the convention, who remembered the veto pledge, and was utterly opposed to nominating its author, broke in upon Butler with the startling exclamation, "D—n his turnips! What are his opinions about the abolition of slavery in the District of Columbia?" "I was just coming to that subject," responded the oily Barnburner, with a suave bow towards the ruffled Whig. "Well, you can't be a moment too quick in coming to it," replied the captious interlocutor. But, as I have already stated, the frank letter of Mr. Van Buren carried him triumphantly over the breakers.

The revolt of the New York Barnburners gave the thirty-six electoral votes of the state to General Taylor, which was his precise majority in the Union.

Some Barnburners have said that the Democratic revolt of 1847-48 was the beginning of the Free-soil movement. This is an error. It is mistaking the rocky cataracts over which the stream fell for the remote fountains whence it rose. The revolt gave a mighty impulse to the current, but did not originate it. Even long before Garrison appeared it had broken forth in the Missouri controversy of 1819-20. Whoever reads the speeches of James Tallmadge, John W. Taylor, and Rufus King in Congress in that troubled period will find that they were as sound in doctrine, as strong in argument, as splendid in diction, as any of the utterances of the following forty-five years, when the Thirteenth Amendment to the Constitution closed the controversy for all time.

In 1849 the Barnburners and Hunkers held separate state conventions at Rome to try to reunite the party. The leaders of each faction were present, and committees of conference exchanged opinions. A resolution offered by me to adhere to the Wilmot Proviso was adopted. We split on that rock, and the conventions adjourned. A pressure from the rank and file brought them together again, when a frail coalition was effected. John Van Buren described it, in his graphic style: "We are asked to compromise our principles," said he. "The day of compromise is past; but, in regard to candidates for state offices, we are still a commercial people. We will unite with our late antagonists," he added. Then, paraphrasing the Declaration of Independence, he said: "And we will hold them as we hold the rest of mankind—enemies in war, in peace friends." This effort to combine incongruous elements failed. A mixed ticket for the five state candidates was nominated. With one exception they were all defeated at the ballot-boxes. This device, so frequently employed by leaders of parties for closing chasms in their ranks when fundamental principles are involved, is rarely successful. The history of political coalitions proves this.

CHAPTER XIX.

The Author Elected to the New York Senate in 1849.—The Canal Bill.—Twelve Senators Resign to Defeat it.—Re-elected in 1851.—The Bill Passes.—The Court of Appeals Pronounce it Unconstitutional.—The Author's Seat Contested.—Dinner at the Astor House.—Speech of Seward and another.—Thurlow Weed.—The Midnight Call.—The Contest Squelched.—Weed's Hand in it.—Members and Measures in the Senate.—Hamilton Fish Elected United States Senator.—James W. Beekman Bolts Fish.—Notices of Hoffman, Loomis, Seymour, Dix, Van Buren, Marcy, and Dickinson.—John Van Buren and the Apple-woman; his Ill-health; the Water-cure Establishment; his Death at Sea.

I WAS elected to the State Senate in 1849, and took my seat in 1850. I was there during the agitation over the compromise measures growing out of the Mexican war. A great variety of resolutions were introduced in the legislature on those questions. While this subject was before the Senate I drew a very radical resolution, by way of amendment to a series then pending. It elicited warm debate, and was put to test on a call of the yeas and nays. It was adopted. Every Whig and every Democrat who voted for this amendment subsequently became a member of the Republican party.

I will here insert two of the resolutions which I assisted to frame, and supported in speeches by my votes. One declared that "the Federal government ought to relieve itself from all responsibility for the existence or continuance of slavery or the slave-trade, wherever it has the constitutional power over these subjects." Another said that "we feel bound to oppose, by all constitutional means, and our Senators in Congress are hereby instructed, and our Representatives requested, to use their best efforts to prevent, *by positive enactment*, whenever necessary, the extension of slavery over any part of our territory, however small, and by whatever pretence of compromise. These sentiments seem commonplace to-day, but it cost a high price to utter them in a legislative body in January, 1850, and to stand up to them before the people. All the Barnburners in the Senate voted for these resolutions, while seven of the seventeen Whigs recorded their names against them.

The Whigs in the legislature, at the session of 1851, introduced an unprecedented bill, which appropriated many millions of money for the purpose of enlarging the canals. The Barnburners deemed it unconstitutional, as did Democrats generally. The bill had passed the Assembly, where the Whigs had a large majority. To prevent the presence of the three-fifths quorum necessary to carry it in the Senate, it was thought best that twelve senators should resort to the desperate expedient of resigning their offices. The consequence was that the bill fell in the Senate.

Elections were ordered on short notice to fill the twelve vacancies, and an extra session of the legislature was called for June. The tide ran against the resigning senators, all of whom stood for re-election. Six, whose districts were far away from the canals, were successful. The other six, who lived in canal districts, were overwhelmed, with one exception.

There were three canals, stretching forty-two miles, in the three counties of my district. There were twelve stump-speakers in the field against me, marshalled by Gerrit Smith. At the close of the savage fight I was re-elected by five majority. The bill was passed at the extra session. I opposed it step by step. The judiciary soon afterwards vindicated the soundness of the doctrines of the resigning senators. The Court of Appeals adjudged the law to be unconstitutional, null, and void. In this contest I was the special target of the "Canal Ring." On both occasions when I ran for the Senate, my district, on a fair test of the strength of parties, was politically opposed to me. I was at each election carried through by a large number of votes from the opposite party in my own town and several adjoining towns, and particularly from the poorer citizens in these towns. To be thus sustained at home in these sharp struggles, and when I had to bear up against great moneyed interests and profligate legislation, I regarded as a higher compliment than to have received the degree of LL.D. from the proudest university in the country.

My opponent in the second election was Hon. Josiah B. Williams, a rich, popular, and highly respectable Whig, of Ithaca. He prepared himself with a pile of petitions and affidavits, for the purpose of contesting my seat before a body wherein his political party had a great majority. I had not armed myself with a single petition or affidavit. The following facts illustrate the tact of one or two Whig leaders who flourished in that era. In the winter previous to the resignation of the twelve senators a public dinner was given in New York city to the legislature. Mr. Seward, then in the Senate at Washington, was confronting, almost single-handed, the assaults of the slave power, in a crisis that was extremely perilous. He attended the dinner. I was required to make a speech. I complimented Mr. Seward for his fidelity to the Free-soil cause in the Senate, and at the close gave a toast like this: "William H. Seward, our eminent Senator in Congress, may prosperity ever attend him." All the Whigs cheered because it was Seward, and all the Barnburners because I said it. In the dead vast and middle of the night, while asleep at the Astor, Thurlow Weed came to my room, awoke me, and said that the manuscript in his hand was an imperfect report of my speech. He wished me to correct it for the newspapers, and be sure and supply some of the eulogies on Seward, which the reporter had omitted. I arose and spent a half hour in revising the speech, and thought no more of the small matter.

In the following June, on the first day when the new Senate assembled, Mr. Weed met me in the lobby before I entered the chamber, and, laying his hand on my shoulder, said, in substance: "Mr. Williams has collected a pile of affidavits, and will contest your seat furiously. You recollect you made a speech in favor of Mr. Seward, at the Astor dinner last winter, and got out of bed at my request and revised it. The Whigs, at this session of the Senate, will change the committee on 'Privileges and Elections,' and (giving my shoulder a squeeze that made me wince), *I think you will like the change!*" The committee was changed. The new member, whereon everything hinged, had served with me in the previous Senate. He was a leading Whig, of the Weed-Seward school. My contestant filed his huge heap of petitions and affidavits. The committee met. I presented two legal points, on a piece of paper about as large as my hand. The new member gave a side glance at them, craved time to examine them, and moved that the committee adjourn one week. Williams flourished his pile of documents, and protested. The motion to adjourn was carried by one majority. The week came around, and the committee again met. The new member assured them that he had been so busy in the Senate that he had not found leisure to look at the papers in my case, and therefore moved an adjournment for two weeks, so that he could examine my two points. Mr. Williams had employed counsel, and there was a tussle over the question of adjournment. The new member again carried his motion. Meanwhile I opposed the canal bill as vigorously as in the session previous to the resignation. When the two weeks came along there was no quorum of the committee present, nor was there at a subsequent meeting, and that was the last I heard of the attempt to unseat me.

It is proper to add that I had not a doubt of the legality of my election, and that I never said a word on the subject to any member of the committee nor to Mr. Weed. But I presume there was not a fool in the legislature so big as to believe that Thurlow Weed's hand was not in the matter.

I was not a candidate for another nomination to the Senate, I could not afford to be a member, and I had no desire to support myself on "the drippings of unclean legislation."

During my membership the presidents of the Senate were Lieutenant-governors Patterson and Church. In the front rank of my colleagues stood Edwin D. Morgan, afterwards Governor and United States Senator; James M. Cook, subsequently Comptroller and Bank Superintendent; Thomas B. Carroll, who became a Canal Appraiser, and Mayor of Troy; George Geddes, the accomplished civil-engineer; William A. Dart, United States District-attorney and Consul-general to Canada; George R. Babcock, Charles A. Mann, Clarkson Crolius, James W. Beekman, and Dr. Brandreth, of medical fame. We were the second senate chosen under the Constitution of 1846. It devolved on us to pass several general statutes for giving effect to provisions of that radical instrument, especially in regard to corporations. Among an unusual number of important measures adopted were the general manufacturing law, the general railroad law, the general school law, and a complete revision of the then very defective code of procedure. I was on the committee that performed this last-mentioned weary task, wherein we were guided by David Dudley Field, Arphaxad Loomis, John C. Spencer, and Nicholas Hill.

I have taken part in the election of five senators in Congress. One of the stormiest conflicts we had in the legislature of 1851 was over the choice of a Senator to succeed Daniel S. Dickinson. The Whigs held the State Senate by a majority of two. In the Assembly they had a good working majority. Their caucus nominated Hamilton Fish for Senator. James

W. Beekman, a Whig Senator, of New York city, threw out the hint that he would not support Fish, because he had fallen too much under the control of Thurlow Weed. The day for electing the Senator arrived. Sixteen Whigs voted for Hamilton Fish, the fifteen Democrats voted for as many different candidates, so that the Fish Whigs could not double over upon them. Beekman voted for Francis Granger. There being no choice, another ballot was taken, with the same result. Thereupon I moved that the Senate adjourn. The roll was called. The sixteen Fish Whigs voted nay, and the fifteen Democrats and Beekman voted yea—a tie. The movement was such a surprise to Lieutenant-governor Church that he forgot to give the casting vote. He was hurrying down the steps, with the gavel in his hand, when somebody pushed him back to the chair, and he announced his vote in the affirmative, and declared the Senate adjourned, amid great excitement. All this while the Assembly was slowly going through the roll, and it was nearly an hour after we had adjourned before they had nominated Governor Fish.

However, our Whig friends lay in wait, and stole a march upon us a few weeks later. One morning, when two Democratic senators were in New York city, they sprung a resolution upon us, to go into the election of a Senator in Congress. After an unbroken struggle of fourteen hours Mr. Fish was elected, the exultant cannon of the victors startling the city from its slumbers, and convincing the Silver Grays that the Woolly Heads still held the capitol.

The Democratic policy in respect to the canals was

mainly due to Michael Hoffman and Arphaxad Loomis, of Herkimer, who represented that county in the Constitutional Convention of 1846, and often appeared as colleagues in the Assembly. In 1843 I spent a week or two in Albany, and frequently dropped into the Assembly, where a bill in regard to the enlargement of the canals was pending. For four days the debate shed darkness rather than light over the subject, and the chamber grew murky. One morning a tallish man, past middle age, with iron-gray locks drooping on his shoulders, and wearing a mixed suit of plain clothes, took the floor on the canal bill. I noticed that pens, newspapers, and all else were laid down, and every eye fixed on the speaker. I supposed he was some quaint old joker from the backwoods, who was going to afford the House a little fun. The first sentences arrested my attention. A beam of light shot through the darkness, and I began to get glimpses of the question at issue. Soon a broad belt of sunshine spread over the chamber. I asked a member, "Who is that?" "Michael Hoffman," was the reply. He spoke for an hour, and though his manner was quiet and his diction simple, he was so methodical and lucid in his argument that, where all had appeared confused before, everything now seemed clear. Mr. Hoffman was at home on this subject, and his speech foreshadowed the articles in the Constitution of 1846 on the canals and the finances.

Judge Loomis was a leader in the Convention of 1846, on the questions pertaining to the judiciary and the legislature. The articles on these subjects were moulded by him. He subsequently bore a conspicuous part in defeating the New York Code of Procedure, whose chief elements were adopted in several other states. The canal law of 1851 having been adjudged unconstitutional, it devolved upon him in the legislature of 1853 to frame and carry through the new constitutional amendment by which the state tided over the difficulty. He and Mr. Hoffman approved the course of the senators who resigned to defeat the measure of 1851.

It has been a disputed point which contained the most men of mark, the Whig Assembly of 1838, chosen in the fall that witnessed the prostration of Van Buren's administration on the Sub-treasury question, or the Democratic Assembly of 1842, elected in the autumn that saw the overthrow of Tyler's administration on the Bank question. In the two there were fifty members that subsequently became distinguished in state and national politics. Horatio Seymour was in the Assembly of 1842. He and Sanford E. Church were the youngest members. Conspicuous among their seniors stood Michael Hoffman and John A. Dix. With a fine address and excellent debating powers, Seymour soon became a leader of one wing of the Democracy. He was in the legislatures of 1844 and 1845, which were agitated by the state issue of the enlargement of the canals and the national issue of the annexation of Texas. These rent the Democrats in New York asunder, the two factions being then generally called Radicals and Conservatives, and not Barnburners and Hunkers, as at a little later date. Seymour was already a chieftain in the ranks of the Conservatives. He measured weapons often with opponents in the legislature like Hoffman, Dix, and Loomis, and attained the high position in the Democratic party as an orator and a manager which he held through his long public career. He was courteous towards opponents in the Assembly, and he gracefully recognized their exhibition of the like treatment of himself. He went into a glow of enthusiasm many years subsequent to the occurrence, as he told me of grim Michael Hoffman's generous course after he had sharply arraigned the veteran Barnburner, during a bitter debate about the canals, and Silas Wright, and kindred themes, which had lasted several days. One morning Hoffman rose to reply to Seymour, but on learning that he was ill he refused to deliver his speech for two or three days, till Seymour was able to be in his seat.

I shall not try to paint a portrait of John Van Buren, the brilliant Barnburner. There could hardly be a wider contrast between two men than the space that divided the Sage of Lindenwald from Prince John. In one particular, however, they were alike. Each had that personal magnetism that binds followers to leaders with hooks of steel. The father was grave, urbane, wary, a safe counsellor, and accustomed to an argumentative and deliberate method of address that befitted the bar and the Senate. Few knew how able a lawyer the elder Van Buren was. The son was enthusiastic, frank, bold, and given to wit, repartee, and a style of oratory admirably adapted to swaying popular assemblies. The younger Van Buren, too, was a sound lawyer. Some of his admirers were wont to tell him that he made a mistake in not aiding to lay the foundations of the Republican party ; " for," said they in 1856, " if you had, you would now have been where Fremont is." " Wait and let us see," was the sarcastic response, " how Fremont turns out."

I heard John Van Buren relate this little anecdote with characteristic humor: When he was Attorney-general he had obtained for an elderly female the valuable monopoly of the right to sell apples, cakes, and candy in the rotunda of the State Capitol. She was an ardent admirer of Prince John, and a vociferous Barnburner. It was admitted that in the campaign of 1848 he had led in the Democratic revolt that gave the thirty-six electoral votes of New York to General Taylor, which defeated General Cass. When the Whigs came into power they threatened to turn the Barnburner woman out of the Capitol. With ruin staring her in the face she repaired to her patron, and begged him to save her. He went to Thurlow Weed, who was supposed to own the Whig party, explained the case, pleaded his services in the Presidential campaign, and said he asked only the single favor of the salvation of the apple-stand. Mr. Weed squeezed the hand of the Prince, shed a sympathizing tear, and hoped he might be able to pull the old woman through. But when the tide of administration reform reached Albany she was swept out of the Capitol, and the apple-stand was bestowed on a female of the Whig persuasion.

The last time I saw John Van Buren was before he left for Europe, to make a final effort to regain his health. I was on the Hudson River Railroad. The conductor said a gentleman in a seat farther forward (pointing to it) wished to see me. As I took the proffered place by his side, and gave him a puzzled look, he said, " You don't know me!" The tones of his voice instantly told me that it was John Van Buren. Though faded, wan, and feeble, the wit remained. He had been at a water-cure establishment. " Think of trying to bring me up by cold water," remarked the Prince, with a quiet smile. " Why," he added, " as they put me in a pack the other night, and stowed me away in an upper loft, where the moonbeams came trickling down upon me through the skylight, I felt as if I were dead and laid out."

When, afterwards, I heard of the sad death of my friend in mid-ocean, I recalled the lines of Scott:

> " Fleet foot on the corrie,
> Sage counsel in cumber,
> Red hand in the foray,
> How sound is thy slumber!"

Mr. Seymour resisted the Barnburner revolt of 1847, and supported General Cass for President in 1848. But he warmly espoused the movement to reunite the party the next year. He was in advance of Governor Marcy in that direction. Seymour pushed forward, while Marcy hung back. Seymour rather liked the Barnburners, except John Van Buren, of whom he was quite jealous and somewhat afraid. But Marcy, after the experiences of 1844 and 1848, denounced them in hard terms, until Seymour's plastic hand kneaded him into a Soft, and the Free-soil Democrats began to talk of him for President in 1852, when the wily old Regency tactician mellowed towards them. Nothing was wanted to carry Marcy clear over except the hostility of Daniel S. Dickinson, who stood in his way to the White House. This he soon encountered, and this reconciled him to the Barnburners. Some of them, however, still distrusted him.

The resignation of senators to defeat the canal bill led to a great meeting in the Capitol grounds at Albany, where Horatio Seymour, who had been beaten for governor the previous fall, made a bold speech in their defence. Mr. Seymour was then among the most effective and eloquent platform orators in New York. Less electrical than John Van Buren, he was more persuasive; less witty, he was more logical; less sarcastic, he was more candid; less denunciatory of antagonists, he was more convincing to opponents. They were rivals—one carrying the standard of the Barnburners, the other bearing the banner of the Hunkers. But on the canal issue they were in accord, each denouncing the unconstitutional measure, and applauding the retiring senators. Both naturally took to statesmanship of a high order.

I frequently spoke on the same platform with Seymour and Van Buren, and attended state and national conventions with each of them. But I never met both of them at the same time on the same platform, nor in the same convention. These two remarkable men had little in common except lofty ambition and rare mental and social gifts. Their salient characteristics were widely dissimilar. Seymour was conciliatory, and cultivated peace. Van Buren was aggressive, and coveted war.

CHAPTER XX.

Whig National Convention of 1852.—Webster's Sad Appearance.—General Scott Nominated for President.—Democratic National Convention of 1852.—Cass, Buchanan, Marcy, Douglas, and Dickinson Aspirants.—An Unexpected Interview by the Virginians.—New York Delegation in Private Conference.—Threats to Throw Seymour out of the Window.—Marcy and Dickinson Slaughter each other.—Pierce Nominated.—Dean Richmond's "Finality."—Pierce's Cabinet.—Dix Cheated, and Marcy Called.—Pierce Approves the Missouri Compromise Repeal.—Rends the Democratic Party Asunder.—Republican Party Formed in 1855-56.—Fremont Nominated for President.—James G. Blaine.—Notices of Horace Greeley, Gerrit Smith, John Jacob Astor, John Brown, and Martin Van Buren.—Brown Handles a Rifle, and Hits the Bull's-eye.—Van Buren Predicts the Overthrow of Slavery amid Convulsions.

THE Whig National Convention met at Baltimore in May, 1852. I was on the train for Washington. At that day we had to cross the mouth of the Susquehanna at Havre de Grace by ferryboat. As the passengers were descending the long, steep stairs into the gorge I saw Mr. Webster, leaning heavily on the arms of two gentlemen, and surrounded by a cavalcade of friends. He was a candidate for the Presidency, in the convention then about to assemble. It was a sad spectacle. The great statesman was then so shattered in health that four months afterwards he sank into his tomb. But though a wreck, he bore up sturdily while clutching at the glittering prize he had so long pursued. He received a mortifyingly small vote in the convention. General Scott carried off the nomination. "Oh, Charles," exclaimed Webster to Mr. Stetson, of the Astor House, a few days afterwards, "what pains me is that the South, for which I had done and sacrificed so much, did not give me a single vote!"

General Scott made a tour of the country, exhibiting his stalwart figure, and discoursing of "the rich Irish brogue and the sweet German accent." He carried only the four states of Massachusetts, Vermont, Kentucky, and Tennessee. It was the end of the Whig party. The slavery controversy destroyed Webster in the convention, Scott at the polls, and precipitated that grand old organization into a fathomless pit. Close behind stood the Democrats, giving three cheers for their victory, on the crumbling edge of the chasm that had engulfed the Whigs. "It is an irrepressible conflict," said Mr. Seward.

The Democratic National Convention at Baltimore, in 1852, was a struggle for the nomination to the Presidency between Cass, Buchanan, Marcy, and Douglas. The New York delegation was divided, in the proportion of twenty-three for Marcy, whose leader was Horatio Seymour, and thirteen for Cass, whose leader was Daniel S. Dickinson. It soon became apparent that Mr. Dickinson himself was a candidate, and was looking for success to a combination between a large share of the supporters of Cass and a smaller contingent of the friends of Buchanan. Indeed, Mr. Dickinson told me so. The ballotings were many and wearisome, each of the aspirants doing his best to pull down his rivals.

At the close of the first or second day I was passing through the hall of Barnum's Hotel, when, to my surprise, I was invited by Dickinson to enter a room where the Virginia delegation (which thus far had voted for Buchanan) was in consultation. After an introduction, and a statement that I was a Barnburner, the chairman asked me whether, if Mr. Dickinson were to receive the nomination, he could carry New York? Never can I forget the anxious look of Dickinson as they waited for the answer. I promptly replied that Mr. Dickinson, and Governor Marcy, and Mr. Douglas, and any other man whom the convention nominated, would receive the electoral vote of New York. I then retired from this very unexpected interview. Dickinson followed me, thanked me, but regretted that I had mentioned any other name than his.

The next morning Virginia voted for Dickinson. I then saw what the interview of the previous day meant. Dickinson rose, made a short speech, thanked Virginia, and begged its delegation to support General Cass. This was the keynote for the combination on Dickinson. He asked me if I thought Virginia would adhere to him, and I frankly told him "No," for I had reasons for regarding its vote merely as a compliment. Mr. Dickinson's friends used to assert that he threw away the Presidency on this occasion. I happened to know better. He never stood for a moment where he could control the Virginia vote— the hinge whereon all was to turn. The convention generally believed that the result in November would depend on New York, and it was ready to accept any candidate upon whom the delegates from that state would unite. In the protracted and weary ballotings Marcy rose steadily, till his vote reached ninety-eight. The New York delegation then retired for consultation. The convention hall and its adjoining rooms were over a market, which was besieged by noisy carts and trucks. One of the rules of the convention authorized the delegates of any state to cast its vote for such candidates as the majority of its delegates might direct. In the retiring-room Seymour moved a resolution that on the next ballot the vote of New York be cast solidly for William L. Marcy. If a bomb had exploded among them it could hardly have caused more excitement. Oliver Charlick, a superheated Hunker from Long Island, threatened to throw Seymour out of the window unless he withdrew the resolution. Seymour saw that it would be unwise to force a united vote for Marcy in the face of so much hostility, and he finally recalled the resolution. Perhaps, too, he did not relish the idea of being thrown into the street among the struggling carts and trucks. Thus ended the chances of Marcy. In this style it was that Dickinson and Marcy, the envenomed rival sachems, scalped each other in the great wigwam at Baltimore.

On the next ballot (I think it was the next) Virginia voted for Franklin Pierce. The convention was weary, and soon the stampede came, and the New Hampshire brigadier was nominated.

The Barnburners did not weep over the defeat of Marcy, rejoiced at the discomfiture of Cass, and were in doubt about Pierce. The convention had adopted resolutions declaring the Pro-slavery Compromise Acts of 1850 a "finality" on that subject. On the way home from Baltimore a Hunker was teasing Dean Richmond, of Buffalo, by telling him that the proceedings were a finality on the Wilmot Proviso. "A finality on Cass," was the swift response of the bluff Dean. Though so destitute of all literary furnishment as to be scarcely able to write grammatically, Mr. Richmond carried on his broad shoulders one of the clearest heads in the ranks of the Barnburners.

Pierce was elected by a majority so large that it turned his weak head. He was a calamity to the Democracy and the nation. He yielded to unwise counsellors, and favored the repeal of the Missouri Compromise, which rent the party asunder during his official term, and arrayed against him a large body of Jacksonian Democrats of the type of Thomas H. Benton, Sam Houston, and Francis P. Blair, senior. This insane measure bore bitter fruits in the perturbed administration of Buchanan, and ultimately plunged the country into one of the most portentous and bloody civil wars in all history. In the construction of his cabinet Pierce was a dissembler. Daniel S. Dickinson was urged upon him for a place by an enthusiastic following, but he spurned the distinguished ex-Senator, and drove him into the ranks of the enemies that prevented his renomination and expelled him from power. Pierce first promised the New York seat in his Cabinet to General Dix. He afterwards gave it to Governor Marcy. Dix was consoled with the pledge that he should soon be sent as Minister to

Paris, but was meanwhile set to watching the vaults of the New York sub-treasury. He sat there wearily through the spring, summer, and fall, waiting for the French mission to turn up. I accidentally met him on Broadway on the morning when Pierce's first annual message appeared, and asked him how he liked it. "It is a good message," said he. He then added, with a spice of bitterness in his tone, "If I can say this I think anybody can afford to." If General Dix had not believed that the holding of some office was essential to his existence he would have thrown his sub-treasury commission in the face of the President who had deceived him. It would be difficult to name any other man in this country who filled so many important offices, and so acceptably, as John A. Dix.

The precise date of the organization of the Republican party in the nation is in dispute. In New York it was reduced to form, at Syracuse, in the fall of 1855. Its component elements were Anti-slavery Whigs, Barnburner Democrats, Abolitionists proper, and Free-soil Know-Nothings. Committees of conference, in which Thurlow Weed and Preston King were prominent figures, settled the preliminaries, and the new party assembled in Weiting Hall, with Reuben E. Fenton, of the Barnburner wing, filling the chair. I helped to launch the new party, and then, on the afternoon train of that day, by request of Henry C. Martindale, who was subsequently Attorney-General of the state and Major-General in the army, I went to Rochester and delivered a Republican speech. Of course, I was quite at home on the slavery topic. My address was reported, and generally copied in New York. I subsequently spoke in Buffalo with Governor Seward, and addressed other large meetings in that campaign. Our first venture on this stormy sea was not successful. Our state ticket was submerged in the Know-Nothing breakers.

The Pierce administration repealed the Missouri Compromise. This precipitated the doom of slavery. The Republican party was the legitimate outcome. I helped to organize it in the state of New York, and was a member of the National Convention at Philadelphia, in 1856, which nominated Fremont and Dayton. I delivered numerous addresses in their support from Maine to Ohio. The Philadelphia Convention was opened with prayer by Rev. Albert Barnes. Colonel Harvey S. Lane, of Indiana, presided, and occasionally rapped on the table with his boot-heels to preserve order. James G. Blaine was one of the secretaries. Lane, afterwards senator in Congress, was nearly as tall as Mr. Lincoln. He led the cheers for Lincoln at Chicago in 1860. "When that fellow Lane," exclaimed a disgusted Seward delegate, "jumped on the table with his hat on his uplifted cane and screamed for Lincoln he looked as if he were thirty feet high."

The feeble cause I had espoused at Cincinnati in 1832 rested, in 1856, on the broad shoulders of a strong party which was marching on to victory.

Whenever I think of Horace Greeley the scene rises before me of a flaxen-haired boy in a log-cabin in a cleft of the Green Mountains, lying on the hearth, after a hard day's work in a scrubby field, reading a book by the blaze of pine-knots. But these pine-knots lighted the barefooted youth to the path that led to great achievements and enduring fame.

I first met Greeley on the front stairs of a Graham boarding-house in New York city, where he was living on bran-bread and cold water. He was then editor of the *New-Yorker*, a journal of which he was justly proud. The encounter on the stairway was accidental. His wife, fresh from North Carolina, had sunk down at that rather inconvenient spot in a sort of hysterical swoon, and seemed so reluctant to yield her vantage-ground that ingress and egress by the boarders were only possible by carefully stepping over her. Mr. Greeley, with a deprecatory air, was bending down, and in soothing tones was trying to persuade her to seek a more comfortable resting-place. Early friends of the wedded pair will recall the fact that they became acquainted at this William Street hostelry, and that their espousals were chronicled in some pleasant verses that bore the refrain, "Maid of the Graham-house, sunny and sweet!"

As an illustration of the vicissitudes of journalism, while at the same time pointing to a great political error, I will relate the following anecdote: The first report that came from the Liberal National Convention of 1872 stated that Charles Francis Adams was nominated for President. Happening to be in the *Sun* office, Mr. Dana asked me to write an article on the subject. I went to my law-office, and spent three hours in preparing three columns of what I thought was excellent matter, including a rather imposing sketch of the Adams family, from the first John down to the alleged Liberal nominee. On returning to the *Sun* rooms with my editorial, imagine my surprise to learn that Horace Greeley, and not an Adams of any sort, was the candidate. I cast my labored production into the waste-basket, and went home.

The campaign of 1872 was a blunder on the part of those who opposed the re-election of Grant. If the bolting Republicans had nominated Greeley, and the regular Democrats had presented a candidate like Horatio Seymour, for instance, General Grant would have been defeated. But it proved to be impossible to persuade a large class of Democrats to vote for "the founder of the *New York Tribune*."

My last glimpse of Horace Greeley was soon after the election of 1872. He darted out of the *Tribune* office, ran against me, and started down Park Row at a rapid pace. I contrived to keep up with him, and followed him into a street-car at the Astor House. On accosting him he gave me a wild stare that alarmed me. I inquired after his health, and he replied, " I have ruined all my friends in the election, and now they are destroying me." A few more words satisfied me that his mind was clouded. How sad was his end!

Gerrit Smith helped to quarry the corner-stone of the Republican party. He was the very friend of the slave. His purse was always open for the promotion of their cause. When I was a secretary of the American Anti-slavery Society he placed in my hands at one time his check for $10,000 for its treasury—a sum equal to $25,000 now. He was the protector and patron of runaway negroes who followed the fortunes of the North Star. Forty years ago, at his palatial mansion in Peterboro', and which looked like the country-seat of an English nobleman, it would be singular if you did not find among the fashionable guests from New York, Albany, and Philadelphia surrounding his hospitable board at least one or two fugitive slaves. Indeed—and especially in the summer season—his visitors were of the most miscellaneous and amusing description. There you might meet a dozen wealthy and refined visitors from the metropolitan cities; a sprinkling of negroes from the sunny South on their way to Canada; a crazy Millerite or two, who, disgusted with the world, thought it destined to be burned up at an early day; an adventurer who wanted Mr. Smith to invest largely in some utterly impracticable patent right, while the throng would be checkered with three or four Indians of the neighborhood, the remnants of the once powerful Oneidas, who remembered the father, and felt pretty sure that they could get something out of his munificent son. The high-born guests had come to enjoy themselves during the summer solstice at this fine rural retreat, and they always had a good time. As to the rest, they were never sent empty away, especially the negroes and the Indians, the former accepting cash in hand and good advice about the best route to Canada, while the latter departed in good time with shoulders stooping under burdens of flour, beef, and other edibles. But Mr. Smith never was known to invest in any of the patent rights, and he took not a single share of stock in the scheme for burning up the world.

I was, many years ago, riding with Gerrit Smith in one of the counties of northern New York. He suddenly stopped the carriage, and, looking around for a few minutes, said, "We are now on some of my poor land, familiarly known as the John Brown tract;" and he then added, "I own eight hundred thousand acres, of which this is a part, and all in one piece." Everybody knows that Judge Peter Smith, his father, purchased the most of this land at sales by the comptroller of the state for unpaid taxes, and left it by will to his son Gerrit. He said that he owned land in fifty-six of the sixty counties in New York. Some of this brought him a handsome income, though he gave a good deal of it away years before he died. He was also a landholder in other states of the Union.

Early in 1837 Mr. Smith's father died, leaving a large estate to Gerrit, charged with heavy legacies and debts. Two or three months after the decease of his father the well-remembered panic of 1837 occurred. The banks had suspended specie payments, and could afford Mr. Smith no loans to meet pressing obligations. So embarrassed was he that his counsel advised him to make an assignment of his property for the benefit of his creditors. Mr. Smith declined to make the assignment until he had first conferred with the elder John Jacob Astor, the old friend of his father. Smith wrote to Astor, and informed him of his situation, and said that, if possible, he would be glad if he could make him a loan, and take such security therefor as he had to offer. Mr. Astor invited him to come to New York and talk the matter over. He came, and dined with the great millionaire. Astor, of course, knew his errand, but, during the protracted dinner, seemed more inclined to tell anecdotes about his excursions thirty and forty years before with Peter Smith up the valley of the Mohawk than to listen to details about Gerrit Smith's present obligations and the value of the property which he could put under mortgage. As they sat at the hospitable board Mr. Astor would frequently break in with the enthusiastic exclamation, "Why, Gerrit, how much you do look as your father used to when he and I went up the Mohawk among the Indians after furs!" At length they came down to business, and Mr. Astor asked Smith how much of a loan he wanted. He told him $250,000. "Do you want it immediately, and all at once?" said Astor. "I do," said Gerrit. "Then you shall have it." It was arranged that Smith should give Astor a mortgage on his Oswego water-power, for which Smith had paid $14,000 about fifteen years before, for this loan of $250,000. Mr. Smith returned to Peterboro', and in three or four days received Mr. Astor's check by mail for $250,000. He made out the mortgage and sent it to Oswego to be recorded, with directions to mail it to Mr. Astor as soon as it was inscribed on the records. Smith went on using the money, and supposed that all had gone right about the forwarding of the mortgage. After a delay of several weeks, judge of his surprise at receiving a letter from Mr. Astor, saying that he was afraid that his friend Smith had forgotten to make out that mortgage which they talked about when he was last in the city. Smith hastened to Oswego, and found that, through some stupidity, the county clerk had forgotten to mail the mortgage to Astor, although it had been duly and seasonably recorded. Of course it was now sent forward, accompanied by an appropriate explanation. Thus, for several weeks, John Jacob Astor had nothing but Gerrit Smith's word for a loan of $250,000. This incident lets in a flood of light upon the characters of these two remarkable men.

I have not space to give even a list of the martyrs who endured pains and penalties unto death in the Anti-slavery cause. The tears of an enfranchised race will bedew their graves, and an appreciative posterity will erect monuments to their memory. One well-remembered figure looms on my vision from his lonely resting-place in the Adirondacks. I met John Brown but once, and then unexpectedly, at Gerrit Smith's. Mr. Smith's son, Green, was a sportsman. He had an assortment of rifles, and was a fair shot. After dinner Green went out with a couple of companions to fire at a target. I was looking on when Captain Brown appeared on the scene. The firing was rather wild. Brown watched awhile, and then closely examined the rifles, selected one, loaded it, and faced the target. He pointed the weapon at the ground, with his eye on the barrel, raised it rapidly, and the instant it came to a level he fired, and hit the bull's eye right in the centre. Handing the rifle to Green Smith, he said, with a grim smile, "Boys, that is the way to shoot," and slowly returned to the house. Soon after Brown's execution an editorial from my pen appeared in the New York *Tribune*, which I am willing should stand as my opinion of his character and deeds. He will fill a unique niche in American history. The echo of his fame will reverberate along the colonnades of the centuries, and preserve from oblivion the names of those who put him to death.

In 1858 I had the pleasure of spending a day at the hospitable mansion of ex-President Van Buren, near Kinderhook. The Sage of Lindenwald was instructive and entertaining. The most interesting portion of his conversation related to slavery. Referring to the campaign of 1848, he said that his utterances on that great evil were his matured convictions. "I have nothing to modify or change," he remarked. With serious earnestness he added, "The end of slavery will come—amid terrible convulsions, I fear, but it will come." A word about Mr. Van Buren's personal following. Has it ever been equalled by any other New York statesman? In the contest of 1848 he carried over, on a bolt from the regular Presidential nominee, more than half the Democratic voters in the state. How few Governor Seward was able to lead over to Andrew Johnson's "policy" in the election of 1866! I feel constrained to pay peculiar honors to Mr. Van Buren for the course he and his followers pursued in 1847–48 in regard to the extension of slavery. Their protest at the ballot-boxes in that crucial emergency was the turning-point in the great controversy that ultimated, fifteen years later, in the overthrow of the "institution" and the preservation of the Union. But for the aid of Democrats who had been trained in the school of Martin Van Buren, Silas Wright, and Samuel J. Tilden, the Union and the Constitution might perhaps have gone to pieces in the terrible epoch of 1861–65.

CHAPTER XXI.

William H. Seward as Senator.—Seward on Weed.—Seward Unbending.—Seward and Judge Sackett.—Weed the "State Fifer."—Seward and Conkling.—Conkling Elected to Congress in 1858.—Seward on Greeley.—John Sherman, Candidate for Speaker.—Tom Corwin as an Orator.—The Jewish Rabbi Prays.—Henry Winter Davis.—Pennington Chosen Speaker.—Slidell's Bill to Purchase Cuba.—Wade and Toombs in Close Contact.—"Land for the Landless *versus* Niggers for the Niggerless."—Scene in the Senate in 1859 between Benjamin and Seward.—Seward Smokes Benjamin's Cigar.—Scene in the Senate in 1834 between Clay and Van Buren.—Van Buren Takes a Pinch of Clay's Snuff.

Mr. SEWARD represented New York in the Senate in a grand and memorable era. He rose to the level of his responsibilities, and was courageous, sagacious, sincere, and earnest. He led a forlorn hope against formidable foes, over which the cause he championed finally triumphed. He was grave in argument and dignified in demeanor, and, though rhetorical and even ornate in style, he never indulged in those flashy flippances that sometimes succeed in palming themselves off as wit, but which legitimate wit repudiates as a bastard progeny.

Since Mr. Dickinson and General Dix left the Senate, New York has sent several respectable members to that body, but no really able men, when measured by a lofty standard, except Mr. Seward and Mr. Conkling. Mr. Evarts is yet to be thoroughly tried on this new field. He doubtless remembers that Erskine. one of the greatest advocates that ever addressed an English jury, and Jeffrey, who shone so brilliantly in the Scotch courts, failed in Parliament. The many-sided men like Brougham and Webster are few in number.

Nobody knew better than Mr. Seward that, if he had been the candidate for the Presidency in 1856, he would have received the same vote that Fremont did, and that his nomination in 1860 would have inevitably followed, and he would have entered the White House instead of Lincoln. Mr. Seward more than hinted to confidential friends that Mr. Weed betrayed him for Fremont.

Mr. Weed himself told the following story : He and Mr. Seward were riding up Broadway, and when passing the bronze statue of Lincoln, in Union Square, Seward said : " Weed, if you had been faithful to me, I should have been there instead of Lincoln." " Seward," replied Weed, " is it not better to be alive in a carriage with me than to be dead and set up in bronze ?"

At the close of the Fremont campaign some money remained in the treasury of the National Committee. William M. Chace, of Providence, the secretary, favored its expenditure on the famous " Helper Book." Edwin D. Morgan, the chairman, would consent to this, if Mr. Weed advised it. Being at Washington in the winter of 1857–58, I met Mr. Chace, who had come there for the rather queer purpose of requesting Mr. Seward to request Mr. Weed to request Mr. Morgan to adopt Chace's plan for the disposal of this money. Chace not knowing Mr. Seward personally, I went one evening to his house to introduce him. The Senator was alone with his after-dinner cigar. Chace explained his case to his attentive listener, I sitting near, reading a newspaper. The Senator puffed out a cloud of smoke and began to talk in that deliberate style so familiar to his friends. "Mr. Chace, I understand you want me to speak to Mr. Weed, and request him to advise Mr. Morgan to make a certain disposition of the funds in question?" Mr. Chace bowed. "Mr. Chace," resumed the Senator, "Mr. Weed is a very peculiar man. He is a very secretive man. He is an unfathomable man. He thinks I am always driving everything to the devil. But throughout my public life he has told me to do this or that particular thing, and I have done it. He has told me not to do this or that, and I have refrained from doing it. Whether in all this he was cheating me or cheating somebody else (for I take it for granted he is always cheating somebody), I don't know." He then suggested to Mr. Chace to go to Senator Simon Cameron, and tell him he had sent him, and take his advice in the matter of the funds. Some congressmen dropped in, and Chace and I left. We did not speak for a block or two. My Rhode Island coadjutor then jerked my arm, burst into a laugh, and said, "Did you ever hear anything equal to that?"

We never know a public man till we see him in undress. Webster in a boat at Marshfield, with a fishing-rod in his hand, was a different person from Webster in the Senate holding spellbound the *élite* of the nation. Mr. Seward was an intense toiler in the thorny field of politics. He delighted to throw off his burden, and unbend in a small circle of friends. At Seneca Falls there resided Garry V. Sackett, whom Seward, when Governor, had appointed a judge of the Common Pleas. He was a gentleman farmer, large and stately in person, and dressed in the style of Webster. He was on familiar terms with Seward, took great liberties with him, and the Senator often came to Seneca, and had a free-and-easy round of fun. Sackett did not know as much as he thought he did, and Seward sometimes made a butt of him and roared with laughter, though the Judge would occasionally make reprisals on the spot. When the Senator visited the Judge, I was generally called in, and sometimes the young people of the village were invited for the evening. The latter looked with awe upon the distinguished statesman from Auburn.

During one afternoon, Seward had been firing his teasing arrows at Sackett. In the evening, the Judge, arrayed in full Websterian costume, posed before a houseful of young people, and went for the Senator. He brought out and pinned on the wall the famous caricature in which, when Seward was Governor, Thurlow Weed is depicted as the state fifer, with the principal state officers marching in Indian file behind him, and straining themselves to the utmost to keep up with the musician, who is blowing at the top of his bent. Indeed, the little Governor, in trying to tread in the tracks of the tall fifer, had torn his trousers at rather a delicate spot. The likenesses were perfect. The picture was widely circulated, and it so closely accorded with the jeers in the Democratic newspapers that it was very annoying to Mr. Seward even after he became Senator, for Mr. Weed, in popular estimation, was still "The Dictator."

On the occasion referred to, Sackett elaborately explained the picture to the youngsters in the presence of Seward, telling what a great leader Weed was, how obediently the Governor followed him, how closely even to that day he kept step with him (at this point seemingly trying to conceal the rent in his trousers), assuring the deeply interested listeners that Seward owed his success in politics wholly to Weed; and then, looking over his shoulder to where Seward sat smoking, exclaimed, "Is not that so, Governor?" The response came back, "Sackett, you are a fool. Go and get me another cigar."

At another time, before Mr. Seward and a like audience, and to "get even" with the teasing Senator, the Judge told the story of his visit to the Anti-renters, in the Helderberg, in company with Seward, soon after he was chosen Governor. The Anti-renters were making an uproar. The legislature had authorized a commission to consider their grievances, and Mr. Seward had appointed Sackett one of the commissioners. The latter proposed that they visit the troubled district, the young Governor assented, notice was sent out three or four days ahead, and they rode to the Helderberg in a stately barouche drawn by four horses. Long afterwards, on due provocation, at Seneca Falls, Sackett took reprisals of the bantering Senator after dinner, by describing the scene at Helderberg. He said that when the barouche arrived, several hundred Anti-renters were on the ground. Sackett, standing six feet two inches high, and dressed in imposing costume, got out first. The crowd rushed upon him, saluted him as Governor, and gave three cheers. The commissioner lifted his gold-headed cane high in air, and exclaimed, " Stop, gentlemen! You have made the same mistake that the people of New York made last fall. They doubtless ought to have chosen me Governor, but, instead, they elected this man, whom I present to you as William H. Seward." Sackett, then addressing the dinner-party, would add, with great relish, " You ought to have seen how the crowd fell back when I introduced Seward as the Governor. He was clambering out of the carriage while they were giving me the three cheers, and many of them said they didn't believe that little man was the Governor." Then turning to the Senator, he said, " Wasn't it a funny scene, Seward!" The Senator replied that when the commissioners went into the Helderberg to take testimony, Sackett wasted all their time in telling preposterous stories that nobody believed.

In 1858 Roscoe Conkling was the Republican candidate for Congress in Oneida. Mr. O. B. Matteson, who had previously represented this district, was zealously opposing him. Matteson had long been a personal friend of Mr. Seward. Hard pressed, Mr. Conkling sent for Mr. Seward and myself to address a county meeting at Rome. I was called to keep the Republican Barnburners in line for Conkling. Mr. Seward was summoned to counteract the effect of Matteson's hostility. Wrapped in a blue broadcloth cloak, with elegant trimmings, Conkling surveyed the large audience with anxious eye. I spoke first, eulogizing Seward and Conkling. The Senator commenced his address with a hearty encomium upon Matteson, by way of preface to the matter in hand. He then spoke generally in support of the Republican cause, and eloquently commended his young friend Conkling to the voters of Oneida. I have been told that this eulogium of Mr. Matteson was retained in the published report of Mr. Seward's speech under the special direction of Mr. Seward, and against the earnest protest of Mr. Conkling's friends. The next morning I went to Utica, and was amused to see that nearly the only notice taken of the Rome meeting, by the general press, was a full report of Mr. Seward's eulogium on Mr. Matteson. This, of course, would go the grand rounds of the newspapers in the state. I met Mr. Conkling. My acquaintance with the English language is not sufficiently intimate to enable me to describe how angry he was. Mr. Conkling was elected. Then commenced those twenty years of service, in the House and Senate, which have left their lustrous mark on the records of Congress.

I was at Mr. Seward's, in Auburn. The conversation ran on public affairs and public men. He remarked that it was a long time before he fathomed one prominent character in New York. This was Horace Greeley. He said he had supposed Greeley was doing his work from philanthropic motives, and had no desire for office; but subsequently he found he was mistaken, and that he was very eager to hold office. I replied, in rather a careless tone, "Senator, do you not think it would have been better for you if you had let him have office?" Mr. Seward looked at me intently, rolled out a cloud of tobacco smoke, and then slowly responded, "I don't know but it would." I was not aware how point-blank a shot I had fired, for I did not then know of the existence of the letter of November 11, 1854, addressed by Greeley to Seward, dissolving the old political firm of "Seward, Weed, and Greeley," by the withdrawal of the junior partner. Greeley's opposition to Seward's nomination to the Presidency, in 1860, brought this unique epistle out of the secret archives of Mr. Seward. It is printed in Greeley's "Recollections of a Busy Life," and will repay perusal by students of fallen human nature.

Thomas Corwin was the prince of orators. He was elected to Congress in 1858. He had long before won fame throughout the Union. No party had an absolute majority in the House that witnessed the terrible era that ushered in the rebellion. The balance of power between the Republicans and Democrats, in the House, was held by a small body of Northern Know-Nothings, Southern Know-Nothings, and Old-line Whigs. John Sherman, on the nomination of Corwin, became the Republican candidate for Speaker. The contest, commencing in December, 1859, continued for eight weeks. The ballotings were interspersed with a variety of speeches. One morning Corwin arose. The House and galleries overflowed with spectators. His address lasted three days. His aim was to prove that in their efforts to prohibit by law the extension of slavery the Republicans were a constitutional party. It was one of the most wonderful speeches I ever heard. All that had gone before it, and all that came after it, in this weary contest of two months, seemed mere chattering in comparison with an effort that was replete with logic, wit, humor, repartee, sarcasm, and pertinent references to history, and sketches of statesmen in early days who held the doctrines of the Wilmot Proviso; and all the while, amid the glitter of the lighter and gayer passages of the speech, the orator was carrying forward the heavy chain of ratiocination.

One day there was an unusual commotion on the floor. The pages were running to and fro, and a hundred quivering pencils were keeping tally to the call of the clerk. It was seen that all the Democrats, and a dangerously large share of the Know-Nothings and Old-line Whigs, were voting for Mr. Smith, of North Carolina, a new candidate. Ere the result was announced, John Sherman rose. "Mr. Clerk, please call my name. "John Sherman," said the clerk. "Thomas Corwin," responded Sherman. On counting the tally list, it was found that the votes cast for Sherman and the one vote for Corwin were precisely equal to the total votes given for Smith. A narrow escape.

That evening Sherman withdrew, and ex-Governor William Pennington, of New Jersey, was named as the Republican candidate. There being no regular chaplain, it had been the custom to invite the Washington clergy in turn to officiate in that capacity. The next morning the Jewish rabbi appeared for the first time. Arrayed in his sacerdotal robes, he lifted his open eyes to the ceiling and prayed that the God of Abraham, Isaac, and Jacob would break the deadlock in the House, and set the wheels of Congress in motion. Winter Davis, who had steadily voted against Sherman, was pacing the hall in the rear of the seats. When the clerk called his name, he answered, in a tone that thrilled the crowd, "Pennington!" The elegant member from Baltimore had a following. After one or two ballots Pennington was chosen, and the Republicans had a speaker. The House took a long breath, and determined to have some sport. A motion to adjourn was voted down, and so was another and another. The new speaker gave the floor to everybody that asked for it, till a dozen members were talking at once, amid screams of laughter. Mr. John Cochrane, a Democrat, crept up the marble steps, and told Mr. Pennington that if he would recognize him he would move an adjournment, and he believed enough Democrats would vote with him to carry the motion. "Oh, no, Mr. Cochrane," said the speaker; let her run." After it had had fun enough the House adjourned, with the clumsiest presiding officer that ever filled the chair.

John Slidell introduced into the Senate a bill to appropriate twenty or thirty millions of dollars (I forget which) for the purchase of Cuba. Of course, the object was to strengthen the slave power. When he moved to take up the bill, it was antagonized by a motion to take up the bill for granting public lands free of cost to settlers, known as the Homestead bill. A debate immediately arose on the merits of the two measures, which ran into the night, and became intensely bitter towards the close. Robert Toombs, of Georgia, whose seat was right beside Benjamin F.

Wade's, was eloquently abusive. He shook his fist at Seward, who at that moment was standing in the door of a cloak-room calmly puffing a cigar, and called him a little demagogue. He accused the Republicans of being afraid of the "lacklanders" (as he styled those who might wish to accept the privileges of the homestead policy), frequently thumping his desk by way of emphasis, and occasionally striking a blow on Wade's. As he took his seat, half a dozen senators sprang to their feet. Vice-President Breckinridge could not but give the floor to Wade, for he leaped clear from the carpet. Turning short on Toombs, he exclaimed, " Afraid, are we? Afraid, are we? I never saw anything or any man under God's heavens that I was afraid of," at the same time smiting Toombs's desk with his fist, which came inconveniently close to the Georgian's nose. Two or three more sentences in this vein were hurled at him, accompanied by heavy thuds on the desk. Toombs rolled back his chair, and said, " I except my friend from Ohio from my too sweeping remark." "Very well," resumed Wade, " if you wish to back out, you can go." He then briefly dissected Slidell's measure, contrasting it with the homestead policy, and exclaimed, " We accept the issue tendered to us, and will go to the people on it, viz., land for the landless *versus* niggers for the niggerless." The excited auditory burst into loud applause, which was not easily suppressed. Slidell's motion was rejected, Mr. Douglas rubbing his hands in great glee at the discomfiture of his sly, sour enemy.

It is rare that we meet a character that embodied

so much rough grandeur as Benjamin Franklin Wade's. He did not know what fear was. Toombs was merely an eloquent bully. He had little of that courage that stands fire.

During the four turbulent years of Buchanan's administration, Mr. Seward was recognized both by coadjutors and opponents as the leader of his party in the Senate. Though always respectful towards antagonists, and never for a moment losing his equanimity in debate, he was so radical in his opinions on negro slavery, and so bold in their utterance, that he drew upon himself the hostility of the Southern senators, and especially such slavery propagandists as Toombs, Slidell, Mason, and Benjamin. The latter had formerly been a Whig, and his seat was on the hereditary Whig side of the chamber, where now sat in adjoining chairs four leaders who had supported General Taylor's administration, namely, Seward and Benjamin, Wade and Toombs, the latter then being in the House. Among the ready, pungent, and eloquent orators in the Senate stood Judah P. Benjamin. One day, at the close of a set speech on the Kansas embroglio, he made an impassioned and bitter attack on Seward. As Benjamin resumed his seat, Seward rose, and, turning to his assailant, said, in a calm and indifferent tone, " Benjamin, give me a cigar, and when your speech is printed send me a copy." Seward then retired to the cloak-room and smoked Benjamin's cigar.

Though this was done without affectation on the part of Seward, it was nevertheless a close copy of the dramatic scene in the Senate a quarter of a century before, wherein Clay and Van Buren were the leading actors. It was in the height of the conflict over the removal, by order of President Jackson, of the Federal funds from the United States Bank and its branches, which had set the country all aflame, particularly in commercial and financial centres. Mr. Van Buren, the Vice-President, was a model of courtesy as a presiding officer. The Whigs in the Senate, led by their great chieftains, Clay and Webster, demanded a return of the moneys to the bank. They daily hurled anathemas against Jackson, declaring that he was a despot of the deepest dye, and that an indignant people would soon rise and hurl him from power. They compared him to Nero, Charles I., and other tyrants of olden times. One morning Mr. Clay, in the course of a vehement harangue, implored the Vice-President to instantly leave the Senate chamber and repair to the White House, and on his bended knees before the despot exert his well-known influence over him, and insist upon the restoration of the deposits to the bank without an hour's delay, as the only means of averting a revolution in the country. As Clay closed his eloquent philippic, Van Buren called a senator to the chair and went straight across the chamber to Clay's seat. The tall Kentuckian rose and stared at the little magician, while the perturbed spectators awaited the result with undisguised anxiety. Van Buren bowed gracefully to Clay, and said, "Mr. Senator, allow me to be indebted to you for another pinch of your aromatic Maccaboy." Clay waved his hand towards the gold snuff-box on his desk, and took his seat, while Van Buren took a delicate pinch and leisurely returned to the Vice-President's chair.

Perhaps some of those who witnessed the Bank-Biddle-Clay-Webster-Jackson-Van Buren "revolution" of 1832–1836, and lived to see the convulsions of 1861–1865, may be tempted to look back upon the financial turmoils of the earlier epoch with feelings akin to contempt. But history would be incomplete unless it took note of many little things that derive all their importance from the magnitude of the men who bore a part in them.

CHAPTER XXII.

Turbulent Scenes in the House in 1859, 1860.—Grow Knocks Keitt Down.—Crawford Threatens Thad. Stevens.—Tribute to Stevens.—Stephen A. Douglas; his Re-election to the Senate over Abraham Lincoln in 1859.—His Reception in the Senate.—Pro-Slavery Democrats Assail him.—Seward Preparing for the Chicago Convention of 1860.—Deluded as to his Strength.—The Senators Opposed to him.—Corwin and Lincoln Speak in New England Early in 1860.—New-Yorkers who Oppose Seward at Chicago.—Lincoln Nominated.—Scene at Auburn when the News Came.—Seward Embittered.—Crushed Presidential Aspirations of Seward, Greeley, Clay, and Webster.—Ira Harris Chosen Senator in 1861.—Defeat of Greeley and Evarts.—Rufus King's Chair in the Senate.—Its Distinguished Occupants.

DURING Buchanan's administration scenes often occurred in the House more dramatic and perilous than any in the Senate. I was present when Galusha A. Grow, of Pennsylvania, knocked down Lawrence M. Keitt, of South Carolina, under circumstances that came near to involving the members, and perhaps the galleries, in bloodshed. It was due to the caution and firmness of Speaker Orr that the catastrophe was averted. At a later day Owen Lovejoy, of Illinois, a brother of the Alton martyr, while delivering a speech, unconsciously advanced step by step across the area in front of the clerk's desk. A Southern member laid his hand on Lovejoy's shoulder, saying, "Go back to your own side." Instantly the area was full of members, the most of whom were armed. The ominous "click" of weapons was heard. Elihu B. Washburne, of Illinois, clutched at the supposed hair of William Barksdale, of Mississippi, and pulled off his wig. High above the din rose the voice of William Kellogg, of Illinois, shouting, "My colleague shall be heard!" The crowd swayed to and fro, the mace of the little sergeant-at-arms dancing about on the surface till it was thrown clear out of the vortex, recalling the scene in Westminster Hall, when Cromwell, who had entered to expel the Rump Parliament, was confronted with the mace, and cried, "Take away that bauble!" The frightened Speaker rapped, rapped, rapped, shouted "Order, order, order!" and the storm finally subsided.

Thaddeus Stevens, clearly within parliamentary rules, was addressing the House on another occasion in his usual pungent style, when Martin J. Crawford, of Georgia, followed by a dozen other Secessionists, rushed towards him, some of them threatening to assassinate him on the spot unless he retracted his words. The brave old commoner maintained his ground, and stood by his words. He was then in his sixty-ninth year, and a cripple. Crawford was forty, and tall, wiry, and athletic. The assault plunged the House into a vortex of excitement. The deliberation and dignity of Stevens cowed Crawford and his caitiffs, who, one after another, slunk into their seats, while the great debater resumed his speech. The steadiness of nerve exhibited by Mr. Stevens probably saved the House from a bloody affray. The subsequent career of Crawford illustrates his colossal impudence. During the civil war he was a member of the rebel congress, and was sent by that assembly to Washington as one of a so-called commission or embassy to negotiate a treaty of peace between the Confederacy and the United States, on the basis that the Union was already dissolved. Could effrontery further go! These tumults were the skirmishes that preceded Bull Run, Antietam, Gettysburg, and Appomattox Court House. Keitt was killed in battle in front of Washington, and Barksdale fell in the last terrible charge of Lee against Cemetery Ridge, at Gettysburg, but Crawford preferred to practise law.

An emancipated race, through the long years to come, will cast wreaths on the grave of Thaddeus Stevens. Born to a low condition, he struggled with adversity till he reached eminence in law, politics, and statesmanship. During the administrations of Lincoln and Johnson he was the leader of the Republican party in the House of Representatives, its most acute and fearless debater, occupying extreme radical ground on the subjects of the emancipation of the slaves, their enlistment in the army in the war period, and their admission to the ballot-boxes in the reconstruction era; while on the other hand he advocated the political disfranchisement and the confiscation of the property of all those who had actively participated in the rebellion.

Rising from obscurity and poverty, Stephen A. Douglas, without adventitious aids, advanced by sheer force of will and perseverance to eminent leadership in the Democratic party. He had little learning, but was endowed with rare oratorical gifts, while his buoyant spirits made him popular with the multitude.

He was a native-born tribune of the people. A little story will illustrate his jovial manner. Beverly Tucker was sitting on his knee, with Douglas's arm around him. "Bev.," said he, "when I get to be President what shall I do for you?" "Doug.," replied Tucker, "when you get to be President all I shall ask of you is to take me on your knee, put your arm around me, and call me 'Bev.'"

In his contest for Senator with Mr. Lincoln, in 1858, he was successful, but did not come to Washington in the following winter until after his re-election to the Senate by the legislature. In his conflict with the "Tall Sucker," of Springfield, the "Little Giant," of Chicago, had been driven to the utterance of opinions on the Free-soil question which were repugnant to the creed of such slavery propagandists in the Senate as Davis, Mason, Toombs, and Slidell. His reception in the Senate, on his first appearance, was a spectacle to be enjoyed. As he entered a select crowd in the galleries applauded. Mason, Slidell, and their bitter clique scowled and did not recognize him. When a distinguished senator approached he rose from his seat and received the greeting with marked cordiality. The lesser lights were content with a hearty shake of the hand, he maintaining a sitting posture. Jefferson Davis came to his chair. Douglas rose, and they bowed and bowed, but seemed to say very little. After some of the minor Republicans had paid their respects to the lion of the hour, Mr. Seward crossed the aisle; Douglas rose, they bowed, and he then gave the leader of the opposition a seat by his side. Since the last session the Senate had removed into its new chamber, where Douglas had never sat. Lest he and Seward should be suspected of conversing about the Illinois contest (which was delicate ground for Mr. Seward to tread), the latter, with spectacles in hand and arm extended, was pointing out the architectural beauties of the new hall, Mr. Douglas following the spectacles with his eye, and twisting around in his chair to keep pace with their meanderings.

For many days Douglas was quiet, content with his victory at home. The Slavery propagandists determined to drive him out of the party. A string of resolutions condemnatory of his Illinois opinions was introduced into the Senate. The debate lasted far into the night. The Republicans generally stood aloof. The attacks upon Douglas were rare specimens of scathing oratory, Mason and Slidell being particularly offensive. Douglas and his few Democratic coadjutors bore up gallantly against their assailants. Charles E. Stuart, of Michigan, a Democratic Senator, was a strong, rough debater. In the evening he converted the Senate Chamber into a threshing-floor and his tongue into a flail. He told the propagandists that instead of receiving the distinguished Senator from Illinois as a victor, they had treated him as if he were a pickpocket. He pointed to the many seats, one by one, now occupied by Republicans, which he had formerly seen filled by Democrats. "And this," he exclaimed, in stentorian tones, and shaking his fist at the antagonists of Douglas, "is due to your detestable doctrines." They quailed under the flagellation of Stuart. It gave them a foretaste of the civil war. The success of the North in the

War of the Rebellion was, strange to say, in part due to the author of the bill that repealed the Missouri Compromise. I refer to the patriotic letter Douglas addressed to his Democratic friends, which was appended to Mr. Lincoln's call for seventy-five thousand volunteers, in April, 1861. It produced an impression through the country almost as profound as the President's proclamation. It extinguished the hope of the South that they were to receive open aid from the Northern Democracy in the attempt to destroy the Union. Indeed, the accession to the patriotic side of the struggle at a critical juncture of six such distinguished Democrats as General Cass, Mr. Dickinson, Robert J. Walker, Jeremiah Black, General Dix, and Mr. Douglas, went far to inspire confidence in the ultimate triumph of the constitutional party.

It so happened that Mr. Douglas and I left Washington in the same railway train in the perilous days of April, 1861. We occupied adjoining seats till we reached the Relay House, where he turned his face towards his Western home. He told me he should spend the spring and summer in rallying the people of Illinois to the support of Lincoln and the Union. Alas! on the third of the following June his sun set to rise no more on earth.

In 1860 Mr. Seward made a speech in the Senate which he thought would remove all obstacles to his nomination to the Presidency at Chicago. He read it to me before it was delivered, and requested me to write a description for the *New York Tribune* of the scene in the chamber during the delivery, which I did. The description was elaborate, the Senator himself suggesting some of the nicer touches, and every line of it was written and on its way to New York before Mr. Seward had uttered a word in the Senate Chamber. Soon a large edition of the speech and the description came to Washington. As he handed me some copies he said, in his liveliest manner, "Here we go down to posterity together." He was in buoyant spirits, seeming not to doubt that his nomination was assured. He would have felt otherwise if he had known that at that critical moment scarcely a half dozen Republican Senators were heartily in favor of his candidacy. It is my own personal knowledge that enables me to state that Fessenden, Hamlin, Hale, Simmons, Foster, Dixon, Cameron, Wade, Trumbull, and Doolittle were among his opponents.

In the early spring of 1860 state contests were pending in Connecticut and Rhode Island whose results might exert a wide influence in the next Presidential campaign. I spoke in Connecticut and several times in Rhode Island. In the latter state a fierce struggle was raging for the governorship between two rich candidates — William Sprague, Democrat, and Seth Paddleford, Republican. Each was flooding that little rotten borough with money. The Republicans urged me to get Mr. Corwin to come from Washington and help them. I told them he was poor, and could not afford to waste money in stump speaking. I demanded a *carte blanche* as to the terms I was to submit to the peerless orator. They gave it. I saw him. In his half-serious, half-comic style he pronounced me a philosopher, and started eastward; and on his return he remarked in the same vein that the Yankees were the most magnificent and munificent people on the face of the globe. A recital of the details of my financial negotiations in behalf of the high contracting parties might be amusing.

When in the House of Representatives, in 1848, I saw a tall, lank, sallow-hued member bending over the chair of another member, scarcely larger than one of the pages, whose dried skin looked like parchment. On inquiry I learned that they were Abraham Lincoln and Alexander H. Stephens, both Whigs.

In the spring of 1860 Mr. Lincoln came eastward. He delivered a wonderful speech in Cooper Institute, and went to Connecticut and Rhode Island, where he addressed tumultuous assemblies in the principal cities. His debate with Douglas, his speech in New York, and his trip to New England, gave him the nomination to the Presidency.

Mr. Seward seemed to be certain of receiving the Presidential nomination at Chicago. He felt that it belonged to him. His flatterers had encouraged him in the error that he was the sole creator of the Republican party, both he and they forgetting that it was the grandchild of the Liberty party, which was the legitimate offspring of the Missouri controversy.

At Chicago, Seward encountered the opposition from his own state of such powerful leaders as Greeley, Dudley Field, Bryant, and Wadsworth. The first two were on the ground and very busy. The two latter sent pungent letters that were circulated among the delegates from various states. The main point of the attack was that Seward could not carry New York. Soon after the adjournment of the convention, William Curtis Noyes, who was a delegate, told me (and there could not have been higher authority for the statement than this learned lawyer) that a careful canvass of the New York delegation showed that nearly one fourth of its members believed it was extremely doubtful if Seward could obtain a majority at the polls in that state. This doubt was an element of great weakness in Seward's canvass at Chicago. The Barnburners in the Republican party were generally against him. Perhaps the main stumbling-block over which he fell in the convention was Thurlow Weed. As events finally culminated, it was clear that Seward could have carried New York, for the Southern conspirators against the Union were determined that the Republican candidate, whoever he was, should be elected.

Mr. Seward was popular among his neighbors. On the day when the convention was to ballot for a candidate, Cayuga county poured itself into Auburn. The streets were full, and Mr. Seward's house and grounds overflowed with his admirers. The trees waved their branches on the lawn as if betokening coming victory. Flags were ready to be raised, and a loaded cannon was placed at the gate, whose pillars bore up two guardian lions. Arrangements had been perfected for the receipt of intelligence with unwonted speed from the scene where the battle was proceeding. At Mr. Seward's right hand, just within the porch, stood his trusty henchman, Christopher Morgan. The rider of a galloping steed dashed through the crowd with a telegram, and handed it to Seward. He read it and passed it to Morgan. For Seward,

173½; for Lincoln, 103; and for other aspirants, 189½. Morgan repeated it to the multitude, who cheered vehemently. Then came the tidings of the second ballot: For Seward, 184½; for Lincoln, 181; and for others, 99½. "I shall be nominated on the next ballot," said Seward, and the throng in the house applauded, and those on the lawn and in the street echoed the cheers. The next messenger from the telegraph office lashed his horse into a run. The telegram read, "Lincoln nominated. T. W." Seward turned as pale as ashes. The sad tidings crept through the vast concourse. The flags were furled, the cannon was rolled away, and Cayuga county went home with a clouded brow. Mr. Seward retired to rest at a late hour, and the night breeze in the tall trees sighed a requiem over the blighted hopes of New York's eminent son.

Mr. Seward felt his defeat at Chicago beyond all power of expression, and he never forgave those who had actively contributed to produce it. In incensed moments he accused some men wrongfully, as he subsequently admitted. He was a good hater, and lay in wait to punish his foes. He doubtless defeated General Wadsworth for Governor of New York in 1862. Wadsworth was then military commander at Washington, and Seward was Secretary of State. Wadsworth told me that Seward was "dead against him" all through the campaign. He rather surprised me by saying that Weed wanted him elected. Perhaps this was due to the fact that thirty-five years before Weed and the father of General Wadsworth had stood shoulder to shoulder in the Anti-Masonic party in western New York. I could relate many marked instances within my own knowledge where Seward's lightning strokes fell on New York Republicans who had opposed his nomination in 1860. If bitter exclamations, welling up from the heart, can prove anything, they demonstrated the depth and intensity of his mortification and anger. More than to any other one man he attributed his failure to reach the goal of his ambition to Horace Greeley. For twenty years they were coadjutors in politics, but in 1854 they became estranged, and never after were in close accord. They descended to their graves in the same autumn, Seward in October and Greeley in November, 1872. Crushed Presidential aspirations paved the path of each to the tomb. It was just twenty years since Clay and Webster had gone to the spirit land by the same dark and dreary road.

Mr. Seward's successor was to be elected to the Senate in 1861, he being about to enter Lincoln's Cabinet. Mr. Seward's and Mr. Weed's candidate was William M. Evarts. His principal antagonist was Horace Greeley, but Ira Harris, whom Weed hated a little less than he did Greeley, held about twenty votes as a balance of power. There were a dozen or more votes floating around loose. The Republican nomination was equivalent to an election. The prize was exceptionably valuable, for the Senator would exert great influence in the distribution of patronage and otherwise under the new administration. Evarts and Harris were on the ground weeks previous to the day of trial, and Albany was full of supporters of the rival aspirants. Greeley was at the

West lecturing. Governor Morgan favored Evarts, and on the evening of the caucus gave Weed the possession of the Executive Chamber for the Evarts headquarters. De Witt C. Littlejohn, tall and lithe, was Weed's lieutenant. Greeley and Evarts ran about neck and neck. Harris held the balance. There were a dozen or fifteen floaters. For three ballots the result hardly changed. Suddenly Greeley shot ahead of Evarts, and it looked as if he would win on the next ballot. Pale as ashes, Weed sat smoking a cigar within earshot of the bustle in the crowded Assembly room, where the caucus sat. Littlejohn stalked over the heads of the spectators, and reported to Weed. Unmindful of the fact that he had a cigar in his mouth, Weed lighted another and put it in, then rose in great excitement, and said to Littlejohn, " Tell the Evarts men to go right over to Harris—to *Harris*—to HARRIS!" The order was given in the caucus. They wheeled into line like Napoleon's Old Guard, and Harris was nominated. Cannon reverberated on Capitol hill. They were not fired by the Weed-Evarts faction.

Mr. Seward occupied the seat in the Senate which, under the constitutional mode of arrangement, is in class number three. From the foundation of the government it had been filled by many statesmen of shining talents, among whom were Rufus King, De Witt Clinton, John Armstrong, Nathan Sanford, William L. Marcy, Silas Wright, and John A. Dix. Its prestige had not been tarnished by Mr. Seward. Though defeated in his attempt to reach this elevated position in 1861, Mr. Evarts achieved it twenty-four years later, but through auspices quite different from those that seconded his effort in the earlier struggle. In the intervening period the country had borne up under colossal events that might suffice to make a century bend. Mr. Seward, Mr. Weed, and Mr. Morgan had gone to the tomb, and Mr. Evarts, in his old age, was lifted into the chair that Roscoe Conkling had voluntarily vacated, by politicians who had probably never heard of Rufus King, and knew little of William H. Seward.

CHAPTER XXIII.

Lincoln's Cabinet.—Chase Pushed in.—David Davis, Confidential Adviser of Lincoln.—Mrs. Lincoln "Sub-President."—Notices of Seward, Chase, Cameron, Bates, Blair, and Welles.—Bickerings in the Cabinet.—Chase and Seward Grapple.—Bray Dickinson and Marcus Curtius.—Down in Dixie in April, 1861.—Narrow Escape from Secessionists.—General Butler and his Troops.—Colonel Jones and his Regiment Going through Baltimore.—First Blood of the War.—Notice of Edwin M. Stanton, the War Secretary.

AFTER it was known that Mr. Seward was to be Secretary of State great efforts were made by Vice-President Hamlin, Mr. Greeley, Mr. Dana, Mr. Wadsworth, the elder Blair, ex-Senator Carroll, and others of that type, to get Mr. Chase into the Treasury Department, as an offset to Mr. Seward. The President and Chase were on the same floor at Willard's Hotel. Mr. Chase had just been chosen a Senator in Congress. In ignorance of the President's intentions, he repaired to the Capitol, and was sworn as Senator, when the message appointing him Secretary of the Treasury was opened in his presence. The case of Gideon Welles was not quite so singular. When Mr. Lincoln was stumping Connecticut, in the spring of 1860, Welles accompanied him through the state. At Washington he told me he was to go into the Cabinet; and when asked what portfolio he was to take, said he was not sure, but supposed he would be Postmaster-general.

I could put on paper many more things which I personally know about Mr. Lincoln's Cabinet than I shall. I am constrained to omit some of the raciest. David Davis, then in his prime, came to Washington in the trail of the new President. In his vigorous style he took an active part in the construction of the Cabinet. He stood closer to Mr. Lincoln than was then generally supposed. In the controversies that already appeared, and which subsequently ripened into bitterness, Judge Davis was understood to lean towards Mr. Seward. Who that witnessed the scene can forget how, in the gusty two weeks that foreboded the storm, Davis stamped back and forth among the male and female politicians that crowded the corridors at Willard's, doing great and small errands for large and little people, with hat cocked awry on his head, in the free-and-easy fashion of the boundless West. Mrs. Lincoln, who arrived at Washington with the idea that she was a sort of sub-President, was suspected of communicating her wishes in respect to the composition of the Cabinet to the much-bored and badgered friend of her husband. She, too, was understood to be on the Seward-Weed side of the pending contest, and opposed to the Chase-Greeley clique. Current gossip reported that, when a protest went up to the President against this intermeddling of the mistress of the robes, he replied, in characteristic phrase, "Tell the gentlemen not to be alarmed, for I myself manage all important matters. In little things I have got along through life by letting my wife run her end of the machine pretty much in her own way."

Perhaps Mr. Lincoln was wise in selecting his Cabinet mainly from rivals whom he had overthrown or absorbed at the Chicago Convention. The former lists included Seward, Chase, Cameron, and Bates, while Blair, Smith, and Welles represented factions that had been at the best his cool friends in that trying emergency. I had often spoken from the platform with such members of the new Cabinet as were accustomed to address public meetings, and knew the others well except Mr. Bates, a quiet, retired gentleman, who would not have been dreamed of for Attorney-General had not Mr. Greeley been supporting him as a make-shift candidate for the Presidential nomination. Nothing but the pressure of the civil war and the patience of Mr. Lincoln kept these incongruous materials together for six months. Nor was the harmony of the Cabinet improved when Edwin M. Stanton, nine months after its creation, took the place of Simon Cameron as Secretary of War. I do not rely on rumors or inferences or information from the newspapers or other outside sources when I say that Chase was stubborn, jealous, and always intriguing against some of his associates, especially Seward. Blair, too, was given to plotting and contention, and what he lacked in capacity to cope with his colleagues was supplied by the cool sagacity of his long-headed father and the hot temper of his courageous brother, Frank, junior. Amid these warring elements Seward usually appeared self-poised, conscious of his power, and satisfied with his superior influence at the White House. He parted with his temper now and then, when friends pressed him to perform impossibilities, as, for example, on the occasion of a visit from leading New York Republicans of his type, who complained that their followers were not receiving a due share of Federal patronage. It was reported and believed that he broke into a rage, exclaiming, in substance, "Why come to me about this? Go to the White House! I, who by every right ought to have been chosen President! what am I now? nothing but Abe Lincoln's little —— clerk." Mr. Welles, the Secretary of the Navy, usually steered clear of these feuds, and minded his own business. Mr. Stanton was sometimes drawn into them. I shall speak more particularly of the great War Secretary in another place.

Notorious was the superiority of Seward over Chase in the handling of Federal patronage, and the consequent mortification of Chase. I will give one illustration of this, out of many that fell under my notice. I must first tell of whom I am speaking. In the winter of 1841, I was an onlooker at a debate, in the Senate at Albany, on the causes of Mr. Van Buren's defeat in 1840. John Hunter, a Democrat, of Westchester, a refined gentleman and a classical scholar, declared that Van Buren's courage in placing himself in the chasm between a corrupt bank and a patriotic people had its fitting historic parallel in the Roman Forum when Marcus Curtius leaped into the abyss to save the republic. Andrew B. Dickinson, familiarly called Bray Dickinson, a Whig, of Steuben, illiterate and rough-hewn, but a strong debater, who doubtless never till then had heard of Marcus Curtius, replied to Hunter. When he came to the classical portion of the speech, he said that the difference between that Roman "feller," Curtis, and Van Buren was, that Curtis jumped into the gap of his own accord, but the people *throw'd* Van Buren in.

When Mr. Lincoln became President, Mr. Dickinson and Edward I. Chase, the brother of Secretary Chase, were rival aspirants for the office of Marshal of Northern New York. Secretary Chase took deep interest in his brother's success. He procured for him the recommendation of Attorney-general Bates, and as this office lay within his department, it was supposed that this ended the controversy. Dickinson had long been a devoted follower of Mr. Seward, and the Secretary of State now put forth every exertion for his old friend. It was a stand up fight between the two secretaries. Seward prevailed, and the badgered President appointed Dickinson. When the news came to Chase, it was a scene for a painter. His eyebrows twitched more nervously than usual, and his breath was short and hot as he spitefully said, "What a place you New York men have got me into!" Having won the day, Dickinson said that Seward advised him to take his commission (if it may be so called) to Secretary Chase, and tell him he felt sorry for him and his brother, and that, as Mr. Seward had offered him (Dickinson) his pick of the foreign missions, he would decline the marshalship in his brother's favor. Dickinson did this; and this in substance, and much more of the same kind, Dickinson detailed before a large circle in the public hall of a Washington hotel, seeming to take special pleasure in telling how badly Secretary Chase felt, and how he pitied him, and how glad Chase was to get the appointment for his brother on these terms, and that Mr. Seward had generously opened his book to him, and he had selected the mission to Nicaragua.

Several contests occurred between the two secretaries over places more important than this marshalship, and their oppugnation rose far above offices, and reached measures and policies, till they gave Mr. Lincoln as much trouble in his Cabinet as General Washington had with Jefferson and Hamilton. The sharp criticisms I heard from Mr. Chase on some of his colleagues, and even on the President, would be interesting reading. Probably Mr. Lincoln was glad to place him at the head of the Supreme Bench, where, doubtless, Mr. Chase was glad to go.

As already stated, I left Washington for New York in April, 1861. I had witnessed the arrival at the Capitol of the first volunteer troops that came to its rescue on the 19th of the month. It was that brave Massachusetts regiment commanded by Colonel Edward F. Jones (now Lieutenant-Governor of New York), some of whose members had been slain while passing through Baltimore, and all of whom, doubtless, remembered that it was the anniversary of the battle of Lexington, fought eighty-six years before. I found Baltimore under the control of a mob. A portion of them were armed with muskets, stolen from an arsenal. While circulating among them (this was on Sunday) their murderous purposes were readily perceived. The telegraph wires and railroad tracks between Baltimore and Havre de Grace (where trains cross the Susquehanna) had been destroyed. Never-

10*

theless, somebody had obtained a copy or two of that number of the *New York Herald* which declared in favor of maintaining the Union by force. The manifesto was read to a great throng, and it was easy to pick out the Secessionists by the fall of their countenances.

On Monday, a small party of us hired at an exorbitant rate a man to carry us to Havre de Grace. He proved to be a deputy sheriff of Harford County, residing at Bel Air, who had just come to Baltimore with passengers from the North. Baltimore was then a nest of rebels, and Maryland was on the verge of secession. The towns we went through were inflamed with excitement. I was on the box with our sheriff, who seemed to know everybody, and would shout to the crowds, "Hurrah for Jeff.!" at the same time punching me and saying, "I'll take care of my load." We stopped at Bel Air to dine. Our wagon stood in the street with half a dozen trunks marked "New York," and so on, which loungers kept curiously inspecting. We waited a couple of hours after dinner; the horses had been stabled; the sheriff could not be found; the landlord, whom we had liberally rewarded for our dinner, was away, and there were no signs of preparation for our departure. The courthouse was near at hand, and I had noticed that a tumultuous meeting was going on within, while a rough crowd hung around the door. After a long delay the landlord appeared, a team was attached to the vehicle, and the landlord shook hands with us, saying, in a significant tone, "Gentlemen, you'll find us all right the next time you venture down into Dixie."

Now for the cause of our detention. The meeting at the court-house had been summoned to decide whether the county should go with the Secessionists. Our arrival had raised a side issue in a small circle of violent men, some of whom wanted to hang us, while others proposed to detain us for examination. The sheriff or landlord interposed, and we were allowed to depart. On arriving at Havre, we found that General B. F. Butler had been there and captured all the ferry-boats for the transportation of Massachusetts troops to Washington *via* Annapolis. We hired a rowboat to take us across the Susquehanna to the railway depot, which a Pennsylvania regiment was at that moment entering, the flags flying and drums beating. Half a dozen fellows tried to prevent our crossing the river. A small scuffle ensued, and we were afloat. They fired muskets at us, but the shades of the evening were gathering, and they missed the mark. I conferred with the commander of the Pennsylvania regiment, giving him the latest information from Baltimore and Washington, whither he was bound, provided he could reach there.

Irrepressible Ben Butler! His prompt seizure of the ferry-boats gave the country a foreshadowing of his stern quality. Clearer than most others he saw the end from the beginning. Baltimore never behaved so well as when cowering under the muzzles of his cannon. But Maryland was slow to take in the situation, and did not come to its senses till General George B. McClellan shut the doors of its legislature to prevent the state being carried out of the Union. And so it was in New Orleans. That turbulent city was kept in good order when ruled by General Butler's pen and sword.

I had previously known of Edwin M. Stanton as the reporter of the Supreme Court of Ohio when I saw him in 1856 at Washington, where he had come to practise law. We held a chatty interview, in which he said we were kindred, his great-grandfather (perchance it was the grandfather), like mine, having been a Rhode-Islander. We acted on this assumption for a good while; but afterwards an expert in genealogy, who volunteered to trace our lineage, informed us that though we sprang from the same stock, our common ancestor lived long before King Philip pitched his tent on Mount Hope, or Roger Williams put his spade into Providence plantations. He ran our line back to *Anno Domini* 1010, which being half a century before William the Conqueror set foot on Saxon soil, I begged him to pause lest he land our progenitors in the Silurian epoch when the first Dr. Darwin electrified the mollusks by foreshadowing the evolution theory of the origin of man.

I met Mr. Stanton many times while he was at the head of the War Department. If he was as brutal an administrator of that office as his enemies were wont to assert, I never discovered it. He discharged its duties according to his own views of right and expediency during a civil war whose magnitude has no parallel in modern times, and when the armies of the belligerents were twice as large as the forces ever commanded by the great Napoleon. A dozen Waterloos were fought by troops which he had summoned to the field, and, like Pitt and Carnot, he was the minister who organized victory. He died, worn out by patriotic labors. While the great secretary was living, Northern demagogues and Southern traitors denounced him. Their calumnies have not ceased since he was laid to rest. I have seen him in very trying and sometimes extremely irritating circumstances, but only once was he rude or even discourteous. I will briefly refer to this rather amusing incident. His office was hung with maps that bore on their surface mysterious marks in inks of various colors. He had left his room unoccupied for a few minutes. On returning to it he found a plainly-dressed countryman lifting up and looking at one or two of the maps. The secretary violently exclaimed, "What rebel emissary do we find here overhauling the secret archives of the War Department? Who are you!" he thundered? "This explains how it is that important intelligence leaks out of this office, and falls into the hands of the enemy. Who are you?" He then pounded the bell for a messenger, and in the uproar the countryman, pale as a ghost, contrived to make his way out of the building. He soon returned from Willard's Hotel, accompanied by his member of Congress, who proceeded to explain that his constituent had two sons in the army, and one had been wounded and was pining in a hospital, and the father wanted permission to go through the lines and take him home; and that he had a letter of introduction in his pocket from the Congressman to the secretary when he stalked accidentally into his empty room half an hour ago; and so on and so forth. Stanton instantly comprehended the situation. He bowed and bowed, shook hands with the Congressman and the countryman, and bowed again to each, but made no allusion to the previous explosion. He listened to a short story about the wounded soldier, and immediately drafted the orders for his father to visit the hospital and take him home. On the way back to Willard's the Congressman offered to bet fifty dollars with his delighted constituent that he would have failed to carry his point if the Secretary had not burst into a passion when he caught him overhauling the maps and called him a rebel emissary.

I witnessed another scene that illustrated the Secretary's proverbial promptness of decision and rapidity of execution. One morning when he came to his office he found a miscellaneous company of thirty or forty men and women (mostly of the middle class) awaiting his arrival. By his direction a messenger conducted them into an adjoining room, in the centre of which was a little desk resting on a pillar. Soon the secretary entered, bowing suavely, and took his stand by the desk, while I settled into a chair and looked on. He called to his side the oldest and plainest-dressed woman in the crowd, and mildly asked, "Madam, what can I do for you?" He listened to a short narrative, drew up and gave her a brief note, and told a messenger to take "this lady" to the Adjutant-general's office. Instantly another aged woman stood at the desk and handed him a letter. He read it, endorsed several lines on the back, and she disappeared under the guidance of a messenger. To the next he said, "Madam, your business belongs to the Navy Department. Messenger, show this lady the way to the Navy Department." To one he gravely remarked, after glancing over her papers, "This is a serious matter. I must examine it carefully. Please step into my office, and wait till I come." And in this manner he went through the entire list, patiently, urbanely, quietly, disposing of every case right on the spot, except three or four that were quite intricate. He cleared the room in forty-five minutes.

A Republican client of mine, a large grocer, had trusted sutlers in the army of the Potomac to the amount of several thousand dollars. He came to me in terror, armed with a letter of Governor Morgan, endorsing his patriotism and integrity, and said I must go to Washington with him in the next train, and procure permission for him to pass through the lines to collect what the sutlers owed him or he should lose it, *for he knew our army was about to attack the enemy*, and the sutlers would be scattered, and perhaps knocked to pieces. We arrived in Washington the next morning. When the Secretary reached the office I humorously remarked that I wished to make a draft on the well-known urbanity of all the Stantons for many generations, "which I am doing so much to dissipate," broke in the Secretary, in the same vein. I explained my business, vouched for the loyalty and prudence of my client, showed the letter of Mr. Morgan, and expressed the hope that, in such an exigency, he would let the grocer pass the lines and collect his dues, or he would be ruined. Stanton struck the table and rose from his chair. "How does this man know that the army is about to move and fight a battle?" "How does *he* know anything about it?" I told him I had not the slightest idea. He then went stamping around the room, wondering why outsiders got up these preposterous reports, but at the same time expressing his indignation at the leaks that were constantly occurring in the War and Navy departments—all of which satisfied me that the army *was* about to attack the enemy. Mr. Stanton resumed his seat, cooled off, sent for Mr. Wolcott, one of his assistants (and his brother-in-law, I believe), and told him to hear me, and do what I wished. My client went through the lines, obtained his money, and was just leaving when our artillery opened fire.

The following anecdote gives a glimpse of the familiar relations subsisting between the President and the Secretary. Owen Lovejoy, a member of Congress from Illinois, obtained from Mr. Lincoln a promise to issue a certain war order, but added, "You must go and tell Stanton about it." He went. "Did the President say he would issue such an order?" inquired the Secretary. "He did," responded Lovejoy. "Then he is a fool—a great fool," replied Stanton. Lovejoy returned to the President, and repeated the conversation between him and the Secretary. "Did Stanton say I was a fool?" inquired Lincoln. "He did," said Lovejoy. "Then I think I am a fool, for Stanton is generally right," was the characteristic reply of the President.

My authority for the following incident was present at the Cabinet meeting where it occurred: Mr. Stanton, the Secretary of War, came in with the details of a foreshadowed plan for a simultaneous attack on the rebels at three points, in which he would want a little assistance from the Navy. Stanton described his first place of attack, and said the troops would need the co-operation of one or two gunboats. The President, addressing Secretary Gideon Welles, asked if they could be furnished. He wriggled around in his chair, and said he couldn't tell, but would inquire, and let them know at the next meeting of the Cabinet. And this, in substance, was his response on all the three points of Stanton's programme. Putting one of his feet on the table, the vexed President said, "Mr. Secretary, will you please tell us all you know about the Navy, and then we shall know all you don't know about it." I have thought that the other members of the Cabinet did not fully appreciate Mr. Welles. I was much with him in the Fremont campaign, and know that he was a gentleman of sound judgment and tireless industry. The Cabinet was torn by factions, which the Secretary of the Navy tried to steer clear of, and mind his own affairs.

Mr. Stanton would sometimes express his weariness of the toils and trials of the War Department, and his strong desire to return to the practice of the law. When consulting with a general of the army, who was a lawyer, about the Military Governorship of Washington, he gave vent to his ardent feelings in that direction, but, suddenly checking the current, he exclaimed, "However, I shall remain here and try our Great Cause through to the end."

CHAPTER XXIV.

Mr. Lincoln and Dr. McPheeters.—Lincoln's Story.—Roscoe Conkling and Noah Davis Candidates for the Senate in 1867.—Conkling Elected.—Defeat of Morgan by Fenton for the Senate in 1869.—Escape of Marshall O. Roberts from the Lobby.—Democratic National Convention of 1868.—Seymour Favors Chase.—Vallandigham's Course.—Seymour Nominated.—Grant Elected.—Seymour Urged to Accept the Senatorship in 1875; Refuses; Why.—Seward's Trip around the World.—Death of Seward in 1872.—R. B. Hayes Running for Governor of Ohio in 1875.—Senator Thurman's Singular Prediction.—Conkling and Platt Resign from the Senate, and Lapham and Miller Succeed them in 1881.—Conkling's Success at the Bar.

My brother, Rev. R. L. Stanton, D.D., was a leader in the Presbyterian Church, and a warm friend of Mr. Lincoln during the war. In the great struggle he was aggressively on the side of the Union, and in favor of the emancipation policy of Mr. Lincoln. In 1862-63 the Rev. Dr. McPheeters, a prominent Presbyterian, was preaching at St. Louis. Major-general Curtis commanded in that military department. One Sunday Dr. McPheeters uttered some sentiments that were deemed disloyal. The next Sunday Dr. McPheeters found the doors of his church closed by order of General Curtis. There was immediate trouble, not alone in St. Louis, but in Washington. A committee, composed of both factions, went to see the President. Finding Dr. Stanton in Washington, they requested him to go with them to the White House and present them to Mr. Lincoln. The President listened patiently, and then spoke as follows:

"I can best illustrate my position in regard to your St. Louis quarrel by telling a story. A man in Illinois had a large watermelon patch, on which he hoped to make money enough to carry him over the year. A big hog broke through the log-fence nearly every night, and the melons were gradually disappearing. At length the farmer told his son John to get out the guns, and they would promptly dispose of the disturber of their melon-patch. They followed the tracks to the neighboring creek, where they disappeared. They discovered them on the opposite bank, and waded through. They kept on the trail a couple of hundred yards, when the tracks again went into the creek, but promptly turned up on the other side. Once more the hunters buffeted the mud and water, and again struck the lead and pushed on a few furlongs, when the tracks made another dive into the creek. Out of breath and patience, the farmer said, 'John, you cross over and go up on that side of the creek, and I'll keep upon this side, for I believe the old fellow is on both sides.' Gentlemen," concluded Mr. Lincoln, "that is just where I stand in regard to your controversies in St. Louis. I am on both sides. I can't allow my generals to run the churches, and I can't allow your ministers to preach rebellion. Go home, preach the Gospel, stand by the Union, and don't disturb the government with any more of your petty quarrels."

Dr. Stanton said that, when the belligerents reached Willard's Hotel, they had a hearty laugh, and made up their minds that they would go home and follow the President's advice.

In January, 1867, Mr. Conkling, having won a high reputation in the House of Representatives, was a candidate for United States Senator. He was supported with fidelity and enthusiasm by a large body of the most skilful politicians in the state. His leading opponent was Noah Davis, then on the Bench of the Supreme Court in the Eighth District. In the contest at Albany Mr. Conkling prevailed over Judge Davis by a narrow majority. The learning, acumen, and versatility displayed by Mr. Davis on the Bench in western New York, and as Presiding Justice of the Supreme Court in the metropolitan city, and while a member of the Forty-first Congress and United States Attorney in the Southern District of New York, are recognized by his fellow-citizens. But it is not so widely known that, in the Free-soil conflict of 1848, he was an active Barnburner. I was on the platform with him before a large out-door meeting in Albion in that campaign. He was then the law partner of Sanford E. Church. He would have ably represented the state as a Senator in Congress.

In 1863 Edwin D. Morgan wielded the influence he had acquired in two gubernatorial terms to secure an election to the Senate. His six years at Washington would expire in March, 1869. He had no doubt that he would be his own successor. He heard that Reuben E. Fenton sought his place. It did not occur to him that the wily Chautauqua sachem had just completed four years' service in the Executive Chamber at Albany, and still tarried in that city to manage his Senatorial canvass. Morgan was cautioned to take heed to the selection of a Speaker of the Assembly, for he would wield great power, especially in the appointment of the committees, most of which in those days were lucrative. Morgan declared himself satisfied with Truman G. Younglove for Speaker. He was under a strange delusion, for Younglove was the fast friend of Fenton.

The new Speaker took the chair at the opening of the session; the Assembly met daily, but no committees were announced. Weeks rolled away, the Speaker's rooms were all the time full of applicants for fat berths, and by and by he proclaimed that no committees would be appointed till after the Senator was chosen. The capital city was crowded with Republicans from every portion of the state. Fenton was as unruffled as Chautauqua lake in summer. Morgan began to be disturbed, broke up his quarters at Washington, came to Albany, and put himself at the head of his forces. Rumor was at fault if plenty of money was not in circulation. It was asserted, and believed, that $12,000 were paid for the sole item of bare rooms at one hotel wherein to bivouac Morgan's troops. So hard pressed were Fenton's lines that he invited his rich and liberal friend, Marshall O. Roberts, of New York, to take his place as a candidate. He came up, but after looking over the ground, and seeing a demand for $250,000 by the lobby staring him in the face, he returned to the city, because it was feared that in an attempt to carry all the Fenton men over to Roberts a few might fall out of line. It was amusing to hear Roberts, in his characteristic style, describe his escape out of the hands of the hungry Albany lobby on this occasion.

The evening for holding the caucus arrived. Nobody who was at the capital during the previous twenty-four hours will ever forget the exciting scene. The caucus assembled. It elected its president, secretaries, and tellers, and now the Republican Speaker, who had all the committees in his brain, rose, and in a fitly framed speech nominated for Senator in Congress Reuben E. Fenton. It hardly need be added that those who had been badgering him for several weeks for first-class places on leading and lucrative committees read between the lines, and were pretty sure that they saw, in clearest words, dropping from the lips of Mr. Younglove:

"Now all you that want me to listen to you two days hence, had better listen to me now."

The result was that Mr. Fenton was nominated on the first ballot. Mr. Morgan paid his bills and went back to Washington, a wiser and a sadder man.

The Democratic Convention of 1868, for nominating a candidate for President, met in Tammany Hall. Mr. Seymour presided, and Mr. Tilden was chairman of the New York delegation. It was the first time the Democracy of the nation had assembled together for eight years. The war was over, slavery had disappeared, and old party lines were faint and feeble. The candidates for the Presidential nomination were numerous, but Mr. Seymour was not among them. He favored Salmon P. Chase. He had prepared a speech which he intended to deliver, when an opportune moment arrived, for presenting Chase's name.

But he failed to bring certain elements in the New York delegation to adopt his plan, and it was quietly dropped. It was asserted and believed that Clement L. Vallandigham, a delegate from Ohio, who was hostile to Chase, feared that Seymour's wishes might finally prevail, and therefore took the lead in the irresistible stampede that forced the nomination on Seymour himself, in spite of his earnest protestations. I have seen some of the private correspondence that passed between the ex-Governor and the Chief-Justice at this period, wherein the latter warmly thanked the former for the efforts he had made to give him the nomination. The light shed on coalitions of this sort by the result of Mr. Greeley's candidacy, four years later, leads to the belief that if Chase had been nominated, in 1868, he would have fared as badly as Seymour did.

Mr. Fenton's term as Senator in Congress expired in 1875. The Democrats controlled the legislature. It was the first time in thirty years that they had been able to elect a Senator. Governor Seymour was pressed to take the office. The Democrats in the Senate and Assembly were eager to confer it upon him. He was urged to accept from all quarters. I plied him through the newspapers and by correspondence. He resolutely refused. He silenced me by a long letter, breathing the noblest sentiments, which I would print here if I could lay my hand upon it. In it he enforced with rare felicity of diction the proposition that to exert great influence in public affairs it is not necessary to hold office. I have ample grounds for supposing that one of the reasons for his peremptory refusal to go to the Senate was that he felt that deafness was creeping upon him, and he did not like to enter an arena with waning powers, where his name for a quarter of a century had ranked so high.

I was strongly in favor of the return of Mr. Conkling and Thomas C. Platt to the Senate in 1881, after their resignation. I had been a resigning Senator, in a very small way, just thirty years before, and knew how it was myself. So I stood by the resigning Senators on this broader and grander field. I had better luck than they, for I was re-elected, while they were defeated. But I would not again resign, to prevent in that way the passage of a fifteen million unconstitutional canal bill. I do not know whether they would again resign, to prevent by that method the appointment of a collector of customs for New York. Their unwise rejection by the legislature, and the election of Elbridge G. Lapham and Warner Miller in their stead, was far-reaching in its consequences. It gave Alonzo B. Cornell leave to retire to private life at the close of his first gubernatorial term, and gave James G. Blaine long-coveted leisure for employing a graphic pen on an interesting period of modern history.

I have no personal knowledge that enables me to penetrate the motives that impelled Mr. Conkling to resign from the Senate. Perhaps he had grown weary of his protracted labors in Congress. Possibly he saw foreshadowed on the horizon factional feuds in the Garfield-Blaine administration, and, as a Republican, had no wish to participate in them. If, however, the chief end he had in view was to resume the undisturbed practice of the law, then the opportune moment he selected for carrying this purpose into effect has already been crowned by a success that has few parallels in the history of the New York bar. By and by Mr. Conkling may return to politics. He has the example of Mr. Seward before him, in the six busy years that intervened between the close of Seward's service as Governor of New York and the commencement of his term as Senator at Washington.

On Mr. Seward's return, in the fall of 1871, from his trip around the globe, Mr. Hugh J. Hastings arranged a plan for my going with the Governor to Auburn, accompanied by a stenographer, to get a condensed report of his journey for publication in the New York *Sun*. Mr. Dana and I conferred, and I went up. The report filled a broadside of the *Sun*, and, as Mr. Seward subsequently told me, it saved him much trouble, for, when any of his friends asked him about his trip, he immediately gave them a copy of the newspaper. Of the many incidents that occurred during this trip to Auburn I will relate but one. The morning after our arrival Mr. Seward was walking in his grounds. The servant was pointing him to this, that, and the other thing, but he kept saying, "Show me the bird." I did not understand what he meant. Soon we stood before the largest eagle I ever saw, enclosed in a great cage. The Governor looked at the eagle; the eagle looked at the Governor. They exchanged winks, as much as to say, "We understand each other." Mr. Seward then exclaimed, with some emotion, "When I was in Alaska they gave me that eagle, and that is all I ever got for my trouble in negotiating the Alaska treaty, except a great deal of undeserved personal abuse."

In the autumn of 1872 Mr. Seward died. In 1828 I had been a member of the Young Men's State Convention, over which Mr. Seward presided. I now stood by his open grave. In the intervening forty-four years he had played a great part in the history of his country.

The contest for the Governorship of Ohio, in 1875, between William Allen and Rutherford B. Hayes, exhibited features of national importance. I spent a few weeks in the state while this extraordinary campaign was in progress. Both candidates were addressing large audiences. Allen was impressive, sagacious, bold. Hayes was respectable, commonplace, feeble. Among other distinguished speakers whom I heard were ex-Governor Noyes, afterwards Minister to France, Senator McDonald, of Indiana; Judge Taft, subsequently Minister to Austria, and Senator Allen G. Thurman. In a conversation with the latter at Columbus he made a prediction which then seemed to me singular. He said that if Hayes defeated Allen in the pending struggle he would be the next Republican candidate for the Presidency. Hayes did defeat Allen, and he was the candidate. The ablest man whom I met in my Western tour was Mr. Thurman. It must have annoyed eminent statesmen like him, aspiring to be President, to see small politicians preferred before them. The Presidency is dwindling in importance with every passing term. Congress controls the administration of the Federal government. The leader of the House and the leader of the Senate exert more influence than presidents in moulding vital measures of public policy.

CHAPTER XXV.

Samuel J. Tilden; his Triumph over the Canal Ring and the Tweed Ring; his Sudden Death; his Note to the Author about "Random Recollections."—State Convention of 1874, when he was Nominated for Governor. — *The* (N. Y.) *Sun's* Editorial Article.—Tilden Elected.—The Presidential Contest of 1876.—Tilden Dies of Heart Disease.—Ex-Governors Clinton, Wright, Marcy, and Fenton Fall by the same Malady under Peculiar Circumstances.—Notice of Robert L. Stanton, D.D.; his Death in Mid-Ocean in May, 1885.—The Presbyterian General Assembly's Tribute to his Memory.

When those animosities, rivalries, and prejudices that spring from party strife have passed away Samuel J. Tilden will be classed among the eminent men of his era. I became associated with him in the memorable contest of 1848, when he stood in the front rank of the Barnburners. In the two rather incompatible qualities of calm, studious, and philosophic statesmanship, and the capacity to gather, classify, and apply the statistics of a political campaign, I do not remember to have met his equal. As the Chairman of the Democratic State Committee, he would deliver an address that might have honored Thomas Jefferson. In the subsequent campaign he would handle the figures of the canvass with a skill that astonished Thurlow Weed. But far above all else rose his genius for administrative reform. While Chief Magistrate of the foremost commonwealth in the Union he broke in pieces the canal ring in the state, and the Tweed ring in the metropolis, which had long been entrenched behind corrupt combinations that had few parallels in our history for the power they had wielded and the audacity they had displayed through a series of years. Mr. Tilden thereby won the confidence of honest and sagacious men in both political parties. The ability and integrity wherewith he performed the duties of the gubernatorial office brought to him the Democratic nomination to the Presidency in 1876. I never met a candid, intelligent Republican, who was thoroughly informed in regard to the facts, that seemed to doubt that he was fairly entitled to a majority of the votes of the electoral college in that famous contest.

I had written the above, and the unfinished manuscript was lying before me, when I received the tidings of Mr. Tilden's sudden death. I need not say that the unexpected event impressed me profoundly. He was my junior by nine years. How many old acquaintances have fallen since I issued the first edition of this small volume. In February last I sent Mr. Tilden a copy of the second edition. He acknowledged it in a brief note, which I should not print if he were living. I insert it simply because it avouches his capacity at so recent a date for devouring books.

"GREYSTONE, YONKERS, N. Y., Feb. 12, 1886.

"DEAR MR. STANTON,—I thank you for the copy of your "Random Recollections," which I found so interesting that I read it through at one sitting.

"With my best wishes for your health and happiness, I remain,

"Very truly yours, S. J. TILDEN."

I was at the State Convention of 1874, in Syracuse, which nominated Mr. Tilden for Governor. He was present as Chairman of the State Committee. Governor Seymour and DeWitt C. Littlejohn (Greeley Liberal in 1872) were delegates. The convention was far from united on the question of the gubernatorial candidate. Many prominent members doubted the expediency of nominating Mr. Tilden. The New York *Sun* had given voice to these doubts. On the 17th of September the convention came to a ballot, when Mr. Tilden received 252 votes, ex-Judge Amasa J. Parker 126, and a few were thrown for others. William Dorsheimer (Greeley Liberal in 1872) was unanimously nominated for Lieutenant-governor, on motion of Mr. Littlejohn. The Democratic campaign opened languidly, and for a while it was believed that General Dix, the Republican candidate for Governor, would be re-elected. The *Sun* looked on, kept its powder dry, and reserved its fire. By and by Mr. Dana suggested that it was time for the *Sun* to hoist its colors. On the 7th of October, three weeks after the nomination, the following article appeared at the head of the editorial columns. If it be in bad taste to quote from one's self, then I am a transgressor. It is only the death of Mr. Tilden that justifies its publication here:

"One of the most essential requisites for making a good Governor of New York is that the man should possess sufficient independence and courage to resist the dictation of the leaders of the party which placed him in office. If Mr. Tilden is elected in November he will be, in the particular we have mentioned, one of the best Democratic governors the state has ever had. Indeed, in the whole list, Silas Wright alone, the most distinguished member of the political school in which Mr. Tilden was raised, can be compared with him.

"Marcy and Seymour were able and upright in the administration of affairs, but they were strong partisans, and never rose to the height of resisting the prevailing current of Democratic opinion. But Governor Wright was a thorough Jeffersonian Democrat. His integrity was above reproach, and his leading characteristic was self-poised independence. On two or three memorable occasions he displayed this quality by pursuing a line of policy in relation to important measures directly hostile to the sentiments and purposes of the great majority of the Democratic party, both in this state and throughout the country. Early in 1844, when the Democracy were running mad in favor of the annexation of Texas, Mr. Wright, then in the Senate, persuaded Mr. Van Buren to write his famous letter against annexation. This letter caused the defeat of Mr. Van Buren's nomination to the Presidency in the National Convention of that year. In the summer of 1846, when Mr. Wright was Governor, and the Democracy were running wild in favor of the conquest of Mexican territory, in order to plant slavery therein, he avowed himself, in the most explicit terms, a supporter of the doctrine of the celebrated Wilmot Proviso. This avowal drove from Wright just enough rabid Hunkers—Bourbons they are now called—to defeat his re-election as Governor in that year.

"For Silas Wright, a prospective candidate for President, to thus set himself in opposition to the great body of his party, exhibited extraordinary fidelity to convictions and a noble moral courage. We have no doubt that under analogous circumstances Mr. Tilden would pursue the same course; for on many occasions he has shown that his mind is made of like metal with that which composed Mr. Wright's. We believe that Mr. Tilden followed the lead of Mr. Wright in 1844 and 1846. We know that he carried the creed of that eminent disciple of Jefferson and Tompkins to its logical conclusions at the Buffalo Convention of 1848, which brought out Van Buren and Adams, in that notable campaign, under the banner of 'Free Soil, Free Speech, Free Press, Free Men.'

"But Mr. Tilden has displayed his courage and his independence of party under far more trying circumstances than those we have detailed; and he has shown these qualities in a very marked manner, and right under the eyes of those who are to pass upon his fitness for the office of Governor. We refer, of course, to his agency in breaking up the Tammany ring in 1871, the subsequent flight of Conolly, and conviction of Tweed and their associates, and many other events which attended or followed that explosion.

Nobody doubts that Mr. Tilden was the leader in this struggle. He elbowed Richard B. Conolly out of the comptroller's office and pushed Andrew H. Green in. He caused the Tammany delegation —stained, but regular—to be rejected by the Democratic State Convention, and he advocated the admission, though without success, of the irregular anti-Tammany delegation. Elected to the Assembly in November of that year, he declined to attend the Democratic caucus for nominating a candidate for Speaker, although he was then chairman of the Democratic State Committee; and he pursued a course quite independent of his party to the end of the session. By this policy he aroused some hostility among a section of the Democratic managers, who were able to send Governor John T. Hoffman, instead of him, as one of the delegates at large to the Baltimore Convention, which nominated Horace Greeley. To Mr. Tilden is largely due the reorganization of Tammany Hall, by turning out the old sachems and installing the new *régime* that now controls a society whose powerful influence has been felt for half a century in the politics of New York, and whose every representative at the recent State Convention cast his vote for Samuel J. Tilden, as the nominee for Governor.

"The fact that Mr. Tilden has done much of what we have recited, in the face of vigorous Democratic influences, raises a strong presumption that if he were Governor of the state he would have the courage to pursue the right path, although in so doing he might sometimes run counter to the wishes of Democratic leaders."

Mr. Tilden knew nothing of this article till his eye fell on it in the *Sun*. I was told that he ordered five thousand copies of the paper for circulation. When the October elections of 1874 were over the Democratic tidal wave set in all through the country. Mr. Tilden carried New York against General Dix by more than fifty thousand majority.

Mr. Tilden died of one of the many forms of what is called "heart disease." It is a rather remarkable coincidence that five of the distinguished statesmen who filled the office of Governor of New York fell by this malady.

On February 11, 1828, De Witt Clinton, then Governor, a man of majestic presence, had been at the Executive Chamber in the Capitol attending to official business, the legislature being in session. In the evening he was sitting in his private library with his son, looking over his afternoon mail. He had a letter in his hand, when his head dropped on his breast, and he immediately expired. He died of heart disease, then little known under that name.

Silas Wright, a totally different man from Clinton, was a part of the time during his public career his contemporary, and always his political opponent. On August 27, 1847, Mr. Wright went to the post-office in his little town of Canton, in the county of St. Lawrence. He was reading a letter when his head sank upon the table and he died of heart disease without a moment's warning. He had retired from the office of Governor the previous January.

William L. Marcy was Governor for three terms, Secretary of War, and Secretary of State. He went out of the latter office on March 4, 1857. On July 4 of that year he was resting at Ballston Spa. He had taken lunch and repaired to his room, where he was found an hour afterwards quite dead, with a volume of Cowper's poems in his hand. He had expired of heart disease.

Ex-Senator Reuben E. Fenton occupied the gubernatorial chair of New York for four years. In August, 1885, while in good health, he was at his desk in the First National Bank of Jamestown, of which he was President, reading his correspondence. Without the slightest premonition he fell backward in his chair, convulsively clutching at a letter he was at that moment answering, gave a long, gasping breath, and soon expired. He died of heart disease.

I have been at a loss in the selection of the most appropriate place in this "random" work for a notice of my last brother. He was a many-sided man, and wrote more than he talked, and studied and thought more than he talked or wrote. He was a scholar, a divine, an author, and an editor; and he was so thoroughly informed in political affairs that this brief tribute to his memory might find a proper place among either of those five classes of citizens.

There were six children in my father's family. All were born in Pachaug. I am the only survivor. My eldest brother, Rev. Robert L. Stanton, D.D., was born in March, 1810. He was living when the first edition of this work was issued. He was graduated at Lane Seminary; was pastor in Mississippi, New Orleans, and Ohio; President of Oakland College, Mississippi, and subsequently President of Miami University, Ohio; Professor of Theology in Danville Seminary, Kentucky; Moderator of the General Assembly of the Presbyterian Church in 1866; and United States Government Visitor at West Point. He wrote much for magazines and newspapers, and was the author of several books and pamphlets. Princeton College conferred upon him the degree of D.D. while he was yet a young man. In May, 1885, he sailed for Europe, as had been his wont before, to recuperate energies exhausted by mental toil. But unmindful of the fact that his health was unusually feeble, and that he was in the seventy-sixth year of his age, he carried the pitcher once too often to the fountain, and it was broken. He died at sea on May 28, and was buried in mid-ocean. When the intelligence of his decease reached America, the Presbyterian General Assembly was in session at Cincinnati. That venerable body placed on its journal this memorial: "The General Assembly records its tribute of respect for the memory of Rev. Robert L. Stanton, D.D., Moderator of the Assembly of 1866. It recognizes the faithfulness and efficiency with which he discharged the duties of the office, and the value to the Church of his services as pastor, editor, and teacher. Sincerely sorrowing for the loss it has sustained, the Assembly hereby expresses its sympathy with the bereaved family, and directs that a copy of the foregoing minute, attested by the Moderator, and Stated and Permanent Clerks, be forwarded to the family of Dr. Stanton.

CHAPTER XXVI.

American Journalism.—Its Rank as a Profession.—Earliest Newspapers.—First Daily Paper.—*Philadelphia Advertiser.*—*Boston Centinel.*—*National Gazette.*—Controversy of Washington and Jefferson over Freneau.—Early Dailies in New York City.—Three Famous Editors.—Bitter Tone of the Press.—List of Distinguished Contributors.—Duels.—Early Journalism in New England.—Rude Methods of Collecting News and Circulating Papers.—Post-riders and Reporters.—The Deacon and the Mohawks.—Dailies in New York, Albany, and Rochester in 1826.—The *Rochester Advertiser* the First Daily Issued West of the Hudson and Delaware Rivers.—Henry O'Reilly.—*Cincinnati Gazette* and Charles Hammond.—*Louisville Journal* and George D. Prentice.—List of Celebrated Contributors in that Era.—Later Editors.—Charles A. Dana.—Henry J. Raymond.—John G. Whittier.—George William Curtis.

It would be wholly aside from the purposes of this publication to give even an outline of the wide field of American journalism. I shall glance at it from my individual standpoint, and jot down little except selections from what I personally know on the subject.

Journalism not only ranks among the learned professions both in respect to the influence it exerts, and the intellectual qualifications necessary to succeed in it, but in peculiar fields it leads all the others. If some of our ablest lawyers were, without disclosing their names, to send editorial articles to the foremost city journals on topics outside of their profession, an impartial hand would frequently consign them to the waste basket. Newspaper reporters of the thoroughly trained school are superior to lawyers of the middle class. It is a fact alike notorious and disgraceful that in some of the chief cities of the Union there are presiding justices in civil and criminal courts of large jurisdiction who can neither speak or write their native language grammatically or clearly. It need hardly be added that such jurists (!) would not be tolerated for a moment as reporters on respectable newspapers.

The press in America rose to its present colossal dimensions from small beginnings. The first newspaper was issued at Boston in 1701. Down to 1725 four others were established in Boston, New York, and Philadelphia. They were little dingy sheets, measuring eight or nine inches by ten, issued weekly or fortnightly, with a very meagre supply of brains, news, advertisements, and subscribers.

The first daily journal in the United States was the *Daily Advertiser*, published in Philadelphia in 1785. The great paper of the period was the *Boston Centinel*, edited by the famous Major Ben Russell. It was intensely Federal, and the leading advocate in after-years of the policy of Washington and Adams in opposition to that of Jefferson and Madison. Its rival was the *National Gazette* issued at Philadelphia, then the seat of government, in 1791. Its editor was the celebrated Philip Freneau, a clerk in the office of Jefferson, Secretary of State in General Washington's Cabinet. Freneau was a caustic writer, voiced the bitter politics of that era, and was highly offensive to

Washington. But, in spite of very direct hints to do so, Jefferson refused to deprive him of his clerkship. In 1793 the *Minerva* was started in New York city, whose first editor was Noah Webster, familiar to us as the distinguished lexicographer. It ultimately bloomed into the *Commercial Advertiser*. The *New York Post* was established in 1801. Both have flourished to this day. In 1801 there were three prominent editors in New York and Philadelphia, namely: Coleman of the *Post*, Cheetham of the *Citizen*, and Duane of the *Aurora*. The first was a Federalist; the two latter were Democrats. Mr. Duane was the father of that Secretary of the Treasury whom General Jackson, a third of a century afterwards, ejected from office because he would not remove the Federal deposits from the United States Bank, and appointed Roger B. Taney to do the work. One morning in 1801 the *Post* assailed its two opponents thus:

> "Lie on, Duane—lie on for pay,
> And Cheetham, lie thou too—
> More against truth you cannot say,
> Than truth can say 'gainst you."

Think of the *Evening Post* of to-day lunging into two of its "esteemed contemporaries" in this style! It seems to take all the originality out of Dr. Greeley's celebrated outburst: "You lie, you villain; you know you lie!"

From the opening of Washington's second Presidential term till the end of Madison's administration, the tone of the press was to the last degree acrimonious. Of the closing five or six years of this period I can speak of my own knowledge. My father was a

Madisonian leader in the eastern portion of Connecticut, and subscribed for several newspapers of that faith. The Federal leaders did the same by their journals. The consequence was, the men, women, and children of the vicinage became peppery partisans. So it was all through the country. Every neighborhood was kept in a broil by the "organs" of the two parties. Others besides their regular managers often contributed to their columns. Among these were John Adams, Timothy Pickering, Joseph Story, Aaron Burr, John Jay, Alexander Hamilton, Edward Livingston, De Witt Clinton, Matthew S. Davis, Washington Irving, and Albert Gallatin. The pens of these prominent men were dipped in gall. Quarrels in those early days meant serious business. The wooded slopes of Hoboken were "the bloody assizes" to which many editors and politicians carried their New York controversies for final arbitrament.

To form a correct notion of the journalism of New England, and, indeed, of any portion of the country, eighty-one years ago, when I was born, we must dismiss all existing ideas on the subject from our minds. Not only the telephone, the telegraph, the railway, and the steamboat must fade into mist, but even the mail, as a means of collecting news and distributing newspapers within circles of fifty or a hundred miles in circumference, must disappear. Editors, of course, existed, but the imagination did not dream of the reporter, now one of the main driving-wheels of American journalism, the essential, useful, and ornamental appendage to every newspaper, whether metropolitan or rural; a class not easily deceived or eluded, capable of painting the tamest scenes in the liveliest colors, and, when in search of truth, may sometimes be tempted to supply deficiencies by inventions, but whose fictions are usually more entertaining than their facts.

In the early days the nearest approach to the modern reporter was the post-rider. When the weekly newspapers were printed at the county seat he took a pile in his "saddle-bags," mounted his horse, and rode into the surrounding towns to dispense his treasures and pick up a little local information for the next number. He usually delivered the sheet in person, but here and there, at cross-roads, was a little box, adapted to shed rain, nailed to a tree, where he deposited a few papers to supply some adjacent hamlet. When he delivered the papers he was often bored to drop an item or two of later intelligence than that in their columns. The following incident occurred in my native county seventy-five years ago: An aged deacon had a confused idea of the upper lakes and a mortal dread of the Mohawk Indians. He hung heavily on the skirts of the post-rider, who resolved to shake him off. One day he handed him the paper, and the deacon bored him for fresh news. With horror depicted on his countenance, he told the deacon that the Mohawks were digging through the banks of the Great Lakes, and that the water would soon pour down from the west, and that all New England would be drowned by a flood as disastrous as that of Noah's time. The post-rider then put spurs to his horse and fled. The terrified deacon ran to the minister and told him the terrible news. The clergyman opened the Bible and read to him, from Genesis, the promise of God that he would never again drown the earth by a flood, and that he had set the bow in the cloud as a seal of this covenant with mankind. "Ah, my beloved pastor," responded the shivering deacon, "that don't apply. It is not God that's going to do it. God's nothing to do with it. It's them infernal Mohawk Injuns that's cutting down the banks!"

A word in passing about the slow pace wherewith intelligence travelled in those days. One of the most important events of modern times was the battle of Waterloo, fought on June 18, 1815. It changed the map of Europe and the face of the civilized world. Napoleon, who there fell to rise no more, had a great party in this country, and the deepest interest was felt in his fortunes after he escaped from Elba, which I remember as vividly as if it had happened in the last month. The battle of Ligny was fought on June 16, when Napoleon defeated tough old Field-marshal Blucher. A slow-sailing packet left Liverpool for New York just in time to bring this news. No other packet was to sail in twenty days. This country, where party spirit ran high for and against the French emperor, was left in terrible suspense. The next packet was forty-five days in crossing, so that we received the news of Waterloo sixty-five days, or more than two months, after the event, when Louis XVIII. was on the throne and Bonaparte was on the way to St. Helena. And how much do you think we got in our papers of the great transactions that followed after Ligny? A leading American journal devoted a third of a column to the subject, sparing five lines for a description of the battle of Waterloo.

I have already said in these pages that I left my birthplace in Connecticut in April, 1826, for Rochester, passing through New York and Albany. At that date New York City contained a population of 155,000, Albany 15,000, Rochester 3500, Buffalo 4500, Cleveland 500, but Chicago was not even a dot on the map. I shall now refer only to daily newspapers. In April, 1826, the dailies in the metropolitan city numbered six or seven. I recall the *Gazette and General Advertiser*, the *Mercantile Advertiser*, the *Commercial Advertiser*, the *Post*, the *Advocate*, the *Enquirer*, and the *American*. Albany then had two dailies—the *Advertiser*, Clintonian in politics, and the *Argus*, Democratic. These nine were then the only dailies in the state. There was not a daily newspaper in the Union west of New York, Albany, and Philadelphia. I have previously stated that, in the fall of 1826, the *Daily Advertiser* was issued at Rochester. It was the earliest daily put forth between the Hudson and Delaware rivers on the East and the Pacific Ocean on the West. Its first editor was Henry O'Reilly, whom I have known and respected for the past sixty years. (The news of his death at Rochester comes to me while I am revising this sheet of manuscript.) The next daily newspaper west of Rochester and Philadelphia was the *Commercial Register*, issued at Cincinnati in 1826, a little later than O'Reilly's *Advertiser*. It lived only six months. The *Cincinnati Gazette* had been published for several years as a weekly and semi-weekly, when, on June 27, 1827, it appeared as a daily. Either then or immediately afterwards it came under the management of Charles Hammond, whom I occasionally met when I dwelt at Cincinnati, in 1832, '33, '34, and '35. Mr. Hammond had been trained in the law. He wielded a keen pen, and stood at the head of the editorial profession in Ohio. All the Whig newspapers of the West and Southwest, however, were destined to be overshadowed by the *Louisville Journal*, founded in 1830, by George D. Prentice, of Pachaug. It is an interesting fact that these three dailies—the *Rochester Advertiser*, the *Cincinnati Gazette*, and the *Louisville Journal*—shine in undimmed lustre to-day. In this later epoch, as in the former, able men besides the regular editors wrote for the newspapers; as, for example, John Quincy Adams, Daniel Webster, Edward Everett, Moses Stuart, Caleb Cushing, William L. Marcy, Silas Wright, Benjamin F. Butler, William H. Seward, John A. Dix, William Wirt, Robert Barnewell Rhett, John C. Calhoun, James Buchanan, Thomas H. Benton, Amos Kendall, Robert J. Walker, James G. Birney, and Salmon P. Chase. Some of these gentlemen were frequent contributors to the press, and took an active share in the political controversies of their times through that powerful agency.

I shall now refer more particularly to some of the editors of newspapers whom I have known, omitting Thurlow Weed, Horace Greeley, and a few familiar names already described in these pages. The number of such editors is so large that a bare catalogue of them would fill a couple of pages. I must make selections from a list to every one of whom I would, did space permit, pay a tribute of respect.

For the past sixty years I have seen much of newspaper editors. During half of this long period I have occasionally contributed to journals mainly or wholly directed by Mr. Charles A. Dana. More thoroughly than any editor I have met he has what I call the true newspaper instinct. Prompt in judgment and rapid in execution; quick to discern what will take with his clientage and what will not; capable of performing a large amount of work in a short space of time; ever welcoming valuable ideas and invoking picturesque diction wherewith to clothe them; fond of variety, pungency, wit, and good-humor, but, on sufficient provocation, hitting when he strikes and leaving a mark where he hits; if this country has produced an abler and more versatile occupant of an editorial chair I have not known or heard of him. It gives me pleasure to add that Mr. Dana was ever on the kindliest relations with his editorial associates, and always courteous to his employees.

On the first of January, 1855, Daniel Cady resigned from the bench of the Supreme Court. Lieutenant-Governor Henry J. Raymond, editor of the *New York Times*, asked me to write him an article on the subject. I complied with his wishes. This rapidly prepared production duly appeared in the *Times*, and, much to my surprise, it subsequently occupied twelve pages in the appendix to the eighteenth volume of "Barbour's Reports of the New York Supreme Court," where it was given the rather high-sounding title of "A Part of the History of the Bar and Bench of New York." Mr. Raymond was a born journalist. He knew how to build up a successful metropolitan newspaper. He wielded a pointed and graceful pen in the editorial chair, wrote with rare intelligence and skill on a great variety of subjects, was thoroughly versed in political questions, enjoyed a wide acquaintance with the public men of the country, was incisive and vigorous in controversy, spoke well on the platform and in deliberative bodies, and was an admirable presiding officer. As an editor, he delighted in perpetual war with Mr. Greeley and the *New York Tribune*. Mr. Raymond was a lively companion, and told a story well. In a familiar conversation at a dinner-table in Washington he was asked why it was that Mr. Greeley called him "The little villain of the *Times*." "Oh," replied Raymond, "That is to distinguish me from the big villain of the *Tribune*."

The person who should propose to introduce John Greenleaf Whittier as a poet, in any place whatever, would find that the name and fame of the Quaker bard had arrived there before him. But he is not so well known to the present generation as an editor of newspapers in his early days. Born in 1807, at Haverhill, on the banks of the beautiful Merrimac, he was eighteen years old when, on a dark evening, he timidly slipped his first communication for the press into the box of the *Gazette*, in his native village, and could hardly believe his dazzled eyes as he afterwards furtively peeped into the columns of the paper and beheld his production staring in his face from the types. From his youth Whittier was an admirer of Henry Clay, and, in 1829, he became the editor of the Boston *American Manufacturer*, a journal that advocated Mr. Clay's doctrines on protection. He succeeded his friend and brother bard, George D. Prentice, in the management of the *New England Weekly Review*, at Hartford, when Prentice went to Kentucky, in 1830, to establish the *Louisville Journal*. In 1832 Whittier returned to his first love, and for about six years was the editor-in-chief of the *Haverhill Gazette*. He removed thence to the city of William Penn, on the shore of the Delaware river, and founded the *Pennsylvania Freeman*, an anti-slavery weekly paper. He promulgated his principles in mild hues and winning ways for a year or two, when one of those unique and summary censors of the press and conservators of the peace, commonly called a mob, sacked the office of the *Freeman* and burned it down, with its contents. In 1840 Mr. Whittier settled in what continued to be for a long time his rural home, at Amesbury, on the lower Merrimac. In 1846 or 1847 he became the corresponding editor of that successful and tasteful journal the *National Era*, established and built up by that able writer, Doctor Gamaliel H. Bailey. It will be remembered that Mrs. Stowe's Uncle Tom's Cabin" first appeared in numbers in the *National Era*.

I became personally acquainted with Mr. Whittier in 1834 or 1835. I speak of him now only as a newspaper man. In the dozen years following 1835 I spent many months in his company, and travelled with him hundreds of miles in eight or ten states. Only those who know my shy friend well are aware how talkative, genial, witty, humorous, sarcastic, and entertaining he is in bright hours with two or three companions. Of course we have exchanged many letters in the past half-century. Peculiar circumstances induce me to break through my rule in respect to such correspondence, and print a recent note, merely as a testimonial of my regard for the author, who, like me, is passing away. It may be well to say that my daughter, Mrs. Harriot Stanton Blatch, of England, did not find Mr. Whittier at home:

"OAK KNOLL, DANVERS, 8*th month*, 23, 1886.

"MY DEAR STANTON,—I have just got back from Holderness, N. H., and find thy letter, introducing thy daughter. I regret that she was not able to see me. I should have been glad to have met her, for my sake as well as thine.

"My dear old friend, how glad I am to see thy writing once more. I wish I could shake the hand that wrote. What times we had together when we fought the wild beasts at Ephesus! I think over the old days a great deal. Life now is all behind me. Most of our early friends have passed away. Sewall and a few others still remain. But we are really getting to be the "Last of the Mohicans!"

"I hope thy health is good. I am only *staying*. I cannot write without suffering.

"God bless thee, old comrade! Ever and faithfully thy friend,
"JOHN G. WHITTIER."

This note from Mr. Whittier enclosed a copy, printed on a fly-sheet, of his poem to the memory of Samuel J. Tilden.

I turn to an editor who joined the guild of journalism just as the veteran we have been contemplating was leaving it. It is difficult to find a niche in which to place so versatile a man as George William Curtis. Is he an author? Yes. Is he an orator? Yes. Is he an editor? Yes. Assign him to any of these positions and the designation would be appropriate. Though an eloquent speaker and debater, fitted to shine in popular and deliberative bodies, he has done the most of his life-work with the pen, and much of it on daily, weekly, and monthly periodical publications. In 1850 he became a regular writer on the *New York Tribune*. He was one of the original editors of *Putnam's Monthly*, and for many years past has been chief editor of the weekly journal of the great publishing house of Harper & Brothers, and a regular contributor to their *Monthly Magazine*. Mr. Curtis was nominated in 1864 for representative in Congress in the First District of New York, in which he resides, and which was strongly opposed to his political views. He was defeated, as he doubtless anticipated, and failed to enter an arena where he would have taken high rank among the able and brilliant members. But, after all, he will perhaps be the longest remembered for his distinguished services with pen and voice in the cause of " Liberty and Union " when it was in extreme peril.

CHAPTER XXVII.

American Journalism.—Vice-President Wilson and Charles Francis Adams.—James and Erastus Brooks.—The *New York Express.*—Lewis Tappan and David Hale.—The *Journal of Commerce.*—Early Modes of Getting News. — William Cullen Bryant and William H. Leggett.—*New York Evening Post.*—Courage of *The Post.*—President Van Buren.—James Watson Webb.—The *Courier and Enquirer.*—Famous Duels of Cilley, Graves, Webb, and Marshall.—Greeley's Comments.—Benjamin Day.—*The* (N. Y.) *Sun.*—James Gordon Bennett.—The *New York Herald.*—"It Does Move."—Brave Editors and Journals. — Joseph Tinker Buckingham and the *Boston Courier.*—Charles King and the *New York American.* — Charles Hammond and the *Cincinnati Gazette.*—James G. Birney.—Gamaliel H. Bailey.—Elijah Parrish Lovejoy.—Cassius M. Clay.

VICE-PRESIDENT WILSON was in early days an editor of a Free-soil newspaper in Boston, in conjunction with Charles Francis Adams. Indeed, the latter was the founder and the leading contributor of the paper. At a later date Wilson wrote an elaborate book, in two volumes, entitled, "The Rise and Fall of the Slave Power." Though the style is heavy, it is a valuable storehouse of facts. Of course, he gathered his materials as others do. He levied contributions among his friends. He assessed me to the amount of one hundred and fifty foolscap pages, which he wrought into the book. In coming years, when some Macaulay shall compose a history of this great epoch, he will find Wilson's work a rich mine from which to draw materials.

In looking back to discover the few, the very few, surviving editors of New York newspapers of early days, the eye naturally falls on the veteran Erastus Brooks. He held a high place in journalism for half a century, and is now an occasional writer for the press. The admirable letters that Mr. James Brooks wrote, in 1835, to the *Portland Advertiser*, describing his tour on foot in Europe, which were extensively copied in this country, deepened the desire in many minds to travel in those enchanting lands. The model letters of Mr. Erastus Brooks, in the same year and the next to the *New York Daily Advertiser*, from Washington, sketching scenes in Congress, in that exciting period, led many young men to visit the National Capital. The two brothers established the New York Daily *Express* in 1836. Under their management it rapidly reached the front rank among the city journals. One of its attractive features were the Washington letters of Erastus Brooks. In a recent communication to the present *Mail and Express*, he says of the founding of the *Express* of 1836, that "the labor of starting a newspaper in New York fifty years ago was intense, and required patience, courage, self-sacrifice, and persistent effort." In this communication the venerable journalist gives the following interesting facts: "In the time of the writer," says Mr. Brooks, "as editor and proprietor, he has seen more than one hundred and twenty journals live and die in the city of New York alone, and he believes that more than twenty millions of dollars was spent in the city papers from 1836 to 1877. Only five of the one hundred and twenty journals in existence in

1836, and since then, survived in 1879, and one hundred and four had disappeared in the space of twenty years. In inexperienced hands the largest collection of sponges will not imbibe water as rapidly as new newspapers will absorb money."

Mr. Brooks achieved distinction as a politician and a legislator. He was a leader in many sessions of the Senate and Assembly of New York, and in the Constitutional Convention of 1867, and the Constitutional Commission of 1872. I have seldom heard his superior in debate in deliberative or partisan bodies. No doubt he was somewhat indebted for his success in this field to his early training and long experience as an editor. He is an expert, too, in one occult branch of law. John C. Spencer, Samuel B. Ruggles, Erastus Brooks, and Horatio Seymour were able to shed valuable light over the ecclesiastical tribunals of the Episcopal Church when they happened to be lay members of its conventions.

Those who have known or heard of Lewis Tappan only as an enterprising merchant, or an Anti-slavery agitator, may be surprised to see him classed among newspaper editors. But this versatile and vigorous man finds an appropriate place there. He and his brother, Arthur, founded the New York *Journal of Commerce* in 1827, Lewis Tappan being editor-in-chief, and David Hale assistant editor. It was established to promote the interests of the mercantile class, and to defend the doctrines of the Christian religion. Mr. Tappan soon became the sole proprietor, and he and Mr. Hale conducted it with so much ability and spirit that it early ranked among the most important newspapers in the commercial metropolis. Mr. Tappan ultimately withdrew from its management, in order to devote his time more exclusively to their mercantile firm, then one of the largest silk houses in the city. The *Journal of Commerce* went into the control of those distinguished editors, Hale and Hallock. In 1828 this paper stationed a swift vessel off Sandy Hook to obtain the European news from inward-bound ships earlier than its contemporaries; and at a subsequent date it ran a horse express from Philadelphia to New York, which enabled it to lay the proceedings of Congress before its readers a day sooner than the other journals. These projects (conceived and executed by Lewis Tappan and David Hale) may seem small to us, but the generation that had not dreamed of the land telegraph, the submarine wire, the telephone, or the railroad, looked upon them as extraordinary achievements.

In those days I knew Mr. Hale slightly. He was born in a lowly, one story, little clapboard house, in Lisbon, just across the Quinnebaug river from Jewett City. I need not say that I was associated with Lewis Tappan all through the struggle for the overthrow of negro slavery. He was one of the bravest men I ever met. I have seen him stand for an hour while a mob was raining a tempest of missiles upon our assembly, and he seemed as cool as if sitting under the shadow of one of the spreading elms of his native Northampton.

The men of to-day have faint conceptions of the bitterness of the controversy over a protective tariff and the rechartering of the United States Bank and cognate questions which raged in Jackson's administration. Party lines sometimes crossed, as in the memorable struggle over the nullification theories, engendered in the fertile brain of John C. Calhoun. On this subject Jackson and Benton were in accord with Webster and Clay. During the whole of this historic crisis the New York *Evening Post* was perhaps the ablest journalistic supporter of the principles and measures espoused by the Jackson party. It was with the hero of the "Hermitage" on the tariff, the bank, and nullification, and was against Clay, Webster, and the Whigs in all these measures except the last. During this troubled period Mr. Bryant controlled the columns of the *Post*, but through a portion of it he was assisted by the more fiery pen of William Leggett. Indeed, it is only stating the exact truth to say that Mr. Leggett was a more vigorous and versatile journalist than Mr. Bryant. Mr. Van Buren was inaugurated as President in March, 1837. The slavery contest was then at its height. Van Buren bent to the storm, and in his inaugural declared that he would veto any act which Congress might pass for the abolition of slavery in the District of Columbia. In an editorial in his own separate paper, just then started, Leggett keenly criticised Van Buren's address, saying that, as to any explicit recommendation of measures, the President might as well have sung "Hail Columbia" or whistled "Yankee Doodle."

And now an event occurred in the history of the *Evening Post* that is worthy of special commendation. Van Buren and Wright had foreshadowed the Sub-treasury scheme. The outbreak against the proposed financial policy was without a precedent in violence. It was to the last degree unpopular with the monetary and trading classes. But the *Post*, though published in the banking and commercial metropolis of the Union, firmly stood by the President and his Sub-treasury scheme, while in the same columns it held up to indignation and contempt his pledge to interpose his veto against any bill that should emancipate the slaves in the district. To fully estimate the courage and fidelity of the *Post* in this conjuncture it must be borne in mind that, probably, no two propositions were ever so unpopular in the city of New York as were the Sub-treasury measure and the project of setting the negroes free at the national capital.

It is wise to contemplate instances of journalistic independence and courage. The Democratic party had imbibed the infatuated idea of strengthening themselves by extending the area of negro slavery. In spite of the longer vision of Van Buren, Benton, Wright, and Blair, the slavery propagandists determined to annex Texas to the Union for the purpose of planting the baleful institution therein. A small band of Democrats resisted this wild scheme from the moment of its inception. Van Buren and his followers in New York looked askance at the project, but hardly dared to speak up like men, and wither it in the bud. But the *Evening Post* did not hesitate to follow where duty led. It denounced the plot, exposed the ulterior objects of the conspirators, and foretold (which subsequently came to pass) that its consummation would prostrate the Democratic party and bring calamity on the country. Week after week the *Post* glowed with indignation against the policy of annexation, so pregnant of present evils, so full of future disasters. Mr. Bryant, in this contest, had many coadjutors at his side, but among Democratic journals the *Post* stood almost alone.

James Watson Webb founded the New York *Courier and Enquirer* in 1829. His career as a journalist and politician are too well known to justify special recital here. For the first twenty years of its long life the *Courier and Enquirer* ranked among influential journals. At the outset it supported the administration of General Jackson in the bold and vehement style so characteristic of its editor-in-chief, and championed the President in the earlier stages of his conflict with Nicholas Biddle and the United States Bank. By and by a change came over the newspaper, and, from being an ardent opponent of the Whig policy of renewing the Charter of the Banks, it became a zealous advocate of that measure. Of the alleged discoveries of a Congressional Committee, and the subsequent charges of corruption by Jonathan Cilley, a Democratic member of the House from Maine, and Colonel Webb's challenge of Cilley to a duel, and Cilley's refusal to meet him for the asserted reason that Webb was not a gentleman, and the taking-up of the quarrel by William J. Graves, a Kentucky Congressman, the second of Webb, and the killing of Cilley in a duel with Graves, when Graves called him to the field because Cilley had said that Graves was the bearer of a hostile message from an individual who was not a gentleman—of this famous, foolish, and fatal fray I shall record nothing, though I was familiar with the transactions at the time they occurred.

The *Courier and Enquirer* now became a prominent Whig journal, under the management of Webb. He was an aggressive editor, indulged in pungent personalities, and courted contradiction and conflict. He charged some of the Kentucky delegation in Congress with corruption respecting the Bankrupt Act. Thomas F. Marshall, a Kentucky member, scarified Webb on the floor of the House. Soon afterwards Marshall came to New York to defend Monroe Edwards, a man of considerable repute, who was arraigned on an indictment for forgery. Webb commented sharply in his newspaper on the conduct of Marshall in leaving his seat in the House to appear at the bar of a criminal court in a distant city. Day by day the *Courier and Enquirer* blazed away at Marshall. The night before he was to sum up for Edwards he addressed a note to Webb, telling him that he should reply to his attacks at the opening of his speech. Colonel Webb appeared in court, and Marshall, by way of exordium, denounced him in a bitter philippic. The result was a challenge to a duel. The parties went to Delaware for the purpose. They fought, and Webb was wounded in the leg. I often saw him on his crutches. The affair created much excitement, and upon his return to New York Webb was indicted for leaving the state to fight a duel. He was found guilty, and sentenced to two years in the state prison. So great was the sympathy expressed for him that his friends, irrespective of party, circulated petitions praying for his pardon. Among the most conspicuous of the seventeen thousand names appended to the petitions was that of Horace Greeley, editor of the *New York Tribune*, then a rival of the *Courier and Enquirer*. Mr. Seward was Governor of the state, and a personal friend of Webb. After Webb had been in the Tombs a few weeks the Governor gave him an unconditional pardon, and saved him from the state prison.

I have related this little piece of history about Marshall, Webb, Greeley, and Seward, as an introduction to a bit of biography concerning Webb and Greeley. I must here draw on my memory for details, and shall give only the substance of the editorial articles in question. Though each was a Whig "organ," the *Tribune* and the *Courier and Enquirer* were constantly in a broil. One morning Webb handled Greeley with severity in a long editorial. He referred to the peculiar dress which Greeley wore, asserting that he appeared on Broadway in an uncouth garb merely to arrest the attention of passers-by. The next morning the *Tribune* contained an elaborate reply, going over Webb's article point by point. The last subject taken up by the philosopher of Spruce Street was Webb's reference to his dress. I give only the substance of Greeley's paragraph relating to this matter. "As to our personal appearance," he said, "it does seem time that we should stay the flood of nonsense with which the town, by this time, must be nauseated." He then went on to tell how he came to New York with scarcely a dollar in his pocket, and worked as a journeyman printer ten or a dozen years, and how he had toiled till he had become the conductor of a leading journal of the country. Greeley closed

12*

his cutting rejoinder by a reference to his efforts to procure Webb's pardon from the state prison, about in these words: "That he" (Greeley) "ever affected eccentricity is most untrue; and certainly no costume he ever appeared in on Broadway or elsewhere would create such a sensation as that which James Watson Webb would have worn but for the clemency of Governor Seward. Heaven grant that our assailant may never hang with such weight on another Whig executive. We drop him."

I heard at the time that when Webb read this outburst of Greeley he broke into a laugh, and said he forgave the irate philosopher.

The *Courier and Enquirer* covered so long a period that its vicissitudes would furnish an epitome of the history of New York journalism. At various times Colonel Webb had for his chief of staff George H. Andrews and Henry J. Raymond. The latter rose till he practically became the principal editor. The old paper waned after Raymond left it to build up the *Times*, and in 1860 it lapsed into the *World*.

I recall the day, in 1835, when the first number of the *New York Herald* was sold in the streets by a dishevelled set of brawling news boys, "price one cent." These greasy and noisy youths were the grandfathers of the lively and audacious gamins of our times. The *Sun*, though, was the first permanent daily penny paper in the Union. It was issued in September, 1833, by Benjamin Day, three years in advance of the *Herald*.

On coming to New York from Lane Seminary, in May, 1834, or 1835, to address the American Anti-slavery Society (I was present in both years), I ascertained that Lewis Tappan had purchased a column in the little *Sun*, with the privilege of using that column as a medium of publishing, at advertising rates, such matter as he pleased. He and Elizur Wright kept it well supplied with anti-slavery facts and figures. When the *Herald* arose it eclipsed the *Sun*. James Gordon Bennett was a canny Scotchman, and possessed the genuine newspaper genius. His unique journal opened a fresh epoch in that department of literature. Some time after its establishment I delivered half a dozen lectures in the city on the Slavery question, especially with reference to the then endangered right of petition and freedom of discussion. They were reported in the *Herald*, after a fashion, accompanied by harmless ridicule of the subject and the speaker. A friend recently sent me those copies of the *Herald*. I was interested in measuring the space the country had passed over in the intervening half-century. "It does move!" said Galileo.

Early remembrances in regard to newspapers are so strong upon me that I must refer to two or three exceptional cases, if it is only to record their names. While I was living in Jewett City, George D. Prentice induced me to subscribe to the *New England Galaxy*, published in Boston by the intrepid Joseph Tinker Buckingham, and to which Prentice was a contributor. I kept the editor in mind through a dozen changing years after I had ceased to read the productions of his pen. Meanwhile he had founded and raised to eminence the *Boston Daily Courier*. When I was mobbed in Massachusetts in the years 1835, '36,

'37, '38, Mr. Buckingham occasionally defended liberty of speech in able articles in the columns of the *Courier*. His caustic pen blistered the enemies of free discussion with stinging epithets. The like meed of praise can be bestowed on the *New York American*, then holding an unusually high literary rank among the daily newspapers of the city. It was conducted by Charles King, the son of Rufus King. In that proscriptive era, when journals issued in commercial centres that traded with the South hardly dared to vindicate even the right of petition, the *Cincinnati Gazette*, under the management of Charles Hammond (previously mentioned), ventured to speak more bravely in support of liberty and law than perhaps any other daily newspaper printed on the banks of the lower affluents of the Mississippi River. Those were indeed troublous days in that portion of the Union. James G. Birney's and Gamaliel H. Bailey's printing presses and types were more than once submerged in the Ohio at Cincinnati, and Elijah Parrish Lovejoy was shot to death by citizens while protecting his press and types from a like fate at Alton. It is painful to hold up to view the dark side of this picture. It is far more agreeable to point to the silver lining that soon afterwards began to tinge the edges of the sombre cloud.

The five brave journalists just mentioned have passed away. One of a later period, who suffered in the same cause, survives to publish the history of his own perils, which, viewed in some aspects, were greater than theirs. I refer to Cassius M. Clay. The freedom of the press never had a more heroic champion than this distinguished son of Kentucky. The first time I saw him was in 1844, at Boston, in a great meeting that he was addressing in support of the election to the Presidency of his relative, Henry Clay. The last time I saw him was at Johnston, N. Y., in 1884, when I was called to the chair of a meeting which he addressed in support of the election of James G. Blaine. In the intervening forty years Mr. Clay had rendered important services in behalf of the slave, especially in his native state, both on the platform and through his newspaper, the *True American*. His life was frequently put to hazard; his blood was shed in encounters with foes whom he contrived to overmaster in more than one hand-to-hand deadly affray. The liberty of speech and of the press owes more to him than to any other citizen of Kentucky. Portions of his recently published autobiography read like a tragic novel.

CHAPTER XXVIII.

American Journalism.—Religious Newspapers.—Albany Journals and Editors: *The Argus, Atlas,* and *Evening Journal;* Croswell, Weed, Cassidy, Van Dyck, Shaw, Dawson, Wilkeson.—Names of Thirty Persons whose Obituary Notices were Written by the Author in Various Journals.—Death of Gerrit Smith in December, 1874.—Several State Conventions.—Tweed Exposes his Persecutors at Rochester in 1871.—Conkling and Fenton Cross Swords at Syracuse in 1871.—Tilden Nominated for Governor in 1874, Robinson in 1876, Cornell and John Kelly in 1879.—Speech-Making and Reporting.—Meeting at Providence in 1856.—The *New York Times.*—Isaac Hill and the *Concord Patriot.*—John M. Niles and the *Hartford Times.*—Newspaper Correspondents Writing Speeches for Senators and Congressmen, and Reports for Committees, and Messages for Governors.—Press Club Receptions in 1885.—Extract from President Amos J. Cumming's Speech; he is Elected to Congress in November, 1886.—The Great Newspaper District he Represents.

Though a little late, I will say, that in the heat of the assault upon the Southern oligarchy, when epithets were not always carefully chosen by the assailants on either side, the charge was made that the religious newspapers in the North were opposed to the anti-slavery enterprise. This was at one period the attitude of journals of that class in large cities, but was never true of those published in the country districts and smaller towns. I occasionally contributed to the religious press, and I affirm that in the later stages of our conflict with the baleful institution, and especially in the civil war, it was a powerful agent in the work of securing the freedom of the slave and the preservation of the Union.

These journals were controlled by clergymen, and what I have said of their newspapers will hold good of the body of the ministers in the North from the opening of the Anti-slavery contest to its close. They were unjustly accused of hostility to emancipation. This was true for a time in a partial sense of those who preached to the wealthy, aristocratic churches of the chief cities, but it was otherwise with those of the rural districts, and with the ministers of two or three of the most populous sects, as, for example, the Methodists and Baptists. I speak from personal observation when I assert that in the trying crisis of our struggle there were no firmer champions of the slave than the mass of the Northern clergy. Indeed, and to state the case exactly, some abolitionists hated ministers more than they hated slave-holders. As Alvan Stewart once quaintly put it in a convention, "Some of our people seem unable to get under way till they have given the ministers a black eye."

In the conflicts between the Barnburners and the Hunkers, the young *Albany Atlas* was the organ of the former, and the venerable *Albany Argus* of the latter. William Cassidy, the editor of the *Atlas*, was a versatile writer. He was assisted by the solid abilities of Henry H. Van Dyck and the sparkling wit of John Van Buren. Edwin Croswell, who had long managed the *Argus*, was trained in the Albany Regency, a political organization that controlled the Democratic party in New York for twenty years. He was an editor of rare gifts. He encountered an opponent worthy of his blade in Mr. Weed, of the *Albany Evening Journal*. The *Argus*, at a later day, came under the able direction of Mr. S. M. Shaw, now of the Cooperstown *Freeman's Journal*, and absorbed the *Atlas*. In those days Governor Marcy wrote occasionally for the *Argus*. The veteran George Dawson took the helm of the *Evening Journal* after the brilliant pen of Mr. Samuel Wilkeson disappeared from its columns. In the vicissitudes of parties from 1848 to 1858, I occasionally wrote as a volunteer for all of these influential newspapers. It would please me to speak of the later days of the *Journal* and the *Argus*, and of those comparatively modern newspapers at the state capital, the *Times*, the *Press*, and the *Express;* but I must move on.

I have never been, in the strict sense of the phrase, on the editorial staff of either the *New York Tribune* or the *New York Sun*. But for the past thirty-two years I have written largely for each in turn, and mostly in the editorial columns. The questions I treated were of every variety. There is one topic, however, to which I will particularly refer. It often devolved upon me to prepare obituary notices of distinguished persons. They exhibit the defects of rapid writing, for they were produced under the pressure of emergencies that would permit of no delay. I recall the following names of subjects, selected at random: Daniel Cady, John Brown, Salmon P. Chase, Charles Sumner, Robert Rantoul, Horace Greeley, Thaddeus Stevens, John A. Dix, William Cullen Bryant, William Lloyd Garrison, Benjamin F. Wade, William Pitt Fessenden, Henry Wilson, Gerrit Smith,

Daniel S. Dickinson, William H. Seward, Sanford E. Church, Thurlow Weed, James Watson Webb, Arphaxad Loomis, Reuben E. Fenton, Robert L. Stanton, Horatio Seymour, Samuel J. Tilden, Henry O'Reilly, Stephen Pearl Andrews, Rev. Thomas S. Shipman, Mrs. Daniel Cady, Mrs. Gerrit Smith, and Mrs. Lucretia Mott. It gave me a melancholy pleasure to strew stray flowers on the graves of some of my coadjutors in a great cause.

On Sunday afternoon, December 28, 1874, I called at the house of General John Cochrane, in New York, and there learned that Gerrit Smith had that morning been stricken with apoplexy, and was lying unconscious in the chamber above. That manly form was waging a desperate battle for life. His attending physician, Dr. Edward Bayard, my brother-in-law, informed me that it was quite possible he might live till the next day. Late in the evening it occurred to me that I would go to the *Sun* office, and prepare an obituary notice of the friend whom I had known for forty years. I dictated it to a shorthand writer. It would fill five columns. The hour of midnight arrived, when it must be decided whether or not it was to go into print. There was no one to confer with but the night editor. I finally sent the article to the composing-room, where they prefixed to it the startling heading, "Gerrit Smith's Deathbed." On Monday morning the *Sun* took the town by surprise. General Cochrane's house was filled with reporters. Mr. Smith died about noon. Towards evening I dropped into the *Sun* office. The night editor rushed up to me, his eyes all aglow, and, seizing my hand, exclaimed: "Mr. Stanton, that was one of the grandest newspaper beats that ever happened in New York! And how fortunate it is for us that Mr. Smith died to-day! The glorious old man did not go back on us. It would have been very embarrassing if he had recovered." The enthusiastic outburst of the night editor may be regarded as the very effervescence of the *esprit de corps* of journalism.

For several years I attended state conventions of both parties in New York, and superintended the reports of their doings for the *Sun*, by a stenographer, who minded his business and let mine alone. It was easy to describe what had transpired to-day, but it was difficult to foreshadow what was to occur to-morrow. I was ofttimes able to do the latter, because I had long been personally acquainted with the leaders of factions, and they would accept my assurance that the information they imparted would not be disclosed to others, though both sides understood that the facts were to appear in the *Sun*.

I was at the Democratic State Convention at Rochester in 1871. The exposures in the *New York Times* of the frauds of the Tweed Ring had startled the country Democrats. Nevertheless, the delegates from the city were, as usual, under the absolute control of Tweed. I am now to speak of the evening before the convention organized. Ultimate results would depend upon whether the Tweed delegation on the morrow demanded seats therein. I knew it was the purpose of such Democrats as Governor Seymour, Mr. Tilden, Chief-Judge Church, and Senator Francis Kernan to exclude them; and Mr. Tilden had counted his followers, and feared no failure. Tweed did not know this. At midnight I met Mr. Tweed alone, by appointment, in his private apartment, where he was to explain to me his programme for the morrow. The scene will long remain in my memory. The chandelier in the large room was turned low, and the elaborate furniture cast ghastly shadows on the walls. The fallen boss, whom I was wont to see in the fulness of his strength, was nervous and sad. In a voice slightly tremulous with emotion, he said the credentials of the Tammany delegates would not be presented. He surprised me with the frankness of his utterances. I will not name those of his persecutors to whom he said he had previously paid money, for a vein of bitterness tinged his conversation. At a later date, Tweed was sacrificed to save others who were as guilty as himself. While in prison, in the fall of 1877, he was drawn into detailed disclosures of the robberies of the Ring by promises which were not kept. Though a public plunderer, he was as honest as some of his prosecutors.

I was at many state conventions on the like errand with that just described. As, for example, at the Republican Convention of 1871, at Syracuse, when Conkling and Fenton crossed swords, and the latter was grievously wounded; and at the Democratic Convention of 1874, where Samuel J. Tilden received authority to break up the Canal Ring, which he afterwards executed; and at the Democratic Convention of 1876, which placed Lucius Robinson in a station that enabled that sour politician to disrupt and almost destroy his party; and at the Republican Convention of 1879, where Alonzo B. Cornell surprised his opponents by winning the Gubernatorial nomination, and afterwards beat his antagonist at the polls by aid of a flank movement of John Kelly.

In the New England campaign of the spring of 1860, which foreshadowed the election of a Republican President (perchance his defeat!), I met in Providence, where I was to speak, Mr. Joseph Howard, Jr., representative of the *New York Times*. Supposing I had prepared a written address, he asked me for a copy for the *Times*. Not a word of my speech was on paper, but, according to my usual habit, the outline was before my eye. We repaired to my room. Mr. Howard posed as the Slave Power. For nearly an hour I upbraided him for his long-continued aggressions upon the liberties of the people and the Constitution of his country. Though evidently a little disturbed in his mind at this vivid portrayal of his manifold iniquities, he nevertheless rallied sufficiently to take down the speech and emphasize its sharp points with "loud applause." This was written out, sent to the *Times*, and put in type before the meeting was held, for, be it remembered, the telegraph was far less used for such purposes then than it is now. The large and tumultuous meeting lasted till near midnight, and the next morning the speech I had hurled at the Slave Power in the person of Joseph Howard three days previously appeared in the *Times*, and several thousand copies of the paper were purchased for circulation in Rhode Island.

An old-time friend in Congress happened to meet me in Washington, and asked me to write a speech for him on the tariff, a subject he said he understood about as well as the average New-Zealander. I did as he requested. He read the speech in the House, and circulated a large edition. It was translated into German, his astonished constituents presented to him a set of silver plate, and he was re-elected.

As pure acts of personal friendship (for I never took a penny for such services), I did this for Representatives and Senators whose names "shone afar" in the Federal councils. I was a little disgusted once when a prominent Senator, by an awkward fumbling of his manuscript, missed a brilliant passage over which I had burned a large amount of midnight gas. I felt as bad, perhaps, as Mrs. Isaac Hill, of New Hampshire, did in Van Buren's day. She was leaning over the rail of the Senate gallery while her husband was reading a speech. She startled the strange ladies around her by exclaiming: "There! Mr. Hill has turned over two leaves at once!" Mr. Hill was an accomplished editor, and therefore able to write his own speeches. So was John M. Niles, of Connecticut. Senator Hill built up the *Concord Patriot;* Senator Niles the *Hartford Times.* Senators and Representatives that can neither write nor speak ought to resign in favor of editors who can do one or both.

What I have stated above is only a sample of a common occurrence at Washington and elsewhere. I am often astounded at the eloquence of some of our public men! Bursting on the country so unexpectedly, too!

Newspaper correspondents do a lucrative business

at Washington in writing speeches for Senators and Representatives. Indeed, so common is this that whenever I see an exceptionally able set speech by an inferior member of either House, I am constrained to exclaim, "That is a good speech; I wonder what newspaper man wrote it?" The enterprising correspondent who sold the same speech to two Congressmen, each of whom delivered it as his own, rather imposed on his victims, especially as he himself hired a third person to write it. So did the reporter who copied the best passages in the speech he furnished to his dupe from an old book in the Congressional library. There should be honor among such people.

This line of remark will now and then apply to reports from Congressional committees and the executive departments, and to Governors' messages and emanations from State Legislatures. Oh, well, if you don't know how to do a thing yourself, is it not best to invoke the aid of somebody who does?

Persons not well informed on this subject are not aware how frequent is the practice of palming on the public writings, and especially speeches and orations, which are the productions of others than their reputed authors. Over and over again men have sent articles to newspapers and magazines, and even books to publishers, claiming them as emanations of their own pens, who, when it came to revising the proofs, were not capable of recasting or rewriting a paragraph.

On June 27, 1885, the day when I completed the eightieth year of my age and the sixtieth since I began to write for newspapers, the New York Press Club gave me a reception at their rooms in the city. The proceedings were elaborately reported. I omit everything except the closing portion of the speech of Mr. Amos J. Cummings, then president of the Club. I print this because it presents some curious information concerning several distinguished editors and authors.

"Glance over Mr. Stanton's past," continued Mr. Cummings. "He was born four years before Abraham Lincoln. When he began to write for newspapers, Lincoln was employed at six dollars a month to manage a ferry across the Ohio, at the mouth of Anderson's Creek. Stephen A. Douglas was a boy twelve years old, living with his widowed mother on a sterile Vermont farm. Fred Douglass was a pickaninny on a Maryland plantation. Horace Greeley had not yet entered a country printing-office. Thurlow Weed was editing a dingy weekly newspaper. Charles Dickens was a boy thirteen years old, employed in an attorney's office. Thackeray was a boy of fourteen, attending school in London. William Cullen Bryant had just come to this city. James Gordon Bennett was trying to establish a commercial school here. Henry J. Raymond and Charles A. Dana were wearing check aprons at district schools. Erastus Brooks was attending a grocery in Boston. James Watson Webb was an adjutant in the regular army. Manton Marble, George W. Childs, and William Henry Hurlbert were enwrapped in the cocoon of futurity. A. K. McClure was just learning to walk. Joseph R. Hawley had just been born in a country town in North Carolina. John W. Forney was a boy nine years old, running around unshod; and scores of other newspaper men who have won fame and fortune were not even literary larvæ."

Mr. Cummings, in November, 1886, was elected by an almost unanimous vote to the Fiftieth Congress from the sixth district of New York. His varied experience as a journalist will enable him to carry to the House of Representatives an amount of rare information, that will be valuable in a body that is always composed very largely of lawyers. For example, the House of the Forty-ninth Congress contains 325 members, of whom 245 belong to the legal profession. The Sixth New York District doubtless issues more newspapers and periodicals than any other Congress district in the United States. The total number is 418, consisting of daily, semi-weekly, weekly, bi-weekly, semi-monthly, monthly, bi-monthly, and quarterly publications, printed in fourteen different languages. This is fifty-five more than are issued in Alabama, Louisiana, and Mississippi combined, which three states send twenty-one members to Congress. The Sixth District, too, is the seat of many of the great book-publishing houses of the country. It is also alive with job printers, who do press-work of all imaginable descriptions. It is entirely appropriate that such a district should be represented in Congress by so competent a journalist as Mr. Cummings.

CHAPTER XXIX.

Conclusion.—Retrospect.—Extract from Thomas Moore's "Oft in the Stilly Night."

As I turn my eye back over the fourscore years covered by this narrative, I am deeply impressed with the sad thought that nearly all the persons of whom I have written are in the spirit-land, and that some of the more distinguished have entered its portals since the first edition of this work was issued. As I approach the goal I may be pardoned for quoting, ere laying down the pen, the familiar lines of Moore:

> "When I remember all
>   The friends, so linked together,
> I've seen around me fall
>   Like leaves in wintry weather,
>   I feel like one
>   Who treads alone
>   Some banquet hall deserted,
>   Whose lights are fled,
>   Whose garlands dead,
>   And all but he departed."

INDEX OF NAMES.

Abinger, Lord, 92.
Adams, Charles Francis, 149, 150, 156, 163, 265.
Adams, John, 72, 255.
Adams, John Quincy, 19, 31, 33, 49, 50, 58–60, 83, 158, 159, 163, 259.
Allen, Charles, 149.
Allen, William, 153, 242.
Andrews, George H., 274.
Andrews, Stephen Pearl, 281.
Anthony, Susan B., 68.
Armstrong, John, 218.
Arnold, Benedict, 5, 6.
Arnold, Matthew, 91.
Astor, John Jacob, 189–191.
Atchinson, David R., 154.
Avery, Ephraim K., 112, 113.

Babcock, George R., 171.
Bailey, E. Prentiss, 66.
Bailey, Gamaliel, 66, 75, 263, 276.
Bailey, Wesley, 66.
Baines, Edward, 76.
Ballantyne, Sergeant, 91.
Banks, Nathaniel P., 61.
Barker, George P., 155, 160.
Barkesdale, William, 208, 209.
Barnard, Daniel D., 35.
Barnes, Albert, 45, 185.
Bates, Edward, 222, 224.
Bayard, Edward, 281.
Beaconsfield, Lord, 83.
Beardsley, Samuel, 51, 161.
Beecher, Harriet, 68.
Beecher, Henry Ward, 44, 45.
Beecher, Lyman, 43–46.
Beekman, James W., 171, 172.
Belknap, Jeremy, 16.
Bellamy, Joseph, 12.

Beman, Nathan S. S., 45.
Benjamin, Judah P., 204.
Bennett, James Gordon, 275, 287.
Bentham, Jeremy, 106.
Benton, Thomas H., 61, 152, 154, 259.
Bickford, Maria, 113, 118, 119, 121.
Biddle, Nicholas, 103, 153, 206.
Bigelow, John, 160.
Binney, Thomas, 76.
Birney, David B., 48.
Birney, James G., 47–49, 58, 65, 75, 259, 276.
Bishop, Joel Prentiss, 126.
Black, Jeremiah, 212.
Blaine, James G., 154, 185.
Blair, Francis P. (Senior), 154, 183, 220.
Blair, Francis P. (Junior), 222.
Blair, Montgomery, 222.
Blatchford, Samuel, 142.
Blucher, Field Marshal, 257.
Booth, Junius Brutus, 96.
Bouck, William C., 30, 161.
Boughton, Selleck, 132, 133.
Bowman, John, 30.
Bowring, John, 76.
Brandreth, Benjamin, 171.
Breckenridge, John C., 203.
Brewster, Henry, 51.
Brewster, Simon, 3, 6.
Brewster, Susan, 3.
Brewster, William, 3, 108.
Bright, John, 76, 101.
Bronson, Greene C., 129.
Brooks, Erastus, 266, 267, 287.
Brooks, James, 266.
Brougham, Henry, 75, 77–81, 85–87, 106.
Brown, John (Capt.), 191, 280.

Brown, Judge, 50.
Brown, Tom, 153.
Brummel, Beau, 90.
Brunswick, Duchess of, 76.
Bryant, William Cullen, 63, 103, 160, 214, 269, 277, 287.
Buchanan, James, 152, 154, 204, 207, 259.
Buckingham, Joseph Tinker, 275.
Buckingham, William A., 54.
Buller, Charles, 76.
Bulwer, Edward Lytton, 85.
Bunyan, John, 108.
Burden, Henry, 141, 142.
Burke, Edmund, 87, 92, 108, 116.
Burleigh, Charles C., 71.
Burleigh, William H., 71.
Burns, Robert, 103, 109.
Burr, Aaron, 255.
Burroughs, Roswell, 13.
Burroughs, Silas, 13.
Butler, Benjamin F. (Albany), 31, 32, 158, 160, 163, 164, 259.
Butler, Benjamin F. (Lowell), 227.
Buxton, Thomas Fowell, 76, 85, 86, 87.
Byron, Ada Augusta, 104.
Byron, Lady, 76, 104.
Byron, Lord, 76, 104.

Cady, Daniel, 35, 74, 130, 131, 139, 140, 260.
Cady, Elizabeth, 74.
Cagger, Peter, 136–138.
Calhoun, John C., 61, 84, 114, 152, 154, 259.
Calvin, Delano C., 145.
Cambreling, Churchill C., 160, 161.
Cameron, Simon, 164, 213, 222.
Campbell, Thomas, 76, 102, 103, 107.
Carlyle, Thomas, 104, 105.
Carnot, L. N. M., 228.
Carroll, Thomas B., 160, 171, 220.
Cass, Lewis, 154, 157, 158, 161, 179–183, 212.
Cassidy, William, 160, 279.
Chace, William M., 194, 195.
Chalmers, Thomas, 105, 106.

Channing, William Ellery, 71.
Chapman, Maria W., 51.
Charlick, Oliver, 182.
Chase, Edward I., 224.
Chase, Salmon P., 66, 154, 163, 220, 222–225, 238, 239, 259.
Cheetham, James, 254.
Child, Lydia Maria, 67.
Childs, George W., 287.
Choate, Joseph H., 90.
Choate, Rufus, 111, 113, 115–119, 121, 124, 151.
Church, Sanford E., 155, 160, 171, 174.
Cilley, Jonathan, 271.
Clark, Daniel, 143.
Clark, Thomas M., 52.
Clarkson, Thomas, 75, 76, 86, 87, 107.
Clay, Cassius M., 66, 276, 277.
Clay, Henry, 19, 20, 28, 32, 38, 39, 61, 84, 152–154, 158, 205, 206, 217.
Clayton, John M., 152.
Cleveland, Chauncey F., 54.
Clinton, De Witt, 23, 31, 32, 132, 218, 249, 255.
Cochrane, John, 202.
Colden, Cadwallader D., 22.
Coleman, William, 254.
Comstock, Oliver C., 40.
Conkling, Roscoe, 32, 154, 193, 198, 199, 236, 240, 241.
Conolly, Richard B., 247.
Cook, James M., 171.
Copley, John, 79.
Cornell, Alonzo B., 240.
Cornell, Maria, 112.
Corning, Erastus, 141.
Corwin, Thomas, 151, 200, 201, 213.
Cottenham, Lord, 92, 93.
Cowen, Eseck, 129, 135, 136.
Cox, F. A. (D.D.), 76.
Crandell, Prudence, 66, 67.
Crawford, Martin J., 208, 209.
Crawford, William H., 19.
Cremieux, Isaac Adolphe, 93.
Crittenden, John J., 151, 152.
Crolius, Clarkson, 171.
Cromwell, Oliver, 92, 97, 98, 208.

INDEX OF NAMES. 293

Croswell, Edwin, 160, 279.
Cummings, Amos J., 287, 288.
Curtis, Benjamin R., 124.
Curtis, George William, 263, 264.
Curtis, Samuel R., 234.
Cushing, Caleb, 57, 58, 259.

Daboll, Nathan, 16, 17.
Dana, Charles A., 186, 220, 241, 246, 260, 287.
Daniels, Alfred, 124.
Daniels, George, 123, 124.
Dart, William A., 171.
Darwin, Doctor (Senior), 228.
Davis, David, 221.
Davis, Henry Winter, 202.
Davis, Jefferson, 210.
Davis, Matthew S., 255.
Davis, Noah, 236.
Dawson, George, 280.
Day, Benjamin, 274.
Decatur, Stephen, 6, 7.
Denio, Hiram, 129, 135.
Denman, Lord, 92.
Derby, Earl, 83.
Dexter, Lord Timothy, 72, 73.
Dickens, Charles, 287.
Dickinson, Andrew B., 223, 224.
Dickinson, Daniel S., 154, 160, 178, 180, 212.
Disraeli, Benjamin, 83, 85.
Dix, John A., 146, 154, 160, 174, 184, 212, 218, 246, 259.
Dixon, James, 213.
Doolittle, James R., 213.
Dorsheimer, William, 246.
Douglas, Stephen A., 154, 203, 209, 212-214, 287.
Douglass, Frederick, 68, 156.
Dow, Lorenzo, 13, 14.
Duane, William, 254.
Durham, Earl, 81.

Edwards, Jonathan, 12.
Edwards, Monroe, 272.
Elliott, Ebenezer, 103.
Emerson, Ralph Waldo, 105.
Emmet, Robert, 84.
Evarts, William M., 115, 193, 217, 218.

Everett, Edward, 259.
Ewing, Thomas, 39.

Fanning, Charles, 19, 20.
Farrar, Canon, 91.
Fenton, Reuben E., 143, 154, 160, 236-239, 249.
Fessenden, Samuel, 54.
Fessenden, William Pitt, 54, 213.
Field, David Dudley, 160, 171, 214.
Fillmore, Millard, 36, 40.
Finney, Charles G., 40-42, 45, 63.
Fish, Hamilton, 171, 172.
Flagg, Azariah C., 30, 158, 160.
Flint, Abel, 16.
Folger, Charles J., 160.
Follett, William, 93.
Folsom, Abigail, 70, 93.
Forney, John W., 287.
Forrest, Edwin, 96.
Forster, William E., 76, 90, 101.
Foster, La Fayette S., 123.
Foster, Stephen S., 70, 213.
Fox, Charles James, 87, 108.
Fox, George, 70.
Franklin, Benjamin, 72, 106.
Fremont, John C., 8, 54.
Freneau, Philip, 253.
Fry, Elizabeth, 76.

Gallatin, Albert, 255.
Gardiner, Addison, 35, 160.
Garfield, James A., 241.
Garrison, William Lloyd, 51, 52, 65, 69, 71, 72, 164.
Geddes, George, 171.
Giddings, Joshua R., 66.
Gladstone, William Ewart, 84, 101.
Goodell, William, 66.
Goodrich, Samuel G., 49.
Gould, Jacob, 32.
Graham, Sylvester, 62, 63.
Granger, Francis, 22.
Grant, Ulysses S., 43.
Graves, William J., 271.
Greeley, Horace, 47, 63, 107, 154, 186, 214, 217, 218, 220, 222, 259, 273, 287.

Green, Andrew H., 160.
Green, Ashbel, Dr., 45.
Green, Beriah, 51, 66.
Grey (Earl, 1st), 77, 79, 80, 81.
Grey (Earl, 2d), 83.
Grey, Lady Jane, 97.
Griffin, John, 134.
Grimke, Angelina, 67.
Grimke, Sarah, 67.
Grow, Galusha A., 143, 207.
Grundy, Felix, 153.
Guizot, F. P. G., 75.
Gurney, Samuel, 76.

Hale, David, 267, 268.
Hale, John P., 127, 128, 213.
Hallett, Benjamin F., 125, 126.
Hamilton, Alexander, 255.
Hamlin, Hannibal, 213, 219.
Hammond, Charles, 258.
Hancock, John, 72.
Hardy, Commodore, 6, 7.
Harris, Ira, 217, 218.
Harrison, William H., 151.
Hart, Levi, 12.
Hastings, Hugh J., 241.
Hastings, Warren, 80, 92, 108.
Hawley, Jesse, 132, 133.
Hawley, Joseph R., 66, 287.
Hawley, Reverend Mr., 66.
Haydon, Benjamin R., 76, 77.
Hayes, Rutherford B., 242.
Hayne, Robert Y., 50.
Head, George, 119, 120, 121.
Hendricks, Thomas A., 154.
Heyrick, Elizabeth, 60.
Hill, Isaac, 285.
Hill, Nicholas, 135, 136, 137, 138, 140, 160, 161.
Hoar, E. Rockwood, 115.
Hoar, George F., 115.
Hoar, Samuel, 113, 114, 115.
Hoffman, John T., 248.
Hoffman, Michael, 155, 160, 173, 175.
Holman, William S., 143.
Hopkins, Samuel, 12.
Houston, Sam, 183.
Howard, Joseph, Jr., 284.
Howick, Lord, 83.

Howitt, Mary, 76.
Hubbard, Samuel, 123.
Hugo, Victor, 104.
Hume, David, 89.
Hunt, Washington, 159.
Hunter, John, 223.
Hurlbert, William Henry, 287.
Hutchinson (The family), 70.

Irving, Washington, 255.
Isambert, François Andre, 93.

Jackson, Andrew, 19, 31–33, 103, 154, 205.
Jackson, Francis, 65.
James, John Angell, 76.
James, William (Senior), 40.
James, William (Junior), 40.
Jay, John, 255.
Jay, William, 65.
Jefferson, Joseph, 13.
Jefferson, Thomas, 3, 142, 148, 149.
Jeffrey, Francis, 106.
Jeffreys, George, 98, 99.
Johnson, Andrew, 209.
Johnson, Richard M., 61.
Johnson, Samuel, 96, 107.
Johnson, William (Law Reporter), 129, 135.
Jones, Edward F., 225.
Judson, Andrew T., 67.

Kean, Charles, 26.
Kean, Edmund, 26, 27.
Keitt, Lawrence M., 207, 209.
Kellogg, William, 208.
Kelly, John, 284.
Kendall, Amos, 259.
Kent, James, 129, 143.
Kernan, Francis, 282.
King, Charles, 62, 276.
King, Preston, 160.
King, Rufus, 164, 218.
King, William R., 152.
Knapp, Frank, 113.
Knapp, Joseph, 113.
Knox, John, 105.

La Fayette, The Marquis, 20.

INDEX OF NAMES. 295

Lamartine, Alphonse, 93.
Lampson, Father, 70.
Lapham, Elbridge G., 240.
Lawrence, Abbott, 114, 115, 150.
Lawrence, James, 9.
Leavitt, Joshua, 65.
Ledyard, William, 6.
Lee, Charles M., 133.
Leggett, William, 269.
Lincoln, Abraham, 134, 209, 212, 214, 216, 221, 222, 232–235, 287.
Lincoln, Mrs. Abraham, 221.
Littlejohn, De Witt C., 218, 246.
Livingston, Edward, 255.
Livingston, Peter R., 22.
Longfellow, Henry W., 103.
Loomis, Arphaxad, 155, 160.
Lord, Hezekiah, 12.
Loring, Charles G., 124.
Lovejoy, Elijah Parrish, 66.
Lovejoy, Owen, 207, 232.
Lovelace, Lady, 76, 104.
Lushington, Stephen, 76.
Lyndhurst, Lord, 78, 79.

McClellan, George B., 227.
McClure, Alexander K., 287.
McDonald, Joseph E., 154, 242.
McPheeters, Dr., 234.
Macaulay, Thomas Babington, 80, 82, 84, 85, 106.
Mackenzie, Alexander Slidell, 145, 146.
Macready, 96.
Madison, James, 7, 9, 10.
Madison, Mrs. James, 152.
Mallory, James, 30.
Mann, Abijah, 160.
Mann, Charles A., 171.
Mann, Horace, 149.
Mansfield, Lord, 129.
Marble, Manton, 287.
Marcy, William L., 30, 37–40, 154, 160, 218, 249, 259.
Marlborough, Duke of, 108.
Marshall, John, 112, 129.
Marshall, Thomas F., 60, 272.
Martindale, Henry C., 184.
Marvin, Dudley, 35.

Mason, James M., 210.
Mason, Jeremiah, 111–113, 118, 204, 210, 211.
Mason, John, 4.
Matteson, Orsamus B., 198, 199.
May, Samuel J., 65, 67.
Melbourne, Lord, 78, 79, 82.
Mellen, George W., 70.
Miantonomoh, 45.
Miller, Warner, 240.
Monro, Timothy, 37.
Montgomery, James, 103.
Moore, Thomas, 23.
Morgan, Christopher, 215.
Morgan, Edwin D., 218, 219, 236–238.
Morgan, William, 24, 36, 37.
Morpeth, Lord, 75.
Morse, Jedediah, 16.
Moses, Franklin J., 114.
Mott, Lucretia, 67, 281.
Murat, Joachim, 83.
Murray, Lindley, 16.

Napoleon I., 79, 228, 257.
Napoleon III., 94.
Neal, John, 54.
Nelson, Horatio, 6.
Nelson, Samuel, 129, 138, 142.
Niles, John M., 285.
Noah, Mordecai M., 22.
Noxen, B. Davis, 35.
Noyes, Edward F., 242.
Noyes, William Curtis, 215.
Nye, James W., 156, 160.

O'Connell, Daniel, 75, 83, 84, 87, 102, 107, 108.
O'Connell, John, 107.
O'Conor, Charles, 161.
Opie, Amelia, 76.
O'Reilly, Henry, 26, 258.
Orr, James L., 207.

Paddleford, Seth, 213.
Parker, Amasa J. (Senior), 246.
Parker, Mary S., 51.
Parker, Samuel Dunn, 119, 121.
Parker, Theodore, 128.
Parley, Peter, 49.

Partridge, Alden, 29.
Patch, Sam, 27.
Patterson, George W., 171.
Payne, Henry B., 154.
Pease, Elizabeth, 76.
Peel, Robert, 83, 84.
Penn, William, 53.
Pennington, William, 61, 201, 202.
Penny, Joseph, 40.
Perry, Oliver Hazard, 8, 9.
Phelps, Amos A., 65.
Phillips, Stephen C., 149.
Phillips, Wendell, 66, 69, 71.
Pickering, Timothy, 255.
Pierce, Franklin, 126, 153.
Pierpont, John, 65.
Pillsbury, Parker, 70.
Pitt, William (Senior), 79, 228.
Pitt, William (Junior), 87, 104.
Platt, Thomas C., 240.
Polk, James K., 60, 157, 158.
Pollock, Frederick, 93.
Porter, John K., 136, 137, 138.
Porter, Peter B., 155.
Porteus, Bishop, 87.
Prentice, George D., 17, 18, 26, 259, 275.
Preston, William C., 152.
Purvis, Robert, 69.

Quincy, Edmund, 70.
Quincy, Josiah, 70.

Randolph, John, 108.
Rantoul, Robert, 280.
Raymond, Henry J., 154, 260, 261, 287.
Redfield, Heman J., 30.
Reynolds, Marcus T., 138, 139.
Rhett, Robert Barnwell, 60, 259.
Richmond, Dean, 156, 160.
Ritchie, Thomas, 154.
Rives, William C., 152.
Roberts, Marshall O., 237.
Robinson, Lucius, 283.
Root, Erastus, 22.
Ruggles, Samuel B., 267.
Russell, Major Ben, 253.
Russell, Lord John, 77, 82.
Russell, Lord William, 108.

Sackett, Garry V., 196–198.
Sanford, Nathan, 218.
Sargeant, John, 152.
Sassacus, 4.
Scarlett, James, 92.
Schofield, John, 19.
Scott, Walter, 108, 177.
Scott, Winfield, 180.
Scribner, Charles, 75.
Selden, Samuel L., 35.
Seward, William H., 33, 34, 36, 142, 154, 169, 170, 203, 204, 210, 212–219, 221–223, 225, 241, 242, 259.
Seymour, Henry, 29, 30.
Seymour, Horatio, 29, 30, 154, 155, 160, 238, 239, 267.
Sharp, Granville, 87, 107.
Shaw, Lemuel, 110, 116.
Shaw, Samuel M., 280.
Sheridan, Richard B., 92, 108.
Sherman, John, 200, 201.
Sherman, Roger, 115.
Sherman, William T., 61.
Shipman, Thomas L., 281.
Simmons, James F., 213.
Slidell, John, 146, 203, 204, 210, 211.
Smith, Caleb B., 222.
Smith, Gerrit, 27, 51, 65, 146, 168, 281, 282.
Smith, Green, 191.
Smith, Horace E., 126.
Smith of N. C., 201.
Smith, Peter, 189, 190.
Smith, Sydney, 80, 81, 106.
Southard, Samuel L., 152.
Southwick, Solomon, 33.
Spencer, Ambrose, 129, 146.
Spencer, John C., 31, 35, 145, 146, 267.
Spencer, Joshua A., 139.
Sprague, Peleg, 110.
Sprague, William, 213.
Stanley, Dean, 91.
Stanley, Lord, 83.
Stanton, Edwin M., 222, 228, 233.
Stanton, Elizabeth Cady, 68.
Stanton, Joseph (Senior), 2.
Stanton, Joseph (Junior), 2.

INDEX OF NAMES.

Stanton, Lodewick, 2.
Stanton, Robert Lodewick, 234, 251.
Stanton, Susan, 3, 4.
Stanton, Thomas, 2.
Stephens, Alexander H., 214.
Stetson, Charles, 180.
Stevens, Samuel. 138–141.
Stephens, Thaddeus, 208, 209.
Stewart, Alvan, 51, 53, 65, 134, 135.
Stone, Lucy, 67, 68.
Storrs, Henry R., 35, 132.
Story, Joseph, 110, 113, 126, 255.
Stowe, Calvin E., 68.
Stowe, Harriet Beecher, 68, 262.
Stuart, Charles E., 211.
Stuart, Moses, 259.
Sturge, Joseph, 76.
Sumner, Charles, 125, 126.
Sutherland, Jacob, 129.
Swift, Jonathan, 108.
Sydney, Algernon, 108.

Taft, Alphonso, 242.
Talfourd, Thomas Noon, 85, 93.
Tallmadge, James, 23, 164.
Tallmadge, Nathaniel P., 152.
Taney, Roger B., 152, 254.
Tappan, Arthur, 65, 267.
Tappan, Lewis, 51, 52, 65, 267, 268, 275.
Taylor, John W., 38, 164.
Taylor, Nathaniel W., 45.
Taylor, Zachary, 159, 162, 164, 204.
Tecumseh, 61.
Temple, William, 108.
Thackeray, William Makepeace, 287.
Thompson, Smith, 33, 129.
Thurman, Allen G., 154, 242.
Tilden, Samuel J., 154, 160–162, 238, 244–248.
Tirrell, Albert J., 113, 118, 119, 120, 121.
Tompkins, Daniel D., 247.
Toombs, Robert, 203, 204, 210.
Tracey, Albert H., 149.
Trumbull, Lyman, 213.
Tucker, Beverly, 210.
Tucker, Ephraim, 7, 8.

Tucker, Luther, 26.
Turner, Nat, 47.
Tweed, William M., 22, 247, 283.
Tyler, John, 151.
Tytler, Alexander Fraser, 16.

Uncas, 4, 5.

Vallandigham, Clement L., 239.
Van Buren, John, 154, 155, 160, 162, 165, 279.
Van Buren, Martin, 31–33, 38, 58, 61, 130, 146, 154, 157–160, 162–164, 205, 223.
Vanderbilt, Cornelius J., 144, 145.
Van Dyck, Henry H., 279.
Van Ness, William W., 130.
Van Rensselaer, Stephen, 31.
Van Vechten, Abraham, 136.
Villiers, C. P., 76.

Wade, Benjamin F., 154, 203, 204, 213.
Wadsworth, James S., 156, 160, 214, 216, 220.
Wait, John T., 123.
Waldo, Horatio, 12.
Walker, Robert J., 153, 212, 259.
Walworth, Reuben H., 142, 143, 161.
Ward, Ferdinand, 43.
Ward, Ferdinand D. W., 43.
Wardlaw, Ralph, 76, 106.
Warren, Samuel, 137.
Washburne, Elihu B., 208.
Washington, George, 70, 72, 148.
Watterson, Henry, 17.
Wayne, Mad Anthony, 133.
Webb, James Watson, 271–274, 287.
Webster, Daniel, 39, 50, 61, 84, 96, 110, 112, 113, 116, 118, 149–152, 154, 205, 206, 217.
Webster, Noah, 16.
Weed, Thurlow, 24–27, 33, 36, 38, 154, 169, 170, 215, 216, 259, 287.
Weld, Theodore D., 57, 65.
Welles, Gideon, 220, 233.
Wellington, Duke of, 77, 79.

13*

INDEX OF NAMES.

Wendell, John L. (Law Reporter), 135.
White, Hugh L., 153.
White, Joseph, 113.
Whitefield, George, 13.
Whitehouse, Henry J., 40.
Whittier, John G., 53, 57, 65, 71, 72, 103, 261–263.
Whittlesey, Frederick, 25.
Wilbar, William, 122, 123.
Wilberforce, William, 87, 107.
Wilde, Judge, 124.
Wiley, John, 75.
Wilkeson, Samuel (Senior), 28.
Wilkeson, Samuel (Junior), 280.
William III., 99, 108.
Williams, Benjamin, 122, 123.
Williams, Elisha, 35, 130–132.
Williams, Josiah B., 168–170.
Williams, Roger, 4, 14, 228.
Williams (Theatre Manager), 26, 27.
Wilmot, Eardley, 76.
Wilmot, David, 40.
Wilson, Henry, 50, 265.
Windham, William, 87.
Winthrop, Robert C., 150, 159.
Wirt, William, 259.
Wise, Henry A., 60.
Wolfe, James, 2.
Woodward, Samuel B., 148, 149.
Wright, Elizur, 48, 65, 275.
Wright, Frances, 28.
Wright, Silas, 22, 38–40, 61, 152, 154, 157–160, 162, 218, 249, 259.

Young, Samuel, 22, 160, 161.
Younglove, Truman G., 237, 238.

THE END.

www.ingramcontent.com/pod-product-compliance
Lightning Source LLC
Chambersburg PA
CBHW030810230426
43667CB00008B/1148